Collins

OCR Gateway GCSE (9–1)
Physics for Combined Science
Student Book

Sandra Mitchell
Charles Golabek
Series editor: Ed Walsh

William Collins' dream of knowledge for all began with the publication of his first book in 1819.

A self-educated mill worker, he not only enriched millions of lives, but also founded a flourishing publishing house. Today, staying true to this spirit, Collins books are packed with inspiration, innovation and practical expertise. They place you at the centre of a world of possibility and give you exactly what you need to explore it.

Collins. Freedom to teach

HarperCollins Publishers
1 London Bridge Street
London SE1 9GF

Browse the complete Collins catalogue at
www.collins.co.uk

First edition 2016

10 9 8 7 6 5 4 3 2 1

© HarperCollins Publishers 2016

ISBN 978-0-00-817501-6

Collins® is a registered trademark of HarperCollins Publishers Limited

www.collins.co.uk

A catalogue record for this book is available from the British Library

Commissioned by Lucy Rowland, Lizzie Catford and Joanna Ramsay

Edited by Hamish Baxter

Project managed by Elektra Media Ltd

With thanks to contributing author Crispin Myerscough

Development edited by Aidan Gill

Copy edited by Gillian Lindsey

Proofread by Jo Kemp and Helen Atkinson

Typeset by Jouve India and Ken Vail Graphic Design

Cover design by We are Laura

Printed by Bell and Bain Ltd, Glasgow

Cover images © Shutterstock/Komsan Loonprom, Shutterstock/Everett Historical

OCR Endorsement statement

This resource is endorsed by OCR for use with specification J250 GCSE (9–1) Gateway Science Suite – Combined Science A. In order to gain OCR endorsement, this resource has undergone an independent quality check. Any references to assessment and/or assessment preparation are the publisher's interpretation of the specification requirements and are not endorsed by OCR. OCR recommends that a range of teaching and learning resources are used in preparing learners for assessment. OCR has not paid for the production of this resource, nor does OCR receive any royalties from its sale. For more information about the endorsement process, please visit the OCR website, www.ocr.org.uk.

ACKNOWLEDGEMENTS

The publishers gratefully acknowledge the permissions granted to reproduce copyright material in this book. Every effort has been made to contact the holders of copyright material, but if any have been inadvertently overlooked, the Publisher will be pleased to make the necessary arrangements at the first opportunity.

Chapter 1

pg. 12 Zmaj88/ Shutterstock; pg. 13 Kekyalyaynen/ Shutterstock, Petr Malyshev/ Shutterstock; pg. 17 SpaceKris/ Shutterstock; pg. 21 Dream79/Shutterstock; pg. 22 Waraphorn Aphai/ Shutterstock; pg. 23 Https://campgourmet.wordpress.com/articles/refrigeration/; pg. 27 Kekyalyaynen/ Shutterstock; pg. 29 Tyler Olson/ Shutterstock; pg. 34 Everett Historical/ Shutterstock;

Chapter 2

pg 42 sippakorn/Shutterstock, ANURAKE SINGTO-ON/Shutterstock; pg 43 dugwy39/Shutterstock, thieury/ Shutterstock, Aleksei Lazukov/Shutterstock; pg 48 Fedor Selivanov/Shutterstock; pg 50 Louise Ann Noeth/ Getty; pg 57 Rustam Shanov / Shutterstock; pg 63 Oleksandr Kalinichenko/Shutterstock; pg 66 MANFRED KAGE/SCIENCE PHOTO LIBRARY; pg 68 Boykov/Shutterstock; pg 70 Mariia Masich/Shutterstock, Jiang Dao Hua/Shutterstock; pg 71 Chris Jenner/Shutterstock; pg 73 lzf /Shutterstock, Viacheslav Lopatin/Shutterstock; pg 74 Georgios Kollidas/Shutterstock, ChameleonsEye/Shutterstock, Vorm in Beeld/Shutterstock; pg 75 Graeme Dawes/Shutterstock; pg. 80 bunnyphoto/Shutterstock, oknoart/Shutterstock, john michael evan potter/shutterstock;

Chapter 3

pg 88 TED KINSMAN/SCIENCE PHOTO LIBRARY, asadykov/shutterstock, Gearstd/Shutterstock; pg 90 Minerva Studio/Shutterstock; pg 91 TED KINSMAN/SCIENCE PHOTO LIBRARY; pg 99 Chones/Shutterstock; pg 104 ANDREW LAMBERT PHOTOGRAPHY/SCIENCE PHOTO LIBRARY; pg 106 cristi180884/Shutterstock, _LeS_/Shutterstock; pg 108 Lilyana Vynogradova; pg. 109 imagedb.com/Shutterstock, you can more/ Shutterstock; pg. 112 Kotkot32/Shutterstock; pg 113 SvedOliver/Shutterstock, Monkey Business Images/ Shutterstock, CPM Photo/Shutterstock; pg 118 ChameleonsEye/Shutterstock; pg 126 Chatchai-Rombix/ Shutterstock; pg 129 goldenjack/Shutterstock

Chapter 4

pg 138 ergii Tverdokhlibov/Shutterstock, Ivan_Sabdo/Shutterstock; pg 139 isarescheewin/Shutterstock; pg 140 James Boardman/Getty; pg 142 Serg64/Shutterstock; pg 148 Joshua Rainey Photography/Shutterstock; pg. 146 Chatchai-Rombix/Shutterstock.com; pg 149 asharkyu/shutterstock.com, Ryan Jorgensen - Jorgo/ Shutterstock; pg 149 tormashka/shutterstock.com; pg 150 Sergii Tverdokhlibov/Shutterstock; pg 152 Denise Lett/Shutterstock, Suttha Burawonk/Shutterstock; pg 153 pg 153 SOVEREIGN/ISM/SCIENCE PHOTO LIBRARY; pg 154 Carlos Arranz/Shutterstock; pg 155 Teodora D/Shutterstock, Ivan Smuk/Shutterstock; pg 156 Hurst Photo/Shutterstock; pg 158 9comeback/Shutterstock; pg 170 Raymond Llewellyn/Shutterstock; pg 175 PUBLIPHOTO DIFFUSION/SCIENCE PHOTO LIBRARY;

Chapter 5

pg 182 Digital Storm/Shutterstock, AlexStaroseltsev/Shutterstock, Christos Siatos/Shutterstock, Kzenon/ Shutterstock; pg 183 Harri Aho/Shutterstock, You can more/Shutterstock, Ivan Smuk /Shutterstock, Filip Fuxa/Shutterstock; pg 184 Digital Storm/Shutterstock; pg 185 DR GARY SETTLES/Shutterstock; pg 186 Mariia Masich/Shutterstock, Faraways/Shutterstock; pg 187 kRie/Shutterstock; pg 189 sasipixel/Shutterstock; pg 190 Petr Malyshev/ Shutterstock; pg 192 rdonar/shutterstock; pg 193 Image Point Fr/Shutterstock; pg 194 Oleksandr Chub/Shutterstock; pg 198 Steve Collender/Shutterstock; pg 199 parinyabinsuk/ shutterstock, Harri Aho/Shutterstock; pg 200 Fouad A. Saad/Shutterstock; pg 205 Ivan Smuk/Shutterstock;

Chapter 6

pg 206 Neil Mitchell/Shutterstock, FooTToo/Shutterstock, StudioFI/Shutterstock; pg 207 Filip Fuxa/ Shutterstock, zhengzaishuru/shutterstock.com, a_v_d/Shutterstock; pg 209 Yauhen_D/Shutterstock; pg 210 Gearstd/Shutterstock; pg 211 michaeljung/Shutterstock; pg 213 GravityLight.org; pg 213 zhu difeng/ shutterstock; pg 215 Michael Wick/Shutterstock; pg 216 a_v_d/Shutterstock;

Contents

How to use this book

Learning objectives which are Higher tier only appear in a purple background box.

Remember! to cover all the content of the OCR Chemistry Specification you should study the text and attempt the End of Chapter Questions.

These tell you what you will be learning about in the lesson and are linked to the OCR specification.

This introduces the topic and puts the science into an interesting context.

Each topic is divided into three sections. The level of challenge gets harder with each section.

Physics – Newton's laws (P2.2)

Forces and acceleration

Learning objectives:

- explain what happens to the motion of an object when the resultant force is not zero
- analyse situations in which a non-zero resultant force is acting
- explain what inertia is.

KEY WORDS

resultant force
Newton's second law
inertia
inertial mass
gravitational mass

The record for the fastest object made by humans is held by the Helios 2 spacecraft, which reached over 246 000 km/h. It has a very elliptical orbit around the Sun which means it accelerates as a result of the Sun's massive gravitational field.

What does a force do?

When the driver presses on the accelerator pedal, it increases the forward **force** of the engine. This makes the car accelerate.

The force of the engine acts forwards and there will be other forces opposing this: friction and air resistance. However, at this point the force from the engine is greater than the opposing forces and so the car accelerates (Figure 2.28). It speeds up.

1. In which direction are the resultant forces acting in Figures 2.26 and 2.29?

2. The driver of the car in Figure 2.29b presses the accelerator harder so that the speed increases. What will happen to the resultant force?

Forward force from engine / Friction and air resistance

Figure 2.28 The car accelerates.

(a)

Forward force from engine / Friction and resistance

(b)

Forward force from engine / Friction and air resistance

Figure 2.29 Forces on a car

Newton's second law

Force, mass and acceleration are linked by the equation

$F = ma$

where F is the **resultant force** in N, m is the mass in kg and a is the acceleration in m/s^2. This is **Newton's second law**.

The resultant force is a single force that has the same effect as all the original forces acting together..

Example:

A car has a mass of 1000 kg. What force is needed to give it an acceleration of 5 m/s^2?

$F = ma$

$= 1000 \text{ kg} \times 5 \text{ m/s}^2$

$= 5000 \text{ N}$

MAKING LINKS

Weight can be considered in terms of Newton's second law: the force is the weight and the acceleration is that due to gravity.

KEY INFORMATION

When using $F = ma$, F is the resultant force.

62   OCR Gateway GCSE Physics for Combined Science: Student Book

③ A car of mass 1200 kg has a resultant forward force acting on it of 4200 N. Determine its acceleration.

④ The weight of an apple is 1 N and it accelerates downwards at 10 m/s². What is its mass?

⑤ What force is needed to accelerate a 4000 kg rocket upwards at 2 m/s²? ($g = 10\,N/kg$)

2.10

HIGHER TIER ONLY

Inertia

Figure 2.30 Once a massive tanker is moving it is difficult to stop.

Massive objects are hard to start to move and also very difficult to stop. (Figure 2.30) They have an inbuilt reluctance to start moving. This is called **inertia** (from the Latin for laziness). Inertia is the natural tendency of objects to resist changes in their velocity.

Inertial mass is a measure of how difficult it is to change the velocity of an object.

Inertial mass is defined by the ratio of force over acceleration:

$$\text{inertial mass} = \frac{\text{force}}{\text{acceleration}}.$$

⑥ What is inertia and how do you calculate inertial mass?

⑦ Another form of mass is **gravitational mass**. Suggest what the difference is between gravitational mass and inertial mass.

⑧ An object has a mass of 2 kg. What are its inertial mass and its gravitational mass?

DID YOU KNOW?

Some large ships can take 10 km to stop from a cruising speed of 12 km/h.

How to use this book   **7**

The first page of a chapter has links to ideas you have met before, which you can now build on.

This page gives a summary of the exciting new ideas you will be learning about in the chapter.

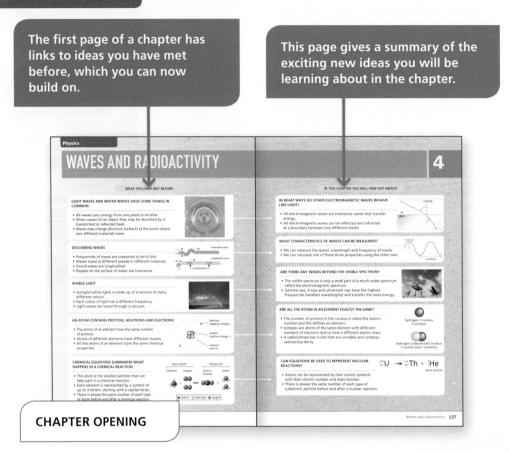

CHAPTER OPENING

The Key Concept pages focus on a core ideas. Once you have understood the key concept in a chapter, it should develop your understanding of the whole topic.

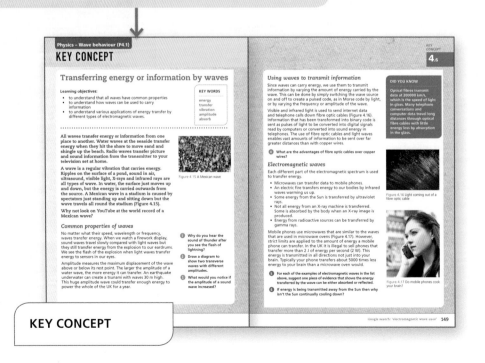

KEY CONCEPT

There are dedicated pages for practicals. They help you to analyse the practical and to answer questions about it.

The tasks – which get a bit more difficult as you go through – challenge you to apply your science skills and knowledge to the new context.

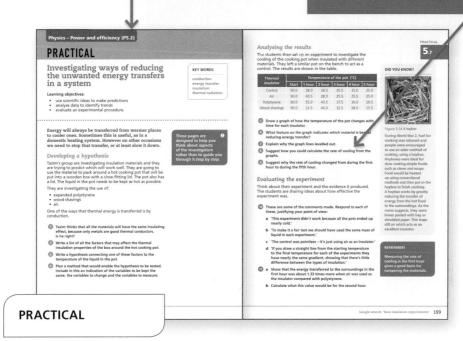

PRACTICAL

The Maths Skills pages focus on the maths requirements in the OCR specification, explaining concepts and providing opportunities to practise.

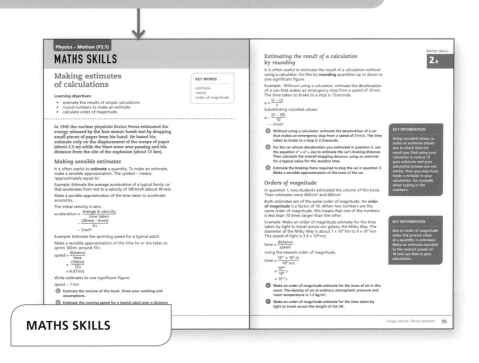

MATHS SKILLS

Physics

These lists at the end of a chapter act as a checklist of the key ideas of the chapter. In each row, the green box gives the ideas or skills that you should master first. Then you can aim to master the ideas and skills in the blue box. Once you have achieved those you can move on to those in the red box.

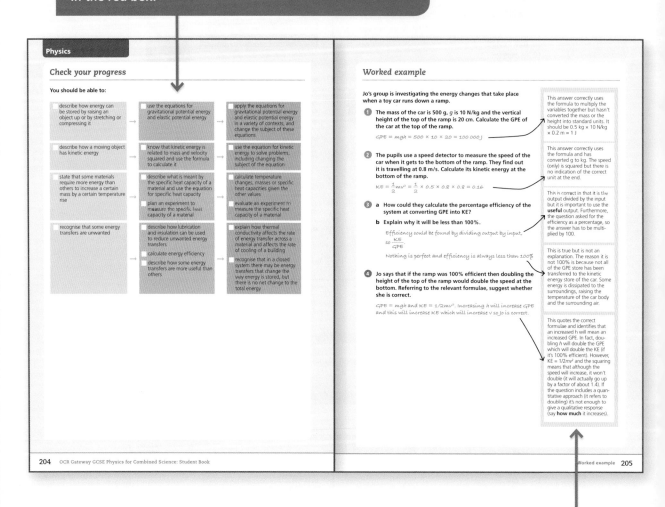

Use the comments to help you understand how to answer questions. Read each question and answer. Try to decide if, and how, the answer can be improved. Finally, read the comments and try to answer the questions yourself.

END OF CHAPTER

The End of Chapter Questions allow you and your teacher to check that you have understood the ideas in the chapter, can apply these to new situations, and can explain new science using the skills and knowledge you have gained. The questions start off easier and get harder. If you are taking Foundation tier try to answer all the questions in the Getting started and Going further sections. If you are taking Higher Tier try to answer all the questions in the Going further, More challenging and Most demanding sections.

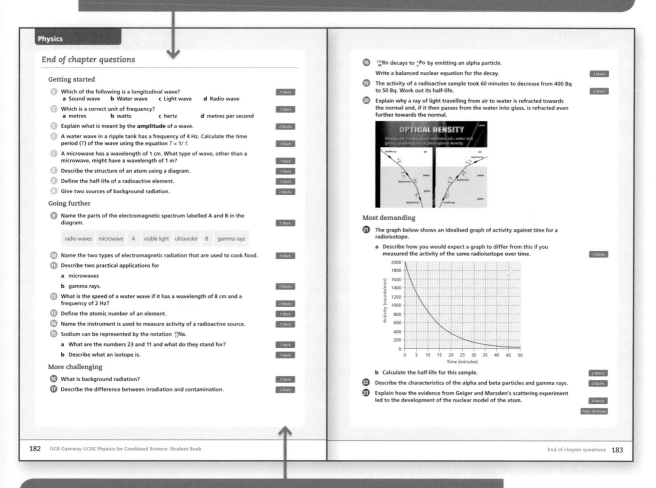

There are questions for each assessment objective (AO) from the final exams. These help you to develop the thinking skills you need to answer each type of question.

AO1 – to answer these questions you should aim to **demonstrate** your knowledge and understanding of scientific ideas, techniques and procedures.

AO2 – to answer these questions you should aim to **apply** your knowledge and understanding of scientific ideas and scientific enquiry, techniques and procedures.

AO3 – to answer these questions you should aim to **analyse** information and ideas to: interpret and evaluate, make judgements and draw conclusions, develop and improve experimental procedures.

MATTER

DENSITY

- Solids usually have a larger density than liquids and gases. The particles are closer together.
- The particles in a gas fill the space available.

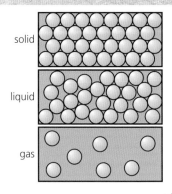

solid

liquid

gas

PRESSURE

- Pressure is equal to the force acting on unit area of a surface. Pressure is equal to force ÷ area. Pressure is measured in pascals (Pa). 1 Pa = 1 N/m^2.
- Atmospheric pressure decreases as the height above sea level increases.
- The weight of air above the Earth's surface decreases as you go higher; this lowers the boiling point of water as you climb a mountain.

PARTICLE MODEL AND PRESSURE OF A GAS

- Every material is made of tiny moving particles.
- The higher the temperature the more energy is stored in the gas and the faster the particles move.
- In a gas the particles are far apart and move freely.

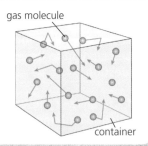

gas molecule

container

IN THIS CHAPTER YOU WILL FIND OUT ABOUT:

WHAT USES ARE MADE OF THE HIGH SPECIFIC HEAT CAPACITY OF WATER?

- The specific heat capacity of a substance, c, is the energy required per unit mass to raise the temperature 1 °C. If the mass is measured in kilograms, the unit for c is J/kg °C.
- Water has a very high specific heat capacity. It needs a lot of energy to heat the water in a radiator or hot water bottle.
- The heating of a substance transfers energy to the substance, which stores that energy.

WHAT ARE THE SPECIFIC LATENT HEAT OF VAPORISATION AND THE SPECIFIC LATENT HEAT OF FUSION?

- A particle model is used to show that mass is conserved when changing state.
- The specific latent heat of fusion is the energy required per unit mass to change a substance from a solid to a liquid without a change in temperature.
- The specific latent heat of vaporisation is the energy required per unit mass to change a substance from a liquid to a gas without a change in temperature.

WHAT HAPPENS TO THE PRESSURE OF A GAS WHEN IT IS HEATED, KEEPING THE VOLUME CONSTANT?

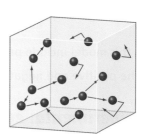

- An increase in temperature increases the energy stored by the gas.
- The particles move faster, colliding more often and with greater force on the walls of their container. The pressure of the gas increases.

KEY CONCEPT

Developing ideas for the structure of the atom

KEY WORDS

atom
alpha particle
electron
neutron
nuclear model
nucleus
plum pudding model
proton

Learning objectives:

- understand how ideas about the structure of the atom have changed
- how evidence is used to test and improve models.

The word 'atom' can be derived from the Greek word for 'indivisible'. The Greek philosopher Democritus developed the idea of the atom around 400 BC. For a long time atoms were thought to be the smallest particles.

The atom

Our theories for the structure of the **atom** have changed as new evidence has emerged.

The idea of an indivisible atom existed for over 2000 years. It was only at the start of the 20th century that scientists began to discover our current model of the atom.

At the end of the 19th century, scientists had started to question that the atom is the smallest particle. In the late 1890s, J. J. Thomson discovered the **electron** and that it is very much lighter than an atom. He proposed the **plum pudding model** of the atom where electrons are surrounded by positive charge (Figure 1.1).

KEY INFORMATION

The radius of an atom is about 10^{-10} m. It would take around 5 million of them placed side by side to cover the distance of 1 mm. The radius of the nucleus is less than 1/10 000th of the radius of the atom!

The radius of the smallest molecules is of the same order of magnitude as an atom. For example, a water molecule is about 2.8×10^{-10} m across its widest point.

1. Does this model include protons, neutrons and electrons?

2. Are the positive and negative charges balanced in this model?

Using experimental evidence to test the model

In 1909, Hans Geiger and Ernest Marsden carried out an experiment where they aimed a beam of **alpha particles** at a thin foil of metal. According to Thomson's model, they should all pass straight through. But some of the alpha particles bounced off the foil in all directions (Figure 1.2).

This led Ernest Rutherford to propose a **nuclear model** of the atom in 1911 with a small central **nucleus** that contained most of the mass and was charged with electrons orbiting it (Figure 1.3).

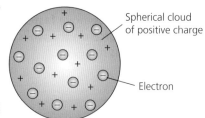

Figure 1.1 Thomson's plum pudding model.

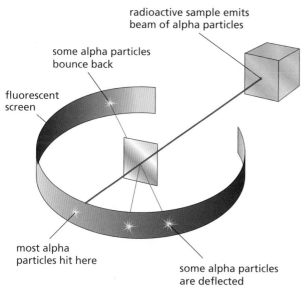

Figure 1.2 Results of the Geiger–Marsden experiment.

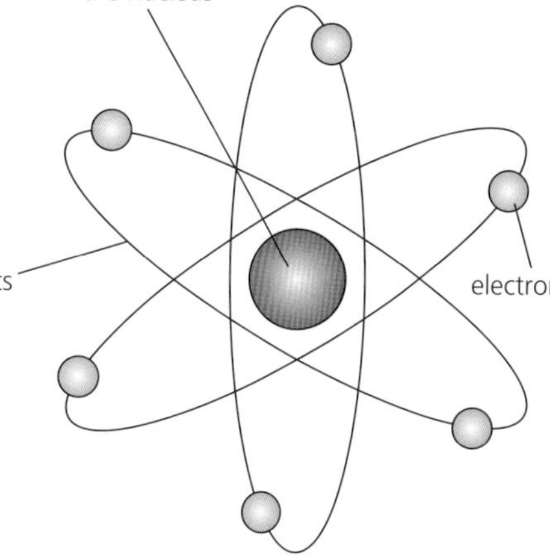

Figure 1.3 Rutherford's model of the atom

There was a problem with this model. Classical mechanics showed that the electrons would not stay in stable orbits and would spiral into the nucleus. So, in 1913, Niels Bohr proposed a refined model in which electrons could only be in certain orbits. This is the model we have today (Figure 1.4).

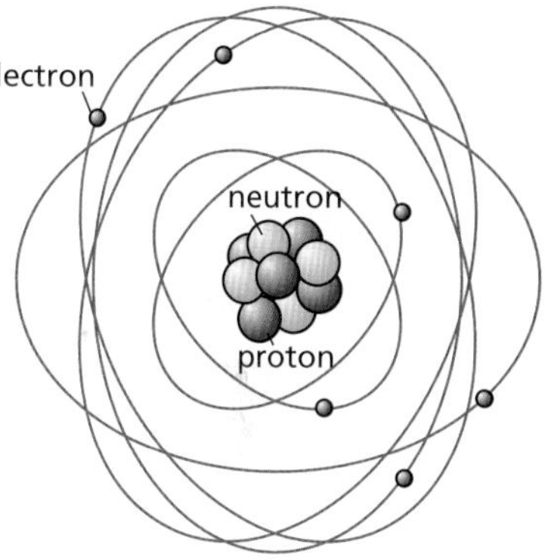

3 **Explain why it was important for Geiger and Marsden to publish the results of their experiment.**

4 **Explain why the model of the atom had to change.**

Developing the model further

Figure 1.4 Bohr's model

The results of further experiments suggested that the positive charge of the nucleus was made up from charged particles that all had the same charge. This led to the idea of the **proton** which was discovered by Rutherford in 1920. In the same year, he suggested that the nucleus was made up of protons and neutral particles. He thought the neutral particles could be a proton and electron combined in some way. The **neutron** was then discovered in 1932 by James Chadwick.

5 **State what Rutherford's model explained.**

6 **Suggest how a theory becomes accepted.**

Density

Learning objectives:

- use the particle model to explain the different states of matter and differences in density
- calculate density.

KEY WORDS

bonds
density
gas
liquid
particle model
solid

Inspectors measure the density of milk and beer to see whether they have been watered down.

States of matter

A **solid** has a fixed volume and shape. The particles vibrate to and fro but cannot change their positions. They are held together by strong forces of attraction called **bonds**.

A **liquid** has a fixed volume but not a fixed shape. It takes the shape of its container. The bonds between particles are less strong than in a solid. The particles are close together and attract each other. They move around but have no regular pattern.

A **gas** has no fixed volume or shape. Its particles move randomly and fill the space available. The particles are well spaced out and virtually free of any attractions. They move quickly, colliding with each other and the walls of their container.

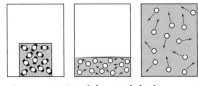

Figure 1.5 **Particle model** of particles in a solid, liquid and gas.

1   Which state does each of the following describe?

   a fixed shape and volume

   b particles move around freely at high speed

   c fixed volume but no fixed shape

Differences in density

Some people say 'lead is heavier than iron'. What they mean is that a piece of lead is heavier than a piece of iron of the same volume. **Density** compares the mass of materials with the same volume. Lead is denser than iron.

Densities of different materials

Substance	Density in kg/m³
gold	19 000
iron	8000
lead	11 000
cork	200
mercury	13 600
water	1000
petrol	800
air	1.3

In general, the liquids in the table above have densities lower than solids but higher than gases, but there are exceptions. The reason for the lower density is that the particles in a liquid are not as tightly packed as the particles of a solid (Figure 1.5).

The particles in a gas are more spread out, unless compressed. Gases have very low densities.

Mercury and cork do not follow the pattern. Mercury is a very dense liquid. Cork is a very light solid.

2 Explain why solids usually have a higher density than liquids and gases.

3 Explain why gases have a low density.

Density

Density is the mass of unit volume of a substance. It is given by the equation:

density = mass (in kg) / volume (in m³)

$\rho = m / V$

where mass is in kg, volume in m³ and density is in kg/m³.

Density is also given in g/cm³ where mass is in g and volume is in cm³.

1 g/cm³ = 1000 kg/m³

Example: Calculate the mass of 3 m³ of water. The density of water is 1000 kg/m³.

$\rho = m / V$

Rearrange the equation to give

$m = \rho V$

   = 1000 kg/m³ × 3 m³

   = 3000 kg

4 **a** Calculate the density of a 5400 kg block of aluminium with a volume of 2 m³.

   b Calculate the mass of steel having the same volume as the aluminium block. Density of steel = 7700 kg/m³.

   c Explain why aluminium is used to build aeroplanes rather than steel (Figure 1.6).

5 Calculate the mass of air in a room 5 m by 4 m by 3 m. The density of air is 1.3 kg/m³.

6 Suggest why cork floats in water, but iron sinks.

7 Explain what happens to the density of air in a bicycle tyre when someone sits on the bicycle.

8 Explain why a density of 1 g/cm³ is the same as a density of 1 kg/m³.

> **DID YOU KNOW?**
>
> Osmium is the densest substance found on Earth. Its density is 22 600 kg/m³.

Figure 1.6 Materials used in aeroplanes have to be light but strong.

KEY CONCEPT

Particle model and changes of state

Learning objectives:

- use the particle model to explain states of matter
- use ideas about energy and bonds to explain changes of state
- explain the relationship between temperature and energy.

KEY WORDS

states of matter
particle model
bonds
internal energy
latent heat
fusion
vaporisation

Everything on Earth is made of matter, but that matter isn't always the same. Matter can exist in three different states: solid, liquid, gas. The particle model of matter helps us understand the differences between those states.

Solids, liquids and gases

All matter is made up of atoms and molecules, but it is the way these atoms and molecules are held together that determines whether a substance is solid, liquid or gas. In a solid the atoms are held tightly together forming strong regular shapes. In a liquid the atoms are held much more loosely, which is why liquids can flow. In a gas the atoms and molecules are free to move about on their own.

What determines the state of matter is the strength with which the atoms and molecules are held together by their bonds. All atoms also vibrate. Even in a solid, where the atoms are held together in a tight structure, every single atom is moving backwards and forwards next to its neighbour.

To get a solid to become a liquid, energy has to be added to the substance (Figure 1.7). Energy increases the vibrations of the atoms. As the vibrations increase, the bonds that hold the atoms are stretched and the atoms are pushed further apart from each other (Figure 1.8).

Adding more energy to the solid increases the vibrations even more until there comes a point where the bonds can no longer hold together. The bonds snap and the atoms are free to move – the solid has become a liquid. Adding yet more energy breaks the bonds completely and the atoms escape into the atmosphere. The liquid becomes a gas.

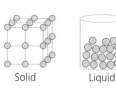

Figure 1.7 States of matter

1. State the difference between a solid and a liquid.

2. Explain why solids expand as they are heated.

3. Explain what happens to the internal energy of a solid (the energy the solid stores) as it is heated.

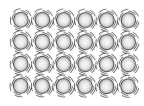

Cold

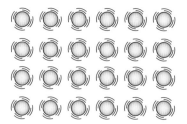

Hot

Figure 1.8 Vibrations in hot and cold solids

Change of state and change in temperature

The state of matter depends on the amount of energy inside it. Heating a substance increases the amount of internal energy and this either raises the temperature of the system or produces a change of state. The process also works in reverse. If you take energy out of the substance it will either decrease the temperature of the system or change state from a gas back to a liquid and then to a solid (Figure 1.9).

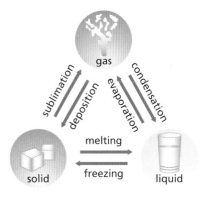

Figure 1.9 Changing between states of matter

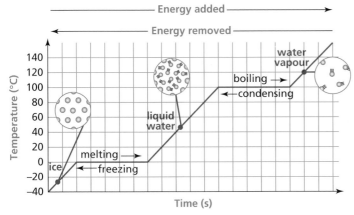

Figure 1.10 Temperature–time graph for heating water

When you heat a substance there are stages where you just get a rise in temperature and then a stage where you get a change of state.

Follow the steps on the graph in Figure 1.10 which shows the three states of water; ice, liquid and water vapour.

Start with ice at −40 °C. As you heat the ice it gets warmer, but is still a solid. The slope of the graph shows the increasing temperature. Then at 0 °C energy is still being put into the ice, but there is no increase in temperature. The graph now shows a level straight line. This is where the energy is being absorbed by the substance to change it into the next state: liquid water. The amount of energy per unit mass needed to change the state from solid to liquid is called the specific latent heat of fusion.

One the ice has melted into water the temperature begins to rise again. The line on the graph is sloping upwards. When the temperature reaches 100 °C we get the second change in state. Energy is absorbed but there is no rise in temperature. The amount of energy required to change the state from liquid to water vapour is called the specific latent heat of vaporisation.

4 Ethanol freezes at −114 °C and boils at 78 °C. Draw a temperature–time diagram for heating ethanol from −120 °C to 100 °C.

5 Explain what a line sloping down from left to right on a temperature–time graph means.

PRACTICAL

To investigate the densities of regular and irregular solid objects and liquids

KEY WORD

density
significant figures
resolution

Learning objectives:

- interpret observations and data
- use spatial models to solve problems
- plan experiments and devise procedures
- use an appropriate number of significant figures in measurements and calculations.

There is a great story about how scientists learned how to measure density. **Density** is worked out knowing the mass of an object and the volume it occupies. Measuring the volume is easy enough if the object is a regular shape such as a cube but what if it was, say, a crown?

This problem was given to Archimedes, a clever man who lived thousands of years ago in Greece. The king had ordered a new crown to be made but suspected the craftsman had mixed a cheaper metal with the gold. Measuring the density would reveal if the gold was pure, but how could the volume be found? Archimedes realised that by carefully immersing the crown in a full can of water, the water that overflowed would have the same volume as the crown.

Apparently he shouted "Eureka!" ("I have found it!") and the cans used in practical investigations are known as Eureka cans in recognition of this.

These pages are designed ❶ to help you think about aspects of the investigation rather than to guide you through it step by step.

Figure 1.11 Archimedes making his discovery

Measuring the density of a liquid

The density of any substance can be worked out using the formula:

density = mass/volume

If mass is measured in grams (g) and volume in cubic centimetres (cm^3) then the density will be in g/cm^3.

Measuring the density of a liquid can be done by pouring the liquid into a measuring cylinder to find its volume and using a balance to find the mass. The results might look rather like those in the table.

Liquid	Mass (g)	Volume (cm^3)
coconut oil	18.5	20
acetone	19.6	25
sea water	51.3	50

Density of different liquids

1. Explain why would not get the mass of the liquid by just putting the measuring cylinder with the liquid on the balance and recording the reading?

2. Suggest what you could do to get the mass of the liquid.

3. Calculate the density of each of the liquids in the table above.

Measuring the density of a regular solid

Solids, of course, have their own shape. If that shape is a regular one, we can calculate the volume by measuring dimensions and then using the correct formula. For example, if the solid was a cuboid, the volume would be length multiplied by width multiplied by height. The mass would be divided by this to get the density.

For example, if a 2.0 cm³ cube of soft rubber had a mass of 8.82 g, its volume would be 2.0 cm × 2.0 cm × 2.0 cm, which is 8.0 cm³, and the density would be 8.82 g/8.0 cm³ which is 1.1 g/cm³.

The answer can only have the same number of **significant figures** as the measurement with the least number of significant figures (in this case 8.0 – it has two significant figures).

Material	Mass (g)	Length (cm)	Width (cm)	Height (cm)
cork	3	2.0	2.0	3.0
oak	17	2.0	3.0	4.0
tin	364	2.5	2.5	8.0

Quantities of three materials

4. Look at the table above. What is the volume of the piece of cork?

5. Determine the its density.

6. What are the densities of the other two materials?

7. Explain why it is incorrect to use 0.70833333 g/cm³ as the answer for the density of oak?

Measuring the density of an irregular solid

This is, of course, the problem that Archimedes was trying to solve and his solution (apparently inspired by getting into a bath tub that was too full) was to use the idea of displacement. The solid will displace the same volume of water as its own volume. If there's room in the container, it rises. If not, it overflows.

Imagine trying to see if a gold necklace was pure. Knowing that the density of gold is 19.29 g/cm³, being able to dangle the necklace on a thread and having a glass of water full to the brim, you could carry out a simple experiment.

8. What procedure would you follow?

9. What measurements would you need to take?

10. What calculation would you then perform?

11. Why might this experiment probably not be very accurate?

Figure 1.12 How could you find out if this is pure gold?

Changes of state

Learning objectives:

- describe how, when substances change state, mass is conserved
- describe energy transfer in changes of state
- explain changes of state in terms of particles.

KEY WORDS

boil
changes of state
condense
conservation of mass
evaporate
freeze
melt
sublimate

When a liquid boils, the energy transferred to the liquid gives all the molecules enough energy to break away from the surface.

Conservation of mass

When substances change state, mass is conserved. If you start with 1 kg of ice and melt it you will have 1 kg of water. Nothing has been added or removed. The process is reversible. If you freeze the 1 kg of water you will end up with 1 kg of ice again.

This is an important idea as it shows that when the state of something is altered, no material has gone away or has been added. There are the same number of particles of the substance there. It is the arrangement that has been changed, not the amount. It also shows that material has the same mass, even though it might have changed state. Boiling 1 kg of water will produce 1 kg of steam.

1 State the type of change from a liquid to a solid.

Changing state

Changes of state occur when substances change from one state to another. The processes of changing from one state to another are:

- **melting:** changing from solid to liquid
- **freezing:** changing from liquid to solid
- **boiling:** changing from liquid to gas at the boiling point
- **evaporating:** changing from liquid to gas when the temperature is lower than the boiling point
- **condensing:** changing from gas to liquid
- **sublimating:** changing from solid to gas without going through the liquid state.

Changes of state are physical changes. Unlike a chemical change the change does not produce a new substance. If the change is reversed, the substance recovers its original properties.

DID YOU KNOW?

Dry ice is frozen carbon dioxide which turns directly from a solid to a gas at a temperature of –78.5 °C. The fog you see is a mixture of cold carbon dioxide gas and cold, humid air, created as the dry ice sublimates (Figure 1.13).

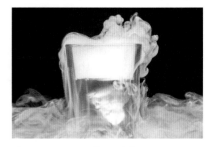

Figure 1.13 Dry ice sublimates

2 Suggest how you could prove that mass is conserved when ice melts.

3 Give an example of a change of state. Specify the material involved.

4 We often say 'it is freezing' when the temperature is cold outside. Explain why this is not an accurate statement.

Explaining changes of state

When a substance changes state, energy is transferred to change the arrangement of the particles.

When a substance melts, such as ice changing to water, energy must be transferred to the ice to change its state from solid to liquid.

In the solid state, such as ice, the particles are close-packed with strong bonds between them. Energy must be provided to weaken these bonds and allow the particles to move more freely in the liquid state (water). To change into a gas (steam) a lot of energy must be provided to break the bonds between the particles and allow the gas particles to spread out, filling the available space.

When a liquid cools down, the energy stored by the particles in the liquid decreases, allowing the particles to come closer together and form bonds (freezing). Energy is released to the surroundings. Energy is also released when a gas condenses to form a liquid.

Evaporation produces cooling (Figure 1.14). As a liquid warms up, the average speed of the particles in it increases. But not all the particles in the liquid will be travelling at the same speed (Figure 1.15). It is the faster particles with more energy which escape from the surface of the liquid, leaving behind the slower particles with less energy.

Figure 1.14 The sand in this pot is wet. Evaporation transfers thermal energy away from the inner pot and keeps the food cool

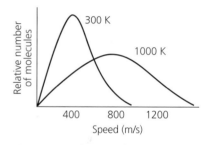

Figure 1.15 The particles in a liquid do not all travel at the same speed

5 Explain why you hang out washing rather than leaving it in a pile to dry.

6 Explain why evaporation produces cooling.

7 Suggest why being burned by steam is worse than being burned by hot water.

8 Explain how sweating can help to reduce body temperature.

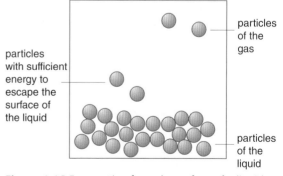

Figure 1.16 Evaporation from the surface of a liquid

Internal energy

Learning objectives:

- describe the particle model of matter
- understand what is meant by the internal energy of a system
- describe the effect of heating on the energy stored within a system.

KEY WORDS

internal energy
particle model

In air, the molecules of the gases hitting your face have an average speed of about 1600 km/h.

Particle model

Everything is made of small particles (atoms or molecules). This is the **particle model**.

The sizes of these particles are different for different materials. The particles are very hard. They cannot be squashed or stretched. But the distance between them can change. The particles are always moving. The higher the temperature the faster they move.

At the same temperature all particles have the same average kinetic energy. This means that heavy particles move slowly and light particles move quickly.

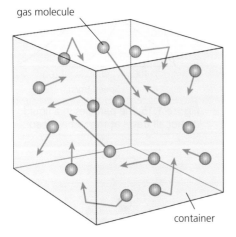

Figure 1.17 The gas particles in this container all have the same average kinetic energy.

1 Explain why the particles in solids, liquids and gases have kinetic energy.

2 Compare the speeds of heavy particles and light particles when they are at the same temperature.

Internal energy

The particles in solids, liquids and gases have kinetic energy because they are always moving. They also have potential energy because their motion keeps them separated. This opposes the forces trying to pull them together. The particles in gases have the most potential energy because they are furthest apart. The **internal energy** of a system is the total kinetic energy and potential energy of all the particles in the system.

3 Explain why the particles in solids, liquids and gases have potential energy.

4 Compare the amount of internal energy in a hot cup of tea with the internal energy in the Pacific Ocean. Justify your answer.

Changes in internal energy

The hotter a material is, the faster its particles move and the more energy it stores. If a hot object is in contact with a cold one, thermal energy is transferred between the two objects. When both are at the same temperature there is no further exchange of thermal energy between them.

You can cool a glass of water by adding ice cubes to it. The faster moving molecules of water transfer energy to the ice. The water decreases its thermal energy store and cools down. The energy stored in the ice increases and the ice melts.

Heating changes the energy stored in a system. It increases the energy of the particles that make it up. The increase in internal energy can have two effects.

When ice melts, the amount of energy stored in the system increases, causing a change of state. When there is a change of state there is no change in temperature. The increase in internal energy is used to weaken the bonds, for instance, changing a solid to a liquid.

If we carried on heating the melted ice, the energy stored in the system increases further. The increase in internal energy causes the temperature of the water to increase.

5 What happens to the internal energy of a system when it is heated?

6 A glass jar containing water is moved from inside a house to outside the house, where the temperature is –2 °C. Describe what happens to the internal energy of the glass and water.

7 Water can exist both in the liquid and the gaseous state at 100 °C.

   a Compare the amount of internal energy in steam at 100 °C with that of water at the same temperature.

   b Justify why using steam to power engines is more useful than using hot water.

DID YOU KNOW?

Water is unusual in that it expands as it freezes. It is most dense at 4 °C (Figure 1.18). When a pond freezes over, there is a layer of denser water at the bottom where fish can survive.

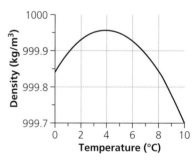

Figure 1.18 Water is most dense at 4 °C

Specific heat capacity

KEY WORDS

specific heat capacity

Learning objectives:

- describe the effect of increasing the temperature of a system in terms of particles
- state the factors that are affected by an increase in temperature of a substance
- explain specific heat capacity.

A cup of water at 50 °C and a bath of water at 50 °C have the same temperature but the bath of water has a greater store of thermal energy.

Heating up

When a liquid is heated, energy is transferred to the liquid and the temperature rises. The particles are close together and attract each other strongly. Their motion opposes the forces of attraction and keeps them separated. As the liquid is heated, it stores energy in this arrangement of particles. Its internal energy has increased.

1 **Describe the energy transfers that take place**

a **when a liquid is heated and**

b **when a liquid is left to cool.**

Increasing temperature

When a liquid is heated, its temperature increases. The temperature rise depends on:

- the mass of liquid heated
- the liquid being heated
- the energy input to the system.

2 **Dan is heating a large saucepan of water to boiling point. Explain why more energy is needed to do this than to heat a cup of water to the same temperature.**

3 **Milk does not need as much energy to raise its temperature by 10 °C as the same mass of water. Will hot milk give out less energy than the same amount of water at the same temperature when it cools down? Explain.**

Specific heat capacity

When an object is heated, energy is transferred and its temperature rises. The amount of energy needed to change the temperature of an object depends on the material the object is made from. This property is called the **specific heat capacity**.

> **MAKING CONNECTIONS**
>
> Chapter 1 has already introduced the idea of calculating the amount of energy in a system's energy store as its temperature changes. This is the same concept, but now we are looking at temperature change within the wider picture of internal energy and energy transfers.

The specific heat capacity of a substance, c, is the energy required per unit mass to raise the temperature by 1 °C. If the mass is measured in kilograms, the unit of c is J/kg °C. It is given by the equation:

change in thermal energy = mass × specific heat capacity
× change in temperature

$$\Delta E = mc\Delta\theta$$

where ΔE = change in thermal energy in J

   m = mass in kg

   c = specific heat capacity in J/kg °C

   $\Delta\theta$ = temperature change in °C.

Example: A change in thermal energy of 18 kJ of energy was supplied to a 2 kg steel block and raised its temperature from 20 °C to 40 °C. Calculate the specific heat capacity of steel.

$$\Delta E = mc\Delta\theta$$

ΔE = 18 kJ = 18 000 J

 m = 2 kg

$\Delta\theta$ = (40 − 20) = 20 °C

Specific heat capacity, $c = \Delta E / (m\Delta\theta)$

= 18 000 / (2 × 20) = 450 J/kg °C

Specific heat capacities of some materials

Material	Specific heat capacity in J/kg °C
water	4200
ice	2100
aluminium	880
copper	380

Water has a very high specific heat capacity. This means that, for a given mass, it absorbs a lot of energy when it warms up by a certain temperature increase. It also gives out a lot of energy when it cools down (Figure 1.19).

4 Calculate how much energy is needed to heat 100 g of water from 10 °C to 40 °C.

5 Water has a very high specific heat capacity. Describe a practical use of this.

6 A 2 kW electric heater supplies energy to a 0.5 kg copper kettle containing 1 kg of water.

   a Calculate the time taken to raise the temperature by 10 °C.

   b What have you assumed in doing this calculation?

7 Suggest why copper saucepans are sometimes used for cooking.

8 A 50 g copper mass is heated to 100 °C. It is then added to cup of 50 g of water. The water has a temperature of 20 °C before the mass is added.

   a Explain what happens to the temperatures of the copper mass and the water after the mass is added.

   b Suggest whether the final temperature of the water is closer to 20 °C or 100 °C. Justify your answer.

17

Figure 1.19 A domestic radiator contains water which is heated by a boiler

DID YOU KNOW?

Water needs lots of energy to heat it up and gives out lots of energy when it cools down. This is why a hot-water bottle is so effective in warming a bed. An equal mass of mercury would store only 1/30th as much energy, but would be 13 times heavier!

KEY INFORMATION

power (W) = work done (J) / time (s).

COMMON MISCONCEPTION

Do not confuse thermal energy transfer and temperature. Temperature is how hot an object is. A change in thermal energy does not always produce the same temperature change.

Specific latent heat

Learning objectives:

- explain what is meant by latent heat
- describe that when a change of state occurs it changes the energy stored but not the temperature
- perform calculations involving specific latent heat.

The latent heat of water is responsible for tornados, hurricanes and the fact that snow takes ages to melt.

Latent heat

When you heat a solid, such as a lump of ice, its temperature rises until it starts to change to a liquid. At its melting point, the temperature stays the same until all the ice has melted (Figure 1.20).

The temperature of the liquid then rises until it starts to change into a gas. At its boiling point, the temperature stays the same until all the liquid has turned into a gas. The temperature then starts to rise again.

Latent heat is the energy needed for a substance to change a state without a change in temperature.

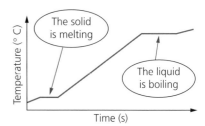

Figure 1.20 Temperature–time graph for heating a substance

1. Describe what is happening when the graph flattens out.

2. Energy is needed to turn water into steam. Suggest how the particle model explains this.

Changes of state

The amount of energy needed to change the state of a substance without a change in temperature depends on the material the substance is made from. All substances have a property called **specific latent heat.**

The specific latent heat is the amount of energy needed per unit mass to change the state of a substance without a change in temperature. Its SI unit is J/kg. It is given by the equation:

energy for a change of state = mass × specific latent heat

$$E = mL$$

where E = energy for a change of state in J

      m = mass in kg

      L = specific latent heat in J/kg.

Specific latent heat of fusion refers to a change of state from solid to liquid. **Specific latent heat of vaporisation** refers to a change of state from liquid to vapour.

Some specific latent heats

Change of state	Specific latent heat in J/kg
ice to water	340 000
water to steam	2 260 000

The specific latent heat of vaporisation is much greater than the specific latent heat of fusion. Most of this energy is used to separate the particles so they can form a gas, but some is required to push back the atmosphere as the gas forms.

3 Explain why is there no change in temperature when a block of ice melts.

4 Why is the specific latent heat of vaporisation much greater than the specific latent heat of fusion?

Latent heat calculations

(In these calculations use the specific heat capacities given in the table earlier on this page.)

Many calculations on specific and latent heat require you to find the energy needed to change the state as well as the temperature of an object. This involves using both specific heat capacity and latent heat equations.

$$\Delta E = m\, c\, \Delta \theta \qquad E = m\, L$$

5 Calculate the energy transferred from a glass of water to just melt 100 g of ice cubes at 0 °C.

6 **a** Calculate the total energy transferred when 200 g of ice cubes at 0 °C are changed to steam at 100 °C.
(Hint: Use the equation for specific heat capacity as well as the equation for specific latent heat.)

b Sketch and label a temperature–time graph for this transfer.

7 A block of ice at –2 °C was heated. After 7304 J of energy was transferred to the ice, the ice had melted and reached a temperature of 5°C. Calculate the mass of the ice.

DID YOU KNOW?

A jet of steam releases latent heat when it condenses (changes to a liquid). This can be used to heat drinks quickly (Figure 1.21).

Figure 1.21 Machines in cafes use steam to heat milk quickly

COMMON MISCONCEPTION

Heating does not always involve a change in temperature. When a change of state occurs, the energy supplied changes the energy stored (internal energy) but not the temperature.

MATHS SKILLS

Drawing and interpreting graphs

Learning objectives:

- plot a graph of temperature against time, choosing a suitable scale
- draw a line of best fit (which may be a curve)
- interpret a graph of temperature against time
- comment on the specific heat capacity and specific latent heat of a substance.

A graph of temperature against time for a substance can show quite a lot about what is going on. If we know how to read a graph we can work out what that might be.

Drawing a graph

To set out the axes for a graph, the **range** of values have to be identified. The maximum and minimum values should be known.

The number of units per square on the graph paper should be chosen with care. It's essential to select a **scale** that is easy to interpret. One that uses five large squares for 100 units is much easier to interpret than a scale that has, say, three large squares for 100 units. Sometimes it is better to use a smaller scale (e.g. two large squares for 100 units) and have a scale that is easier to interpret than to try to fill the page.

KEY INFORMATION

Suitable scales are 1, 2, 5 and 10 (or multiples of 10) units per square.

A group of students conducted an experiment where they recorded the temperature of stearic acid every minute as it cooled down from 90 °C. The results are shown in Table 1.1.

Table 1.1 Results from experiment on cooling stearic acid

Time (min)	Temperature (°C)	Time (min)	Temperature in (°C)
0:00	95.0	8:00	68.1
1:00	90.9	9:00	68.1
2:00	86.3	10:00	67.9
3:00	80.7	11:00	67.3
4:00	73.0	12:00	64.2
5:00	68.1	13:00	58.4
6:00	68.0	14:00	48.2
7:00	68.1	15:00	35.9
		16:00	25.0

MATHS

Some graphs will have a line or curve of best fit. A line of best fit goes roughly through the centre of all the plotted points. It does not go through all the points. The line of best fit could be a curve. If all the points fall close to the line (or curve), it suggests that the variables are closely linked. Look at the points carefully and see what would fit them well.

1. What are the maximum and minimum values that need to be plotted?

2. Draw and label axes for plotting this dataset.

3. Plot the points and draw a line of best fit.

4. Describe the features of the line of best fit.

Interpreting a graph

The graph in Figure 1.22 shows temperature against time for heating a lump of paraffin wax. The temperature was recorded using a datalogger. The rate at which energy was supplied to the wax stayed constant. The graph shows that the temperature of the solid wax increased until about 7 minutes and then stopped rising. It then started rising again at about 15 minutes.

5 Why is there a curve and not a straight line when the energy is being supplied at a constant rate?

6 What is happening between 7 and 15 minutes?

7 What is the melting point of paraffin wax?

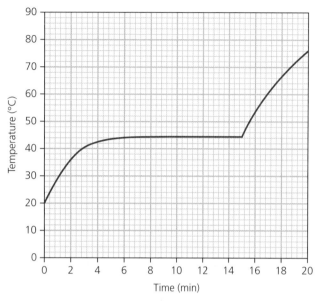

Figure 1.22 Graph of temperature against time for heating paraffin wax

Understanding the shape of the line

This graph shows a really important point. While the wax is melting, energy is being supplied but the temperature isn't changing. The energy being supplied is being used to change the state of the wax and while this is happening the temperature stays the same.

Now look at the graph you drew of temperature against time for stearic acid. This was cooling down but there are similarities.

8 Suggest an explanation for the shape of the graph.

9 What is happening between about 5 and 9 minutes?

10 What is the melting point of stearic acid?

11 Describe the shape of the graph with reference to what is happening with regard to the internal energy of the stearic acid.

12 Label the regions of the graphs for stearic acid and paraffin wax to show what is happening to the energy stored by the particles of the substances.

13 Explain how the shape of the graph in Figure 1.22 would change for a substance that had the same melting point but had a smaller specific heat capacity and a larger latent heat of fusion. Assume everything else (such as the mass of the substance and the heater) remains the same.

PRACTICAL

Investigating specific heat capacity

Learning objectives:

- use theories to develop a hypothesis
- evaluate a method and suggest improvements
- perform calculations to support conclusions.

KEY WORDS

energy store
energy transferred
specific heat
  capacity

A useful way of thinking about energy and energy transfers is the concept of stores. Energy can be stored in a variety of ways and one of those is by heating something up. If this object is put somewhere cooler then energy will be transferred from one store (the object) to another store (the surroundings).

These pages are designed to help you think about aspects of the investigation rather than to guide you through it step by step.

Using scientific ideas to plan an investigation

When a lump of brass is immersed in ice-cold water its temperature decreases. It would end up at 0°C (as long as we left it in contact with the ice for long enough). If we then take the brass out of the ice-cold water and put it into another beaker of hot water, thermal energy transfers from the store in the water to the brass. The brass warms up and the water cools down until they are both at the same temperature.

DID YOU KNOW?

Stone age man, Native American Indians and backwoodsmen all have used hot stones to boil water. Hot stones from a fire are dropped into a wooden bowl of cold water. Thermal energy stored in the stones is transferred to the water, making it hot enough to boil. This is an example of a decrease in one **energy store** producing an increase in another. You can make use of this method to find the specific heat capacity of different materials.

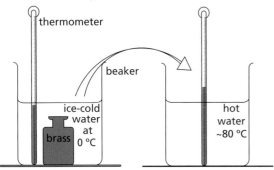

Figure 1.23 The lump of brass is transferred from the water at 0 °C to the hot water

KEY INFORMATION

~ 21 °C means about 21 °C

1. How could we find out what the temperature of the water became when the brass was added to it?

2. How could we calculate the decrease in temperature of the water?

3. How could we calculate the temperature rise of the brass?

4. What would happen to the temperature of the water and the brass in the second beaker if we left them for a long time (e.g. an hour)?

Evaluating the method

This experiment is used to find the **specific heat capacity** of brass by assuming that all the thermal energy transferred from the hot water increases the temperature of the lump of brass. We are equating the decrease in thermal energy store of the water to the increase in thermal energy store of the brass. If this assumption is not true, the method will not be valid.

5 The lump of brass has to be moved from one beaker to the other. Consider how this step in the method could affect the accuracy of the results.

6 The energy transferred from the water to the brass will cause the lump of brass in the second beaker to get hotter. Why will the energy transferred to the lump of brass not be stored there permanently?

7 What are the implications of your answers to questions 5 and 6 for the way the experiment is carried out?

8 Why is it important that the lump of brass is covered in water in the second beaker?

KEY INFORMATION

When thinking about this experiment, remember that energy tends to move from hotter regions to cooler ones.

Using the data to calculate a value for SHC

We find the specific heat capacity of brass by calculating the energy transferred into the water when its temperature increases and equating that to energy transferred out of the brass when its temperature decreases.

Decrease in energy stored by brass = increase in energy stored by water

$$m_{water} \times c_{water} \times \text{temperature increase}_{water}$$

$$= m_{brass} \times c_{brass} \times \text{temperature decrease}_{brass}$$

The final temperature of the water and brass is the same (they reach thermal equilibrium). As long as we know the values of the mass of water, mass of brass, specific heat capacity of water and initial temperatures of the water and brass, we can find the unknown value for the specific heat capacity of brass.

9 There is 250g of water (c_{water} = 4200 J/kg°C) in the second beaker and its temperature rises from 17°C to 26°C. Determine how much energy has been transferred into it.

10 How much energy can we assume has been transferred out of the brass when it is put into the second beaker?

11 If the brass had been in boiling water, by how much would its temperature have decreased?

12 The lump of brass has a mass of 150g. Calculate the specific heat capacity of brass.

13 Explain why is this method likely to give a lower value for the specific heat capacity than its true value.

Particle motion in gases

Learning objectives:

- relate the temperature of a gas to the average kinetic energy of the particles
- explain how a gas has a pressure
- explain that changing the temperature of a gas held at constant volume changes its pressure.

Inside a rocket, the fast-moving gas particles colliding with the walls create a force. The fast-moving gas particles moving out of the bottom of the rocket propel the rocket upwards like in Figure 1.24. For a gas completely enclosed in a container, the forces arising from the collisions cause a pressure.

Figure 1.24 The Space Shuttle taking off

Temperature and pressure of a gas

The particles in a gas move around **randomly**. These particles have kinetic energy. They move about freely at high speed.

The higher the temperature, the faster the particles move and the more kinetic energy they have. The temperature of a gas is related to the average kinetic energy of the molecules. As the temperature increases, the particles move faster. They gain more kinetic energy.

1. **What happens to the molecules of a gas when the gas is heated?**

2. **How does the particle model explain temperature?**

The molecules of a gas collide with each other as well as with the walls of their container (Figure 1.25). When they hit a wall there is a force on the wall. Pressure is equal to the force on the wall divided by the area over which the force acts. The total force exerted by all the molecules inside the container that strike a unit area of the wall is the **gas pressure**.

(3) Describe, in terms of particles, how a gas exerts a pressure.

(4) Suggest why the pressure inside a bicycle tyre increases when you pump more air into it.

Changing the temperature of a gas

Air is sealed in a container (Figure 1.26). If we keep the mass and volume of the air constant, an increase in the temperature will increase the pressure of the gas.

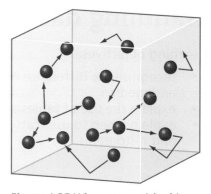

Figure 1.25 When gas particles hit a wall of their container there is a force on the wall. This force is the pressure of the gas

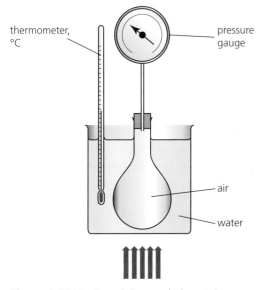

thermometer, °C

pressure gauge

air

water

Figure 1.26 Heating air in a sealed container

DID YOU KNOW?

The internal energy of a compressed gas can be used as an energy store. When the pressure is released in a controlled way, the expanding gas can be used to turn a turbine to generate electricity when needed.

There are the same number of particles because the container is sealed, and there is the same mass of gas. As the container is sealed the volume of gas is also constant. As the particles have more energy, they move faster, hitting the walls more often and with greater force, increasing the pressure.

(5) How do we know that the mass of gas is constant?

(6) Explain, using ideas about energy, why the pressure of gas increases if it gets hotter.

REMEMBER!

Gas particles collide with each other and with the walls of their container, but only collisions with walls contribute to the pressure of the gas.

Handling data

Learning objectives:

- recognise the difference between mean, mode and median
- explain the use of tables and frequency tables
- explain when to use scatter diagrams, bar charts and histograms.

KEY WORDS

continuous data	independent
frequency table	variable
scatter diagram	dependent
correlation	variable
line of best fit	mean
bar chart	median
histogram	mode
	anomalous

The purpose of an experiment is to find out the relationship, if there is any, between the variables you are investigating. You do this by looking for a pattern in the data that is collected. It is difficult to spot a pattern from a mass of numbers, but it is much easier from a picture – a graph or a chart.

Tables and frequency tables

Tables are used to capture the information from an experiment and from graphs. A simple table is used for **continuous data**, where information is measured on a continuous scale – for example, when loading a spring with different weights and measuring the extension produced (Table 1.2).

Force (N)	Extension of spring (mm)		
	1st reading	2nd reading	3rd reading
10	8	9	7
20	19	16	15
30	23	21	29
40	34	32	33
50	35	44	39

Table 1.2 Investigating the relationship between force and the extension of a spring

Another way of collecting data is to use tally marks and make a **frequency table**. This method is best where your data can only have certain values such as shoe sizes, or the information can be categorised such as the names of countries.

Using scatter diagrams, bar charts and histograms

The data in Table 1.1 is continuous and is best displayed by using a **scatter diagram** (Figure 1.27). Plotting the data points will give a clearer picture of the relationship between the two variables, to see if there is a **correlation**. If there is

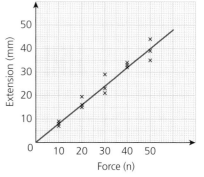

Figure 1.27 Data from Table 1.2 A scatter graph with a line of best fit

Age	Tally	Number of people
11–20	ЖНТ IIII	9
21–30	ЖНТ ЖНТ ЖНТ I	16
31–40	ЖНТ ЖНТ II	12
41–50	IIII	4
51–60	ЖНТ I	6
61–70	I	1

Table 1.3 Frequency distribution of the ages of people on a street

a correlation, you can draw a **line of best fit** (this may be a curve) and then use this to extrapolate further trends and information.

The data in Table 1.4 is not continuous. It is best represented by a bar chart (Figure 1.28).

The data in Table 1.3 is grouped. It is best represented by a **histogram**. Each column represents a group of data, and the frequency of the data is shown by the area of each bar (Figure 1.29).

Country	Tally marks	Number of new nuclear power stations being built
Russia	IIII II	7
UK	IIII	5
India	IIII I	6
USA	IIII	5
Pakistan	III	3

Table 1.4 Number of new nuclear power stations being built in selected countries

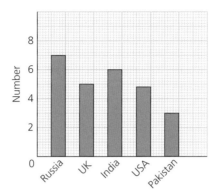

Figure 1.28 Data from Table 1.3: A bar chart

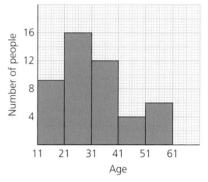

Figure 1.29

Renewable energy resource with the greatest share of total renewable energy production	Frequency
Solar	2
Biomass & renewable waste	31
Geothermal	0
Hydropower	0
Wind	1

Table 1.5 Renewable energy sources in the EU for 2013

Mean, median and mode

To find the **mean**, add up all the values and divide by the number of values.

Example: The mean of four repeated measurements of temperature, 7°C, 12°C, 9°C and 11°C, is

$$\frac{7°C + 12°C + 9°C + 11°C}{4} = 9.75°C$$

or 10°C, rounded to the nearest whole number.

The **median** is the middle value when the values are rearranged in sequence. For example, from the data set above:

7°C, 9°C, 11°C, 12°C

When there are an odd number of data points, it is easy to spot the median. If there is an even number of data points, calculate the median as the midpoint of the two middle values. In this example, the median is halfway between 9°C and 11°C. So the median is 10°C, even though that is not one of the data points.

The **mode** is the value, or item, that occurs most frequently in a set of data. It is easy to spot the mode in a frequency table. In Table 1.5 the mode is 'Biomass & renewable waste'.

When should you use which average? In the repeated measurements of temperature above, the mean and the median turn out to be the same value. But if one of the measurements was **anomalous**, for example, 22°C instead of 12°C, this would skew the mean.

Example: The mean of 7°C, 22°C, 9°C and 11°C is

$$\frac{7°C + 22°C + 9°C + 11°C}{4}$$

$$= 12.25°C$$

or 12°C, rounded to the nearest whole number.

The median, 10°C, is unchanged, so it is the more accurate representation of your data set when there are some anomalous results (or 'outliers').

Check your progress

You should be able to:

☐ Use density = mass/volume to calculate density → ☐ Use particle diagrams to communicate ideas about relative densities of different states
☐ Use the density equation to calculate mass and volume → ☐ Link the particle model for solids, liquids and gases with density values in terms of the arrangements of the atoms or molecules

☐ Describe changes of state as physical changes → ☐ Describe how mass is conserved when substances change state
☐ Explain that changes of state are physical, not chemical, changes because the material recovers its original properties if the change is reversed → ☐ Explain that changes of state conserve mass

☐ Describe how heating raises the temperature of a system → ☐ Describe that heating raises the temperature or changes the state of a system but not at the same time → ☐ Explain that internal energy is the total energy stored by all the particles that make up a system

☐ Describe the effect of an increase in temperature on the motion of the particles → ☐ Use the specific heat capacity equation to calculate the energy required to change the temperature of a certain mass of a substance → ☐ Use the specific heat capacity equation to calculate mass, specific heat capacity or temperature change

☐ State that when an object changes state there is no change in temperature → ☐ Describe the latent heats of fusion and of vaporisation
☐ Use the equation $E = mL$ → ☐ Use the particle model to explain why the latent heat of vaporisation is much larger than the latent heat of fusion

☐ In the particle model the higher the temperature the faster the molecules move. → ☐ Use the particle model to explain the effect on temperature of increasing the pressure of a gas at constant volume → ☐ Describe that the temperature of a gas is related to the average kinetic energy of the molecules

Worked example

1 **Alex is heating a beaker of water by the rays of a sunlamp. The energy transferred was 21 000 J. The time taken for the water to increase by 10 °C was 6000 seconds. Calculate the power supplied by the sunlamp.**

3.5

This is the correct numerical answer, but

a You have not given any units to the number. Always give the unit to the quantity.

b You have not shown any working. When working a calculation; write the equation, and show step by step how you do the calculation.

2 **Explain how raising the temperature of a gas, keeping the volume constant, increases the pressure exerted by the gas.**

The high temperature makes the molecules vibrate faster so there is a stronger force on the side of the container.

You are on the right lines. It is the force of the molecules hitting the side of the container that creates the pressure. With a gas, the molecules are no longer vibrating but they are free to move around at speed. Heating increases the energy they store.

3 **What does it mean to say that the changes of state are reversible?**

It means that the changes go both ways.

Correct, but you should give an example as well. Give an example of a change that goes both ways, e.g. water turns to steam and steam turns back to water.

4 **Explain what heating does to the energy stores of a system.**

Heating raises the total energy inside the system.

Yes it does, but again you should aim to give more specific information about the system. You need to mention the energy transfers that have taken place.

End of chapter questions

Getting started

1. Label these diagrams as solid, liquid and gas. `1 Mark`

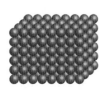

2. Describe how these models represent a solid, liquid and gas. `2 Marks`

3. Give the state that a gas turns into when it condenses. `1 Mark`

4. Describe how energy is needed to change the state of a substance. `1 Mark`

5. Write the relationship between mass, volume and density. `1 Mark`

6. An object has a mass of 100 g and a volume of 25 cm³. Calculate its density. `1 Mark`

7. The specific latent heat of fusion of water = 340 000 J/kg. Explain carefully what this means. `2 Marks`

8. Calculate the amount of energy needed to change the temperature of 2 kg of water by 10 °C using the equation $\Delta E = mc\Delta\theta$. The specific heat capacity of water is 4200 J/kg°C. `1 Mark`

Going further

9. How do we describe the energy that equals the total kinetic and potential energies of the particles in a substance? `1 Mark`

10. Explain why there are two different latent heats for each substance. `1 Mark`

11. What is meant by the internal energy of a system? `2 Marks`

12. 2.0 kg of water was placed in a saucepan and heated to 100 °C. The water then completely boiled into steam.

    Here is some data about water and steam:

    density of water = 1000 kg/m³

    density of steam = 0.59 kg/m³

    The latent heat of vaporisation of water = 2 260 000 J/kg

    a Explain why the density of steam is much smaller than the density of the water. `1 Mark`

    b Calculate the volume of the steam that was produced once all of the water had boiled. `1 Mark`

    c Use the equation $E = mL$ to calculate how much energy was needed to boil the water into steam at 100 °C. `1 Mark`

13. Water in an ice cube tray is put into a freezer. Explain what happens the energy stored inside the system. `2 Marks`

14 Which of these is the correct unit for density? `1 Mark`

   a kg

   b m³

   c m³/kg

   d kg/m³

More challenging

15 When a substance changes state, one energy store increases and another decreases.

   a What part of the substance is always conserved? `1 Mark`

   b State what the two possible results are when a substance is heated. `1 Mark`

16 Explain how raising the temperature of a gas, keeping the volume constant, increases the pressure exerted by the gas. `2 Marks`

17 A block of material has dimensions of 6cm × 4cm × 3cm and a mass of 60g. Explain whether it float in water (which has a density of 1g/cm³)? `3 Marks`

18 Explain how sweating transfers energy. `3 Marks`

Most demanding

19 A 2 kg block of copper is given 8.88 kJ of energy to raise its temperature by 10 °C. Calculate the specific heat capacity of copper. `2 Marks`

20 A science demonstrator poured some liquid nitrogen into a plastic bottle until it was about 1/3 full. She then screwed the lid tightly on the bottle and dropped the bottle into a bucket of warm water. She then quickly ran to a safe distance before the bottle exploded.

Use ideas about energy and particles to explain the physics behind this demonstration. The boiling point of nitrogen is −196 °C. `6 Marks`

21 The latent heat of fusion of water is 3.3×10^5 J/kg and the latent heat of vaporisation of water is 2.5×10^6 J/kg. Suggest why these values are significantly different. `2 Marks`

`Total: 40 Marks`

FORCES

SPEED AND CHANGE OF SPEED

- Average speed can be calculated by dividing the distance travelled by the time taken.
- If the speed of a car is changing it is accelerating.
- A journey can be represented on a distance–time graph.

FORCES CAUSE ACCELERATION

- Forces can speed things up or slow them down.
- The bigger the force the bigger the change in speed.
- Forces can be contact forces, such as an engine powering a car, or non-contact forces, such as gravity.

FALLING SAFELY

- Falling objects accelerate due to the force of gravity.
- Their acceleration is reduced due to the upward force of air resistance or drag.
- When a parachute opens the drag force increases.

IN THIS CHAPTER YOU WILL FIND OUT ABOUT:

HOW CAN WE DESCRIBE MOTION?

- Acceleration is a useful way of showing how speed is changing.
- When a car changes velocity it is accelerating.
- Circular motion needs a force towards the centre of the circle even if the speed is constant.

HOW CAN UNDERSTANDING FORCES MAKE DRIVING SAFER?

- Safety features such as seat belts and air bags reduce the force acting on the human body in an impact.
- This is because they reduce the body's rate of change of momentum.

HOW DOES THE MOTION OF A FALLING OBJECT CHANGE AS IT FALLS?

- In the absence of air resistance, all falling objects accelerate at the same rate.
- An object falling through water or the atmosphere reaches a terminal velocity when the resultant force is zero.

Scalars and vectors

Learning objectives:

- define distance, displacement, speed, velocity and accleration
- recognise the difference between scalar and vector quantities
- state examples of scalar and vector quantities.

People sometimes use terms like distance and speed in a wide range of ways. We may often talk about the speed of a car or of our walking without thinking about the importance of direction. However, in science we use these terms in a very particular way. We're interested in direction and size.

What are distance and speed?

Distance is a measure of how far apart two objects are. In science we measure distance using the SI unit of the metre, symbol m.

Speed is a measure of the distance travelled in a particular time, measured in metres per second (m/s).

Both of these quantities are scalar, meaning that they have a size but no particular direction. In many situations in science it is important to take the direction of a quantity into account – we need a different measurement quantity called a vector.

Figure 2.1 shows an everyday situation in which direction is important. Imagine taking a walk through a woodland. You need to change direction frequently to walk around trees or other plants. From point A to point B is 100 m in a particular direction, north east. However, to walk from A to B involves covering a much greater distance with many changes of direction.

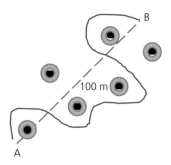

Figure 2.1 A walk in a woodland – the change in your position when walking from A to B is different from the total distance you walk

1. If you walked in a circle of radius 10 m (see Figure 2.2), what distance would you cover in one complete circle?

2. When you have completed your circular walk, what is your position?

Calculating distance and speed from measurements

Remember that

distance = speed × time

and so

$$\text{speed} = \frac{\text{distance}}{\text{time}}$$

In a laboratory experiment, two light gates are set up at a measured distance of 2 m apart on a smooth, flat surface. A trolley is pushed so it moves in a straight line along the surface. When the trolley breaks the first light gate beam, the datalogger starts a timer. When the trolley breaks the second light gate beam, the timer is stopped.

3. If the measured time is 0.5 s, what is the average speed of the trolley?

Scalar and vector quantities

A **scalar** quantity has magnitude (size) only.

A **vector** quantity has magnitude and direction.

A vector quantity can be represented by an arrow. The length of the arrow represents the magnitude and the direction of the arrow shows its direction.

Force is an example of a vector quantity.

Scalar	speed, distance
Vector	velocity, displacement

For example: speed = 10 m/s but velocity = 10 m/s due north.

Distance is a measure of how far an object moves but doesn't indicate the direction it has moved in; it is therefore a scalar quantity. **Displacement** is sometimes used instead. It includes both the distance moved and the direction so it is a vector quantity. It is measured as a straight line from the start point to the end point.

4. a Which of the following are vector quantities?

    mass   acceleration   force

    temperature   energy   momentum

  b Explain your answers.

5. Draw two arrows to represent vectors of 20 m/s due south and 10 m/s due north.

6. A runner runs a 400 m race around a track. If he finishes at the same place as he started, what is his final distance and displacement?

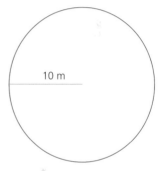

Figure 2.2 Circular walk of radius 10 m

KEY INFORMATION

Velocity is speed in a particular direction.

Speed

Learning objectives:

- calculate speed using distance travelled divided by time taken
- calculate speed from a distance–time graph
- recall that distance = speed × time
- measure the gradient of a distance–time graph at any point.

The astronauts who landed on the Moon travelled at an average speed of 8000 km/h to get there.

Speed and average speed

Speed tells us how fast something is moving.

If a car has a speed of 50 km/h it means it travels 50 km in 1 hour.

$$\text{speed } (v) = \frac{\text{distance } (d)}{\text{time } (t)} = \frac{d}{t}$$

You can convert a speed in km/h to m/s.

$$50 \text{ km/h} = \frac{50\,000 \text{ m}}{3600 \text{ s}} = 13.9 \text{ m/s}$$

We usually calculate its **average** speed because speed changes during a journey. It is rarely constant.

$$\text{average speed} = \frac{\text{total distance}}{\text{total time}}$$

Example: A Formula 1 racing car driver completes a 520 km race in 2 hours. Calculate the average speed.

$$\text{average speed} = \frac{\text{total distance}}{\text{total time}} = \frac{520 \text{ km}}{2 \text{ h}} = 260 \text{ km/h}$$

1 Explain why it is usually impossible to maintain a constant (steady) speed during a car journey.

2 Abi swam 50 m in $2\frac{1}{2}$ minutes. Calculate her average speed in m/s.

3 Farah walks 10 km in one and three quarter hours. What is her average speed in m/s?

The distance travelled in a specific time can be calculated using the equation:

distance travelled = speed × time

4 A snail travels at an average speed of 0.5 mm/s. How far does it travel in 1 hour?

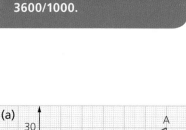

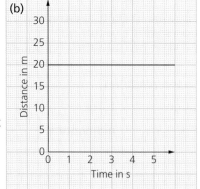

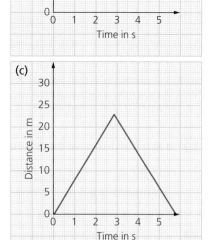

Figure 2.3 Distance–time graphs (a) object travelling at a constant speed (b) object stationary (c) object travelling and returning to its original place

Distance–time graphs

Drawing a graph of distance against time shows how the distance moved by a car from its starting point changes over time. It is easier to interpret than simply looking at a table of results. Look at the graphs shown in Figures 2.3a–c.

The **gradient** of a **distance–time graph** is equal to the speed of the object.

The gradient of the graph in Figure 2.4a

$$= \frac{AC}{BC} = \frac{(30\text{ m} - 15\text{ m})}{(6\text{ s} - 0)} = \frac{15\text{ m}}{6\text{ s}} = 2.5\text{ m/s}$$

So the speed is 2.5 m/s.

5 How would the graph change if the object went faster?

- **A straight line indicates the speed is constant. A curved line shows the speed is changing.**
- **When the gradient increases the speed increases.**
- **When the gradient decreases the speed decreases.**

6 **a** Sketch a distance–time graph for a car that is slowing down.

b Describe how the speed changes for the car in Figure 2.4.

Tangents to a distance–time graph

If an object is travelling at a steady speed, its distance–time graph will be a straight line (Figure 2.3a). However, if its speed is changing the line of the graph will be curved (Figure 2.5). We can find the speed at any particular point by drawing a **tangent** to the line and measuring the gradient of the tangent.

For example, if we wanted to know the speed of this object after it had travelled 80 m, we would draw a tangent to the line at the point for 80 m and find its gradient.

The gradient of the tangent to the curve

$$= \frac{(140\text{ m} - 20\text{ m})}{(9\text{ s} - 4\text{ s})} = \frac{120\text{ m}}{5\text{ s}} = 24\text{ m/s}$$

So the speed at this time is 24 m/s.

7 For the distance–time graph in Figure 2.5, describe how the gradient of the graph changes from 0 to 10 s. What does this tell you about how the speed changes?

We can also determine the average speed for the whole journey, by connecting the start point and the end point and drawing a straight line. The gradient of this line is the average speed.

8 Calculate the average speed for the entire journey shown by the distance–time graph in Figure 2.5.

> **KEY INFORMATION**
>
> Typical speeds are
> - 1 m/s walking
> - 3 m/s running
> - 6 m/s cycling
> - 0 to 34 m/s wind (11 m/s is a strong breeze, 34 m/s is a hurricane!)
> - 330 m/s sound (in air, near sea level)

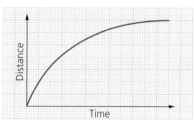

Figure 2.4 A distance–time graph for a car

> **KEY INFORMATION**
>
> **If the speed is changing, we say the motion is non-uniform.**

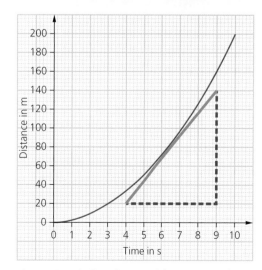

Figure 2.5 Finding the speed from a curved distance–time graph

Acceleration

Learning objectives:
- describe acceleration
- calculate acceleration

KEY WORDS
....
acceleration
deceleration
air resistance
(or drag)

A car may go around a roundabout at a constant speed but it is accelerating.

Acceleration

- When the velocity of a car is increasing it is **accelerating**.
- When the velocity of a car is decreasing it is **decelerating**. Its acceleration is negative.

The faster the velocity changes the greater the acceleration. A car which has a high acceleration reaches a high speed in a short time.

1 Car A accelerates from 10 m/s to 40 m/s in 6 s. Car B accelerates from 20 m/s to 30 m/s in 5 s. Determine which car has the greater acceleration.

DID YOU KNOW?

On the Moon the acceleration of free fall is only 1.6 m/s^2. As there is no atmosphere a feather would fall with the same acceleration as a lump of lead.

There is a story that a famous scientist called Galileo dropped two cannon balls – one large and one small – at the same time from the top of the leaning tower of Pisa (Figure 2.7). The balls reached the ground at the same time. This showed that both objects accelerated at the same rate and so the acceleration due to gravity does not depend on size. From this experiment, scientists deduced that all objects accelerate at the same rate under gravity (about 10 m/s^2).

Figure 2.6 The leaning tower of Pisa

If an object is dropped its speed increases as it falls. It accelerates because it is pulled towards the centre of the Earth due to the force of gravity.

If a ball and a feather are dropped the ball reaches the ground first because the feather has a large surface area. This slowing down force is called **air resistance** or **drag**.

2 Explain why a ball accelerates when you drop it.

3 Why does a feather fall more slowly than a ball?

4 What happens when you throw a ball upwards?

Calculating acceleration

A sports car speeds up to 40 km/h in 5 s and a van speeds up to 40 km/h in 10 s. The acceleration of the car is twice as big as the acceleration of the van.

You can work out the acceleration of the car or van using the equation:

$$\text{acceleration} = \frac{\text{change in velocity}}{\text{time taken}}$$

$$a = \frac{\Delta v}{t}$$

If change of velocity Δv is in m/s and time t is in s, acceleration a is in m/s².

Example: A car accelerates from 10 m/s to 30 m/s in 8 s. Calculate its acceleration.

$$\text{Acceleration} = \frac{\text{change in velocity}}{\text{time taken}}$$

$$= \frac{(30 \text{ m/s} - 10 \text{ m/s})}{8 \text{ s}}$$

$$= 2.5 \text{ m/s}^2$$

MATHS

The symbol Δ means the difference or change in a quantity. Δv means a change in velocity.

5 A car takes 8 s to increase its velocity from 10 m/s to 30 m/s. What is its average acceleration?

6 A car has an acceleration of +2 m/s²

   a What does this tell you about the velocity of the car?

   b What is meant by an acceleration of –2 m/s²?

7 Kevin is driving his car at 24 m/s. He brakes and stops in 3 s. Find his acceleration.

8 Jane is driving at a speed of 72 km/h. She accelerates to 108 km/h in 5 s. Find her acceleration in m/s².

9 A glacier is accelerating at 4mm/s/year. Explain carefully what this means.

MATHS

Remember – to change a speed in km/h to m/s: $\times \frac{1000}{3600}$.

E.g. 180 km/h

$$= \frac{(180 \times 1000)}{3600}$$

$$= 50 \text{ m/s}.$$

Calculations of motion

KEY WORDS

uniform motion

Learning objectives:

- describe motion with uniform acceleration
- use an equation for motion with uniform acceleration
- apply this equation to vertical motion.

On 15 October 1997 Thrust SSC (Figure 2.8), driven by Andy Green, broke the land speed record, reaching a speed of 763 mph, measured over a distance of 1 mile.

Describing motion

Uniform acceleration is a situation in which acceleration is defined as constant.

We use these symbols when we are describing motion:

s = displacement in m
u = initial velocity in m/s
v = final velocity in m/s
a = acceleration in m/s^2

Figure 2.8 Andy Green was required to do two 1 mile runs in opposite directions

1 What is meant by:

  a initial velocity?
  b final velocity?

2 Why are the units for acceleration different from those for velocity?

An equation for uniform acceleration

When an object accelerates uniformly you can use this equation to link initial and final velocities, acceleration and distance:

(final velocity (m/s))^2 – (initial velocity (m/s))^2 = 2 × acceleration (m/s^2) × displacement (m)

$$v^2 = u^2 + 2as$$

Example: A car accelerates from 8.0 m/s at 2.5 m/s^2 for the next 11 m. What is its final velocity?

u = initial velocity = 8.0 m/s
a = acceleration = 2.5 m/s^2
s = displacement = 11 m

Substitute the values into the equation:

$$v^2 = 8^2 + (2 \times 2.5 \times 11) = 64 + 55 = 119$$
Therefore $v = \sqrt{119}$
$$= 11 \text{ m/s (to 2 significant figures)}$$

Example:

A train approaching a red signal has a speed of 10 m/s. The signal then changes to green and the train accelerates. By the

ADVICE

Remember that s means displacement. Make sure you don't confuse this with speed.

KEY INFORMATION

To use this equation, we need to substitute values into it. We need to know three values and from these we can work out the fourth.

MATHS

Notice that it is only u that is squared and that the multiplication has to be done before the addition; you must then take the square root to get v. Also notice that the answer is rounded to 2 significant figures, because the data is to 2 significant figures.

time it has travelled another 1000 m it is now travelling at 20 m/s. What is its acceleration?

Rearrange $v^2 = u^2 + 2as$ to give $2as = v^2 - u^2$

$$a = \frac{(v^2 - u^2)}{2s}$$

Substituting values:

$$a = \frac{(20^2 - 10^2)}{2 \times 1000}$$
$$= \frac{(400 - 100)}{2000}$$
$$= \frac{300}{2000} = 0.15 \, \text{m/s}^2$$

3 An aircraft accelerates from rest at 2.5 m/s². Its take-off speed is 60 m/s. What length of runway does it need to take off?

4 A car accelerates from rest at 3 m/s² along a straight road. How far has the car travelled after 4 s?

5 A train is travelling at 40 m/s when its brakes are applied. This produces a deceleration of 2 m/s². Determine the distance the train travels before stopping.

> **REMEMBER!**
> ....
> When the object is slowing down, v will have a smaller value than u.

Applying the equation to vertical motion

Useful points to remember:

- If there is no air resistance, gravity gives a falling object an acceleration of approximately 10 m/s² downwards. When a ball is thrown upwards it decelerates. Acceleration is then equal to –10 m/s². Acceleration is negative.
- When the ball falls back to the ground it accelerates. Acceleration = +10 m/s².
- The equation can only be used when an object travels with constant uniform acceleration in a straight line.

Example:

A ball is thrown vertically upwards at 20 m/s. Ignoring air resistance and taking $g = 10$ m/s² calculate how high it goes.

We know that when it reaches the highest point it will be (momentarily) stationary, so velocity, $v = 0$.

$u = 20$ m/s
$v = 0$ m/s
$a = -10$ m/s²
$v^2 = u^2 + 2as$
$0 = (20)^2 + (2 \times -10 \times s)$
$0 = 400 - 20s$
$20s = 400$, so $s = 20$ m

6 A ball is thrown upwards with a velocity of 10 m/s. How high does it go? Assume $g = 10$ m/s².

7 An apple drops from a tree and falls 2.5 m to the ground. What is its speed when it hits the ground? Assume $g = 10$ m/s² and ignore air resistance.

Velocity–time graphs

Learning objectives:

- draw velocity–time graphs
- calculate acceleration using a velocity–time graph
- calculate displacement using a velocity–time graph.

KEY WORDS

velocity–time
  graph
sketch graph
gradient
rate of change
displacement

Constant acceleration does not mean constant velocity.

Velocity–time graphs

A **velocity–time graph** shows how the velocity of a moving object changes over time.

1 The table gives some velocities of a racing car at different times from the start of a race. Draw a velocity–time graph for the racing car.

> **REMEMBER!**
>
> Don't confuse distance–time and velocity–time graphs. Look at the axis labels carefully.

Time (s)	0	1	2	3	4	6	8	10	12
Velocity (m/s)	0	10	20	29	36	50	59	64	64

A graph is easier to interpret than a table of results.

When drawing velocity–time graphs remember that the velocity scale will have positive and negative values if there is a change in direction.

A **sketch graph** does not have plotted points, just the shape of the graph and the parts of the journey where the velocity is positive or negative (Figure 2.9). A sketch graph does not usually need numbers or units on the axes.

2 A car brakes and reverses. Which of the graphs in Figure 2.9 shows this? Describe what the other two graphs show.

3 A tube train travels between two stations, A and B. Sketch a velocity–time graph for a journey from A to B and back to A.

Acceleration

The **gradient** of a velocity–time graph (Figure 2.10) shows how velocity changes with time. This is the **rate of change** of velocity or acceleration. A steep gradient means the acceleration is large. The object's velocity is changing rapidly.

$$\text{Acceleration} = \frac{\text{change in velocity}}{\text{time taken}}$$

$$= \text{gradient of a velocity–time graph.}$$

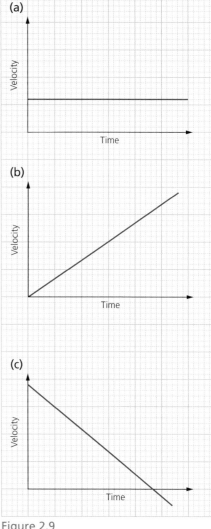

Figure 2.9

4 Calculate the acceleration in each of the graphs in Figure 2.10.

5 A motor cycle travelling at 20 m/s takes 5 s to stop. What is its average acceleration?

6 A truck travelling at 25 m/s puts on its brakes for 4 s. This produces an acceleration of −2 m/s². What is the truck's velocity after braking?

HIGHER TIER ONLY

Displacement

Displacement is equal to the area under a velocity–time graph.

If we have a velocity–time graph and want to know the displacement of the object, we can find this out by measuring the area under the line.

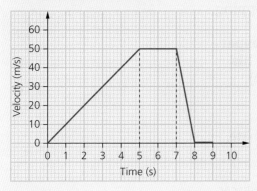

Figure 2.11

Example:

For the journey shown in Figure 2.11 we can divide the area under the line into three simple shapes.

The area of the triangle on the left is $\frac{1}{2} \times 5$ s $\times 50$ m/s = 125 m, the area of the rectangle is 2 s $\times 50$ m/s = 100 m and the area of the second triangle is $\frac{1}{2} \times 1$ s $\times 50$ m/s = 25 m. So the total distance travelled by the object is 250 m.

7 **a** Describe the motion of a train that has the graph shown in Figure 2.12.

b How far did the train travel?

8 Amy is cycling through a town.

- For the first 10 s she travelled at a constant velocity.
- She started to climb a hill so she slowed down.
- At the top of the hill she had to stop for some traffic lights.
- When the lights turned green she accelerated away. Sketch a velocity–time graph for Amy's journey.

9 A stone was thrown upwards. Which of the graphs in Figure 2.10 could represent the motion of the stone? Describe how the graph could be extended to show the motion of the stone as it fell back down.

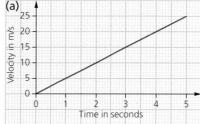

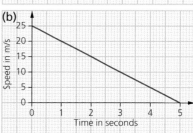

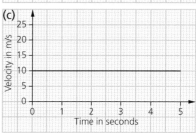

Figure 2.10 Velocity–time graphs

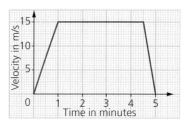

Figure 2.12 Velocity–time graph for a train

DID YOU KNOW?

Acceleration is a change in velocity over time. But we often use change of speed over time when calculating acceleration in situations where the direction is not important.

MATHS SKILLS

Making estimates of calculations

Learning objectives:

- estimate the results of simple calculations
- round numbers to make an estimate
- calculate order of magnitude.

In 1945 the nuclear physicist Enrico Fermi estimated the energy released by the first atomic bomb test by dropping small pieces of paper from his hand. He based his estimate only on the displacement of the scraps of paper (about 2.5 m) while the blast wave was passing and his distance from the site of the explosion (about 15 km).

Making sensible estimates

It is often useful to **estimate** a quantity. To make an estimate, make a sensible approximation. The symbol ~ means 'approximately equal to'.

Example: Estimate the average acceleration of a typical family car that accelerates from rest to a velocity of 100 km/h (about 30 m/s).

Make a sensible approximation of the time taken to accelerate: around 6 s.

The initial velocity is zero.

$$\text{acceleration} = \frac{\text{change in velocity}}{\text{time taken}}$$
$$\sim \frac{(30\,\text{m/s} - 0\,\text{m/s})}{6\,\text{s}}$$
$$\sim 5\,\text{m/s}^2$$

Example: Estimate the sprinting speed for a typical adult.

Make a sensible approximation of the time he or she takes to sprint 100 m: around 15 s.

$$\text{speed} = \frac{\text{distance}}{\text{time}}$$
$$= \frac{(100\,\text{m})}{15\,\text{s}}$$
$$= 6.67\,\text{m/s}$$

Write estimates to one significant figure.

speed ~ 7 m/s

1. Estimate the volume of this book. Show your working and assumptions.

2. Estimate the running speed for a typical adult over a distance of 500 m. Show your working and assumptions.

Estimating the result of a calculation by rounding

It is often useful to estimate the result of a calculation without using a calculator. Do this by **rounding** quantities up or down to one significant figure.

Example: Without using a calculator, estimate the deceleration of a van that makes an emergency stop from a speed of 33 m/s. The time taken to brake to a stop is 13 seconds.

$$a = \frac{(v - u)}{t}$$

Substituting rounded values:

$$a \sim \frac{(0 - 30)}{10}$$
$$\sim -3 \text{ m/s}^2$$

3 Without using a calculator, estimate the deceleration of a car that makes an emergency stop from a speed of 21 m/s. The time taken to brake to a stop is 3.5 seconds.

4 For the car whose deceleration you estimated in question 3, use the equation $v^2 = u^2 + 2as$ to estimate the car's braking distance. Then calculate the overall stopping distance, using an estimate for a typical value for the reaction time.

5 Estimate the braking force required to stop the car in question 3. Make a sensible approximation of the mass of the car.

Orders of magnitude

In question 1, two students estimated the volume of this book. Their estimates were 400 cm³ and 600 cm³.

Both estimates are of the same order of magnitude. An **order of magnitude** is a factor of 10. When two numbers are the same order of magnitude, this means that one of the numbers is less than 10 times larger than the other.

Example: Make an order of magnitude estimate for the time taken by light to travel across our galaxy, the Milky Way. The diameter of the Milky Way is about 7×10^{17} km to 9×10^{17} km. The speed of light is 3.0×10^8 m/s.

$$\text{time} = \frac{\text{distance}}{\text{speed}}$$

Using the nearest order of magnitude,

$$\text{time} = \frac{10^{17} \times 10^3 \text{ m}}{10^8 \text{ m/s}}$$
$$= \frac{10^{20}}{10^8} \text{ s}$$
$$= 10^{12} \text{ s}$$

6 Make an order of magnitude estimate for the mass of air in this room. The density of air at ordinary atmospheric pressure and room temperature is 1.2 kg/m³.

7 Make an order of magnitude estimate for the time taken by light to travel across the length of the UK.

> **KEY INFORMATION**
>
> Using rounded values to make an estimate allows you to check that the result you find using your calculator is correct. If your estimate and your calculated answer are not similar, then you may have made a mistake in your calculation, for example when typing in the numbers.

> **KEY INFORMATION**
>
> Use an order of magnitude when the precise value of a quantity is unknown. Make an estimate rounded to the nearest power of 10 and use that in your calculation.

Forces explain how objects interact

Learning objectives:

- describe a force
- recognise the difference between contact and non-contact forces
- state examples of scalar and vector quantities.

KEY WORDS

newtons (N)
contact force
non-contact force
displacement
velocity
scalar
vector

People sometimes use force in a wide range of ways – we talk about someone having a 'forceful personality' or the 'force of their argument'. However, in science we use force in a very particular way. We're interested in direction, size and contact.

What is a force?

A force is a push or a pull that is applied by one object on another.

Force is measured in **newtons (N)**. The force needed to pick up a bag of sugar is 20 N. The pulling force required to open a drinks can is about 20 N.

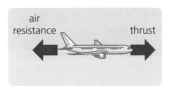

Figure 2.13 The aeroplane's engines give it a forward force or thrust. Air resistance is a frictional force that resists movement in air.

Contact and non-contact forces

All forces between objects are either contact or non-contact forces.

Contact forces – the objects are physically touching, such as a parachute in contact with air (Figure 2.14).

Non-contact forces – the objects are physically separated (Figure 2.15).

Figure 2.14 Air resistance – a contact force

Contact forces	Non-contact forces
friction	gravitational force
air resistance	electrostatic force
tension	magnetic force
normal contact force	

KEY INFORMATION

When you stand on the floor there is a force from the floor pushing up on you, called the normal contact force.

Figure 2.15 Attraction and repulsion between charged objects is an example of a non-contact force.

1. **Give an example of a contact force (other than the one in Figure 2.14).**

2. **Give an example of a non-contact force (other than the one in Figure 2.15).**

Force diagrams

You will often see forces represented using diagrams, which help us to understand how forces combine. Figure 2.X shows the forces acting on a heavy block being pulled across a floor.

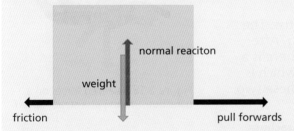

Figure 2.16 Forces on a block

The size and direction of each force is shown to scale. Forces are vectors, so direction is important. The weight acting downwards is exactly balanced by the normal reaction of the floor on the block. There is some friction pulling the block back, but the forwards pull on the block is greater. The forces combine to produce a force in the direction of the pull.

3. **In Figure 2.16, in which direction do you think the block will move?**

Forces and motion

Learning objectives:

* understand what a force does
* explain what happens to an object if all the forces acting on it cancel each other out
* analyse how this applies to everyday situations.

ABS (anti-lock braking system) brakes stop a car more quickly by rapidly pumping the brakes and preventing skidding.

Thinking about forces

If we think about an object, we can usually identify the forces that are acting on it. For example, an apple growing on a tree (Figure 2.17) has the force of gravity acting downwards; this is its weight. There is another force acting, vertically upwards, through the stalk. These two forces are equal and opposite. They cancel out and the apple doesn't move.

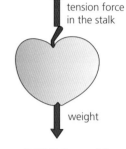

Figure 2.17 **Balanced forces** on an apple hanging from a stalk

1. The weight of the apple in Figure 2.17 is 1 N. What is the force upwards in the stalk?

2. Is it *always* true that when all the forces on an object balance out it will be stationary?

HIGHER TIER ONLY

Terminal velocity

Let's think of another situation: that of a parachutist. The parachutist jumped out of an aircraft and is falling. After a while, the parachutist reaches a steady speed. There is a downwards force weight, and an upwards force, which is called drag, or air resistance (Figure 2.18). When these two forces are equal and opposite, they cancel out.

Figure 2.18 Balanced forces on a parachutist falling at a steady speed

3. When the parachutist in Figure 2.18 opens the parachute:

   a What will happen to the size of the drag force?

   b Will the two forces still be in balance immediately after the parachute opens?

DID YOU KNOW?

Anything falling through the atmosphere will reach a terminal velocity for the space capsules that bring astronauts back from the International Space Station, the terminal velocity is about 230 m/s. This reduces to 80 m/s when parachutes are deployed.

Newton's first law

An object may have several forces acting on it (Figure 2.19). A number of forces acting on an object may be replaced by a single force that has the same effect as all the original forces acting together. This single force is called the **resultant force**. If the forces are in balance they cancel each other out and the resultant force is zero. The object behaves as if there is no force on it at all. The object will be in **equilibrium**; it will not accelerate.

Newton's first law says that, if the resultant force acting on an object is zero it will

- if stationary, remain stationary
- if moving, keep moving at a steady speed in a straight line.

drag
friction
forward force from engine

Figure 2.19 If the forces cancel out the resultant force is zero.

4 If the resultant of two forces is zero, what must be true about their size and direction?

5 Look at the three forces shown in Figure 2.19. If the resultant of the three forces is zero, what must be true about the sizes of those forces?

6 In addition to the forces shown in Figure 2.19, there will also be weight, acting downwards, and a reaction force, acting upwards. How do these also obey Newton's first law?

Applying Newton's first law

One of the most important questions to ask about a situation in which forces are acting on an object is whether the resultant force in a certain direction is zero. In this case Newton's first law applies and a stationary object will remain at rest and if the object is moving it will continue to move in a straight line and at constant velocity. Examples of this are a boulder resting on the ground and a bicycle being pedalled along a level road at steady speed in a straight line.

7 Explain why there is a zero resultant force for a boulder on the ground.

8 Explain why there is a zero resultant force in the horizontal direction for a bicycle being pedalled along a level road at steady speed in a straight line.

9 Explain why, in the example of the bicycle, if the cyclist gets tired, the resultant force may no longer be zero.

10 Describe the motion of the Earth if the Sun suddenly vanished.

HIGHER TIER ONLY

Motion in a circle

When a vehicle goes round a roundabout at a constant speed its direction of movement is changing. This means that its velocity is changing because velocity is a vector. When the velocity of an object is changing, it is accelerating. There is a force towards the centre of the roundabout in the same direction as the acceleration which causes the change in velocity.

11 Dan and Karen are riding on a carousel at a fairground. They are moving at a constant speed. Why are they accelerating?

DID YOU KNOW?

Deep in space, with no drag or gravitational forces to affect it, a spacecraft moving with its rockets off will keep moving forever without slowing down or speeding up.

REMEMBER!

A normal contact force is exerted on an object by, for example, the surface of a floor or wall it is in contact with. The force is at right angles to the surface. In physics, 'normal to' means 'at right angles to'.

KEY INFORMATION

Planets orbiting the Sun display motion in a circle or ellipse. The force of gravity acts on the planet, towards the Sun. The velocity of the planet is constantly changing as it moves in its orbit.

Resultant forces

Learning objectives:

- calculate the resultant of a number of forces
- draw free-body diagrams to find resultant forces
- understand that a force can be resolved into two components acting at right angles to each other.

There's always more than one force acting in a situation. For example, when you pull a box across the floor the friction force acts in the opposite direction to the pulling force on the box.

Combining forces

When there are several forces acting on an object, we can work out what their combined effect is. If one child is behind a sledge, pushing it along, and another is in front, pulling it, we can combine these forces by adding them. In a tug-of-war, two teams are pulling in opposite directions. The force applied by one team should be subtracted from that applied by the other team to find out what the combined force is. The combined force is called the **resultant force**.

Figure 2.20 The forces are balanced. The resultant force is zero.

Figure 2.21 The forces are **unbalanced**. The resultant force is not zero.

1. **Gemma and Alan are pushing a packing case across the floor, each applying a force of 40 N. The friction opposing the motion is 50 N. What is the resultant force?**

2. **Jo is driving her car along a level road. The engine is providing 1500 N of force. Air resistance is opposing the motion with a value of 1000 N and friction accounts for another 500 N. What is the resultant force?**

Free-body diagrams

A **free-body diagram** shows the magnitude and direction of the forces acting on an object. This saves us from having to spend a lot of time drawing the exact shape. The object (such as the aircraft shown in Figure 2.22) is represented by a point. The force arrows all start from the centre of the point.

A free-body diagram for the jet aircraft is shown in Figure 2.23. It shows all the forces acting. The direction of the forces is shown by the direction of the arrows and the size of the forces by the length of the arrows.

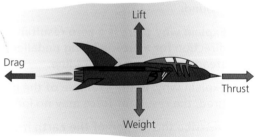

Figure 2.22 Forces on an aircraft

3. **Draw a free-body diagram for a stationary car.**

4. **Draw a free-body diagram for an aeroplane flying horizontally with positive acceleration.**

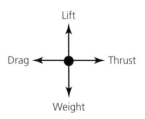

Figure 2.23 The free-body diagram for the jet aeroplane

Finding forces from a vector diagram

You can determine the magnitude and direction of a resultant force by drawing a scale diagram.

To work out the resultant of the forces in Figure 2.25, draw the 3N force as shown in Figure 2.26. Then draw the 4N force with its tail joining on to the head of the 3N force. The lengths of the arrows represent the magnitudes of the forces. Choose a suitable scale, such as 1 cm = 1 N.

The resultant force is the imaginary line that goes from A to B in Figure 2.26. The magnitude of the resultant is found by measuring the length of the line and the direction is found by measuring the angle θ. In this case you should find that the resultant force is 5N at an angle of 37° above the horizontal.

5 Two forces act on an object. One force is 5N to the right and the other force is 12N upwards. Draw a scale diagram to find the magnitude and direction of the resultant force.

6 A 12N force is pulling an object to the right and a 16N force is pulling it downwards. A third force is needed to keep the object still, so that there is no resultant force. Determine the size of the third force by drawing a scale diagram.

Looking at this the other way round, if you take a single force you can find two forces which, when combined, will produce a resultant force with the same magnitude and direction as the original. This is called **resolving the force** into **components**. It is useful to resolve a force into two perpendicular components, such as the horizontal and vertical components of the force. For example the 5N force in Figure 2.25 has the same effect as the 3N and 4N forces acting together at right angles. You can use a scale diagram to determine the size of the components.

Example: A force of magnitude 100N acts in a direction of 40° to the horizontal. Resolve this force into horizontal and vertical components.

Draw a scale diagram with the 100N force at 40° to the horizontal. Choose a scale that will give a large triangle. At 5N:1cm the force arrow is 20cm long.

Draw a straight line down to the x-axis and measure the length of the line. This is the horizontal component of the force.

Length = 15.4cm so horizontal component = 77N

Draw a straight line across to the y-axis and measure the length of the line. This is the vertical component of the force.

Length = 12.8cm so vertical component = 64N

7 A 14.1N force acts at 45° above the horizontal to the right. Determine the vertical and horizontal components of this force.

8 The 14.1N force in question 7 points together with a 14.1N force which points at 45° below the horizontal. Determine the resultant force produced by these two forces.

KEY INFORMATION

When drawing free-body diagrams the weight of an object is considered to act at a single point. We call this point the object's centre of mass.

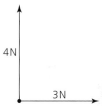

Figure 2.24 The weight is shown as a force vector passing through the object's centre of mass, X

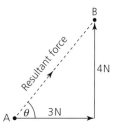

Figure 2.25 Free-body diagram for two forces acting at right angles

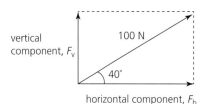

Figure 2.26 A scale diagram to calculate the resultant force

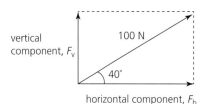

Figure 2.27

Forces and acceleration

Learning objectives:

- explain what happens to the motion of an object when the resultant force is not zero
- analyse situations in which a non-zero resultant force is acting
- explain what inertia is.

KEY WORDS

resultant force
Newton's second
    law
inertia
inertial mass
gravitational mass

The record for the fastest object made by humans is held by the Helios 2 spacecraft, which reached over 246 000 km/h. It has a very elliptical orbit around the Sun which means it accelerates as a result of the Sun's massive gravitational field.

What does a force do?

When the driver presses on the accelerator pedal, it increases the forward **force** of the engine. This makes the car accelerate.

The force of the engine acts forwards and there will be other forces opposing this: friction and air resistance. However, at this point the force from the engine is greater than the opposing forces and so the car accelerates (Figure 2.28). It speeds up.

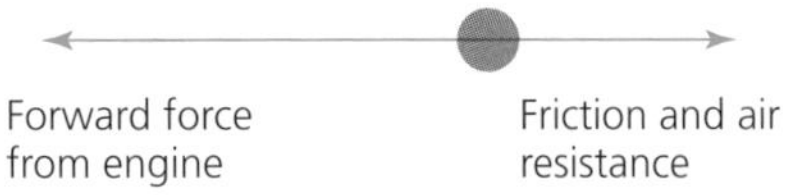

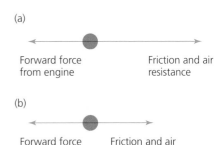

Forward force   Friction and air
from engine   resistance

Figure 2.28 The car accelerates.

(a)

Forward force   Friction and air
from engine   resistance

(b)

Forward force   Friction and air
from engine   resistance

Figure 2.29 Forces on a car

1. In which direction are the resultant forces acting in Figures 2.26 and 2.29?

2. The driver of the car in Figure 2.29b presses the accelerator harder so that the speed increases. What will happen to the resultant force?

Newton's second law

Force, mass and acceleration are linked by the equation

$F = ma$

where F is the **resultant force** in N, m is the mass in kg and a is the acceleration in m/s^2. This is **Newton's second law.**

The resultant force is a single force that has the same effect as all the original forces acting together..

Example:

A car has a mass of 1000 kg. What force is needed to give it an acceleration of 5 m/s^2?

$F = ma$

$= 1000 \text{ kg} \times 5 \text{ m/s}^2$

$= 5000 \text{ N}$

MAKING LINKS

Weight can be considered in terms of Newton's second law: the force is the weight and the acceleration is that due to gravity.

KEY INFORMATION

When using $F = ma$, F is the resultant force.

3 A car of mass 1200 kg has a resultant forward force acting on it of 4200 N. Determine its acceleration.

4 The weight of an apple is 1 N and it accelerates downwards at 10 m/s². What is its mass?

5 What force is needed to accelerate a 4000 kg rocket upwards at 2 m/s²? (g = 10 N/kg)

HIGHER TIER ONLY

Inertia

Figure 2.30 Once a massive tanker is moving it is difficult to stop.

Massive objects are hard to start to move and also very difficult to stop. (Figure 2.30) They have an inbuilt reluctance to start moving. This is called **inertia** (from the Latin for laziness). Inertia is the natural tendency of objects to resist changes in their velocity.

Inertial mass is a measure of how difficult it is to change the velocity of an object.

Inertial mass is defined by the ratio of force over acceleration:

$$\text{inertial mass} = \frac{\text{force}}{\text{acceleration}}.$$

6 What is inertia and how do you calculate inertial mass?

7 Another form of mass is **gravitational mass**. Suggest what the difference is between gravitational mass and inertial mass.

8 An object has a mass of 2 kg. What are its inertial mass and its gravitational mass?

DID YOU KNOW?

Some large ships can take 10 km to stop from a cruising speed of 12 km/h.

Momentum

Learning objectives:

- explain what is meant by momentum
- apply ideas about rate of change of momentum to safety features in cars
- use momentum calculations to predict what happens in a collision.

Understanding momentum enables car designers to save lives.

HIGHER TIER ONLY

Understanding momentum

A moving object has **momentum**. The amount of momentum an object has depends on its mass and its velocity.

momentum = mass × velocity

$p = mv$

where p is the momentum in kg m/s, m is the mass in kg and v is the velocity in m/s.

Example:

Evie has a mass of 60 kg. Her momentum is 120 kg m/s. How fast is she moving?

momentum = mass × velocity

$$\text{velocity} = \frac{\text{momentum}}{\text{mass}} = \frac{120 \text{ kg m/s}}{60 \text{ kg}} = 2 \text{ m/s}$$

KEY INFORMATION

Velocity is a vector so momentum is also a vector.

1 Calculate the momentum of a car with a mass of 1000 kg travelling at 20 m/s.

2 Tom has a mass of 60 kg. His momentum is 240 kg m/s. How fast is he moving?

Changes in momentum

In an accident a car stops suddenly. Its momentum becomes zero. The larger the force applied to the car, the quicker its momentum becomes zero.

We can calculate this by combining ideas we have met already:

force, $F = ma$ (Newton's second law)

$$\text{acceleration} = \frac{\text{change in velocity}}{\text{time}} = \frac{(v - u)}{t}$$

Therefore, $F = \dfrac{m(v - u)}{t}$ or $F = \dfrac{m\Delta v}{\Delta t}$

since momentum = mv

MATHS

$m\Delta v$ is a change in momentum (we assume the mass stays the same). $m\Delta v/t$ is the **rate of change** of momentum – how quickly the momentum changes.

Example:

A car of mass 1000 kg is moving at 12 m/s when it hits a wall. The force on the car is 4800 N. Calculate the stopping time.

$$F = \frac{m\Delta v}{\Delta t}$$

$$Ft = m(v - u)$$

$$t = \frac{(mv - mu)}{m(v - u)}$$

$$= \frac{1000 \text{ kg } (12 \text{ m/s} - 0)}{4800 \text{ N}} = \frac{12\,000 \text{ kg m/s}}{4800 \text{ N}} = 2.5 \text{ s}$$

Figure 2.31 Crumple zones in a car

Safety features are designed to increase the time a car or its passengers takes to stop. It means that momentum has not been changed as quickly. The longer the time the smaller the force on the car's occupants.

Crumple zones increase the time between first impact and the car stopping (Figure 2.31). The rate of change of momentum is smaller, reducing the force on the car's occupants.

3 An airbag inflates on impact. Explain with reference to momentum how this improves safety.

4 Suggest why there is a greater risk to the driver and front seat passenger if a back seat passenger fails to wear a seat belt.

5 A car of mass 800 kg is moving at 12 m/s when it collides with a wall. The force on the car is 3000 N. Calculate the stopping time.

Conservation of momentum

We can use the principle of **conservation of momentum** to calculate velocities before and after a collision. The principle states that in a closed system, the total momentum before a collision is equal to the total momentum after the collision.

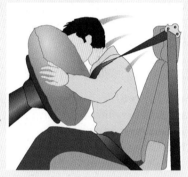

Figure 2.32 A seat belt stretches a little so the passenger's rate of change of momentum is reduced in a crash.

In Figure 2.33, the total momentum of the two trolleys before the collision is equal to the total momentum of the two trolleys after the collision, as long as the system is closed.

Figure 2.33: An inelastic collision

Example:

A trolley has a mass of 3 kg and is travelling at 3 m/s. It collides with a second trolley which has a mass of 2 kg and is travelling at 2 m/s. They stick together. Find their common velocity.

$$m_1u_1 + m_2 u_2 = (m_1 + m_2)v$$

where v = common velocity after the collision.

$$(3 \text{ kg} \times 3 \text{ m/s}) + (2 \text{ kg} \times 2 \text{ m/s}) = (3 \text{ kg} + 2 \text{ kg})v$$

$$13 \text{ kg m/s} = 5v \text{ kg}$$

$$v = \frac{13}{5} \text{ m/s} = 2.6 \text{ m/s to the right}$$

6 A car of mass 1200 kg travelling at 30 m/s runs into the back of a stationary lorry. The car and lorry move at 4 m/s after impact. Determine the mass of the lorry.

7 A truck of mass 2 kg travels at 8 m/s towards a stationary truck of mass 6 kg. After colliding the trucks move off together. Calculate their common velocity.

PRACTICAL

Investigating the acceleration of an object

Learning objectives:

- plan an investigation to explore an idea
- analysing results to identify patterns and draw conclusions
- compare results with scientific theory.

KEY WORDS

Newton's second law
direct proportion
inverse proportion

There is a very important relationship between force, mass and acceleration. This is a fundamental idea in Physics, yet it is possible to demonstrate it using fairly straightforward apparatus and analysing the results with care.

Planning your investigation

The relationship being explored here is the one between force, mass and acceleration. The acceleration can be determined in several ways; for example, light gates and a data logger or a ticker timer could be used. The effects of varying either force or acceleration can then be investigated.

Figure 2.34 A smart phone accelerometer chip

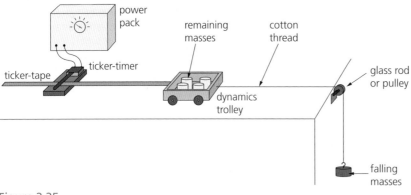

Figure 2.35

Look at Figure 2.35. The weight is attached to the trolley by a thread. If the trolley moves to the right it will pull the tape through the timer so the speed can be measured.

1 Describe the motion of the trolley when the weight is released.

2 What is true about the size of the force during this experiment?

3 How could the force on the trolley be altered?

4 When we are altering the force, what can we do with the weights to make sure the mass of the system doesn't change?

5 Explain how the mass of the trolley could be altered.

These pages are designed to help you think about aspects of the investigation rather than to guide you through it step by step.

DID YOU KNOW?

An accelerometer is a device which measures acceleration. You find them in smart phones and game handsets such as the Wii. In a smart phone they enable the auto-rotate to turn your screen display vertical or horizontal when the phone is moved. The accelerometer in the Wii remote can sense a change in speed or direction.

Analysing the results

When analysing results we look for patterns or similarities and draw these together in a conclusion. Adam's group are seeing if their data confirmed that the acceleration of the trolley was proportional to the force acting on it. They used the equipment in Figure 2.30, altering the force on the trolley but keeping the mass constant. The table shows their results.

Force (N)	Acceleration (m/s²)
1	0.5
2	0.9
3	1.4
4	2.1
5	2.5
6	3.0
7	3.6
8	4.1

6 **What would you expect Adam to find happened to the acceleration when he increased the force and kept the mass constant?**

7 **Do his group's results show this?**

8 **Plot a graph of force against acceleration. What shape is it?**

9 **What does this show?**

Amy's group were doing a different investigation. They kept the force constant but altered the mass of the trolley. Their results are shown in the table below.

Mass of trolley (g)	Acceleration (m/s²)
20	5.0
30	3.3
40	2.5
50	2.0
60	1.7
70	1.4
80	1.2

10 **What is happening to the acceleration of the trolley as its mass is increased?**

11 **What shape would the graph of mass against acceleration have?**

REMEMBER!

We can show relationships of direct or inverse proportionality both by calculation and by graphing.

Exploring the connection with accepted theory

Newton's second law of motion says that if a force accelerates an object, the acceleration is directly proportional to the force and inversely proportional to the mass of the object. We should be able to analyse the results to see if they show this relationship.

12 **Explain how Adam's and Amy's results support this.**

13 **If the force is tripled and the mass is doubled, what happens to the acceleration?**

Newton's third law

Learning objectives:

- identify force pairs
- understand and be able to apply Newton's third law.

KEY WORDS

weight
Newton's third law

Soldiers firing a large gun never stand behind the gun because the gun moves backwards when it is fired (Figure 2.36).

Force pairs

When a force acts on an object in equilibrium, another force arises as a result. The forces are equal in size but act in opposite directions and on different objects.

Some examples of force pairs:

- When you walk, your foot pushes the ground backwards; the ground pushes your foot forwards.
- If you stand on a skateboard next to a wall and push on the wall, the wall pushes back on you.
- In a small boat, if you push on the quayside, it pushes back on you and you and the boat moves away.

Figure 2.36 A cannon being fired

1 **What can you say about each pair of forces?**

2 **The tyres of a car push on the road. Name the other force in the force pair.**

Newton's third law

Newton's third law states that whenever two objects interact, the forces they exert on each other are equal and opposite. When two cars collide, the forces on each are of equal size but in opposite directions (Figure 2.37)

$F_1 = F_2$.

Figure 2.37 Forces in a collision

The forces in the pair:

- are the same size
- act in opposite directions
- act on *different* objects.

COMMON MISCONCEPTION

When a pair of objects produce a force on each other we draw the forces as vectors.
But unlike the forces in a free-body diagram, the forces in a Newton's third law pair act on *different* objects.

3 Imagine two people, each sitting on an office chair with wheels. One pushes against the other.

   a Describe what happens next.

   b Explain how this illustrates Newton's third law.

4 Kim and Ben are standing on ice. Kim pushes Ben with a force of 50 N. What force acts on Kim? Describe what happens next.

5 A lorry collides head on with a small car. Compare:

   a the resultant forces acting on the lorry and the car

   b the decelerations of the lorry and the car.

6 An astronaut is floating in space and has become detached from her spaceship. She is wearing a backpack that she is able to remove from her suit. Suggest what she could do to get back to the ship.

Further ideas about force pairs

It is often useful to realise that the pair of forces in Newton's third law are between two objects only. If object A exerts a force on object B then object B exerts a force of equal size but in the opposite direction on object A. The two forces must be the same type of force.

7 A cat is falling to the ground having jumped out of a tree. Ignoring air resistance, the only force acting on the cat is its weight.

   a Complete the sentence by selecting the correct word.

     The force on the cat is due to the Earth pulling on the cat. This type of force is a **magnetic / electrostatic / gravitational** force.

   b Describe the other force in the force pair in this situation.

8 The cat is now sitting on a table.

   a What is the other force in the force pair to the cat's weight?

   b State the other pair of forces which involve the cat.

9 The cat jumps off the table and falls to the ground. Describe how the cat affects the motion of the Earth as it is falling.

10 Describe all of the forces that occur between your body and the Earth when you jump upwards, reach a maximum height and land again.

> **REMEMBER!**
> ·······················
> Remember that two vehicles experiencing the same braking force will decelerate by different amounts if they have different masses.

> **KEY INFORMATION**
> ·······················
> The normal contact force when two surfaces are in contact is one of a force pair. But Newton's third law also applies for non-contact forces, for example due to gravitational attraction.
>
>
>
> Figure 2.38 By Newton's third law, the boy exerts a gravitational force upwards on the Earth of the same size as the gravitational force downwards on the boy (weight).

Work done and energy transfer

Learning objectives:

- understand what is meant by work done
- explain the relationship between work done and force applied
- identify the transfers between energy stores when work is done against friction.

KEY WORDS

energy transfer
force
kinetic energy
work

People on a roller coaster experience rapid energy changes and experience G-forces similar to those experienced by astronauts.

Work done by a force

In science, **work** is only done by a **force** when an object **moves**.

More work is done when

- the force is bigger
- the object moves further – its displacement is bigger.

Sam's car has broken down. He tries to push it but the car does not move. He is not doing any work though. Work is only done when a force *moves*. Sam gets some friends to help. Together, they can push with a larger force and the car moves. They are all doing work.

① What affects the amount of work done by a force?

② What force moves when someone jumps off a wall?

> **REMEMBER!**
>
> Work is only done when a force causes a displacement of the object (that is, movement along the line of action of the force).

Figure 2.39 These men are doing work

Calculating work done

The equation that links work, force and distance is:

Work done = force × distance moved along the line of action of the force where work, W, is in joules, force, F, is in newtons and distance, s, is in metres.

$W = F \times s$

When a person climbs stairs or jumps in the air the force moved is their weight.

Example: Dev climbs a flight of stairs rising a vertical height of 5 m. He weighs 600 N. Calculate the work Dev does by lifting his weight up the stairs.

Work done = force × distance moved along the line of action of the force.

Work done = 600 N × 5 m = 3000 J.

③ A gymnast (Figure 2.9) weighs 400 N. How much work does she do when she jumps from the ground onto a beam 1.5 m above the ground?

> **ADVICE**
>
> One joule of work is done when a force of one newton causes a displacement of one metre.

Figure 2.40 The gymnast does work when she jumps up onto the beam from the floor

4. Mia is holding a 20 N weight without moving. How much work is she doing?

5. Amrita does 300 J of work in lifting a box with a force of 200 N. How high does she lift it?

Energy calculations

When work is done on an object there can also be a change in its **kinetic energy.** We can use this to calculate the force needed to stop a car when the distance it travels while coming to rest is known.

Example: A car of mass 1000 kg does an emergency stop when travelling at 15 m/s. It stops in a distance of 20 m. Calculate the braking force.

E_k of car $= \frac{1}{2}mv^2$

$\qquad = \frac{1}{2} \times 1000$ kg $\times (15$ m/s$)^2$

$\qquad = 112\ 500$ J.

Work has to be done to reduce the kinetic energy of the car and bring it to a stop. The force that does the work is the friction force between the brakes and the wheel. The work done by the braking force is 112 500 J.

$W = F \times s$, where F is the braking force and s is the distance moved during braking. We can rearrange this to make F the subject of the equation.

$F = \dfrac{W}{s}$

$\quad = \dfrac{112\ 500\,\text{J}}{20\,\text{m}}$

$\quad = 5625$ N.

Work done against the frictional forces acting on an object causes a rise in the temperature of the object. The temperature of the brakes increases.

6. Tom does 3000 J of work against friction in pushing a small van a distance of 12 m. How big is the friction force he has to push against?

7. A car of mass 800 kg is travelling at 12 m/s.

   a Calculate its kinetic energy.

   b The brakes are applied. What force from the brakes is needed if the car stops after travelling 8 m?

8. A pole-vaulter has a weight of 500 N.

   a She vaults to a height of 4 m. How much work does she do?

   b How much kinetic energy does she have just before she lands?

   c When she lands, her trainers compress by 1 cm. Calculate the average force acting on her trainers as she is landing.

DID YOU KNOW?

A water-powered inclined railway has no engine. The top car has a water tank which makes it slightly heavier than the car at the bottom. The two cars are attached by a cable going over a pulley. The extra weight of the top car does work to lift the lower car up the slope. Work is also done to overcome the force of friction.

Figure 2.41 Inclined railway

MAKING LINKS

You will need to link the information given here to the forces topic 2.13, where you will look at the factors that affect stopping distance.

Understanding power

Learning objectives:

- define power
- compare the rate of energy transfer by various machines and electrical appliances
- calculate power.

A human being can be considered an energy transfer device. Our energy comes from our food, about 10 MJ (10 million joules) every day.

Power

Imagine a tall office block with two lifts, the same mass. One lift takes 40 s to go up to the tenth floor; the other, newer lift, takes 25 s. Both lifts do the same amount of work but the newer one does it more quickly. The transfer of energy is more rapid; the new lift has more **power**.

Power is the rate of doing work or transferring energy. A machine that is more powerful than another machine transfers more energy each second.

Power is measured in watts (W). If one joule of energy is transferred in one second this is one watt of power. 1 W = 1 J/s.

The table shows the typical power of various electrical appliances.

	Power / W
Kettle	2500
Microwave oven	1100
Iron	1000
Hairdryer	2000
Vacuum cleaner	1600
Television	114
Food blender	150

1 Which appliance is the most powerful?

2 Explain why a television might do more work than a food blender.

Calculating power

$$\text{Power} = \frac{\text{work done in J}}{\text{time in s}} \text{ or } \frac{\text{energy transferred in J}}{\text{time in s}}$$

These formulae can be written as:

$P = W/t$ and

$P = E/t$

Example: A machine does 1000 J of work in 8 seconds. What power does it develop?

$$\text{Power} = \frac{\text{work done}}{\text{time}} = \frac{1000\,\text{J}}{8\,\text{s}} = 125\,\text{W}$$

3 A toaster transferred 108 000 J of energy in 2 minutes. What is the power of the toaster?

4 An electric kettle is rated at 2 kW (2000 W). How much energy is transferred in 30 s?

5 A crane lifts a load weighing 4000 N through a height of 6 m in 20 s.

    a How much work does the crane do to lift the load, assuming there is no friction?

    b What is the power of the crane?

Personal power

Mel decides to work out her leg power. She runs up 16 stairs each 20 cm high in 10 s (Figure 2.11). Mel's mass is 50 kg.

Work done = force × distance moved **in the direction of the force**.

The force moved is Mel's weight = 50 × 10 = 500 N.

The **vertical** height of the stairs (in m) = 16 × 0.2 = 3.2 m

Work done = 500 N × 3.2 m = 1600 J.

$$\text{Power} = \frac{\text{work done}}{\text{time}} = \frac{1600\,\text{J}}{10\text{s}} = 160\,\text{W}$$

Figure 2.42 How can Mel measure the vertical height?

6 Al weighs 800 N. He climbs 5 m vertically in 10 s when he runs up the stairs of an office block.

    a How much work does he do?

    b Calculate his power.

7 The Eiffel Tower in Paris (Figure 2.12) is 300 m high. Louis took 15 minutes to climb its 1792 steps. He has a mass of 60 kg. What was his average power output during the climb?

8 Emma decides to measure her personal leg power doing step-ups. The step is 10 cm high. Emma does 20 step ups in 30 s. Her mass is 60 kg. Calculate her leg power.

9 A car is moving at 108 km/h and the engine provides a constant force of 1000N. Calculate:

Figure 2.43 The Eiffel Tower

    a the distance the car moves in 1 second

    b the power of the engine.

KEY CONCEPT

Forces and acceleration

Learning objectives:

- to recognise examples of balanced and unbalanced forces
- to apply ideas about speed and acceleration to explain sensations of movement
- to apply ideas about inertia and circular motion to explain braking and cornering.

KEY WORDS

force
speed
acceleration
balanced
inertia
velocity

The reason why scientists study forces is that they tell us about how things move. If you know all the forces acting on something you can predict very accurately if and how it will move. Newton's laws of motion are very simple but the situations you can apply them to can be complex. The laws were first suggested by Isaac Newton (Figure 2.59) and published in 1686. NASA used these simple laws to get men safely to the Moon and back, and theme parks use them to thrill us on their rides.

Balanced and unbalanced forces

People who design rides for theme parks understand what will make a ride exciting. It's not just speed. Stealth, at Thorpe Park, is the UK's fastest roller coaster and reaches 128 km/h, which is not much faster than a car on a motorway, but is much more exciting. You need high acceleration for a good ride and that requires force, or, to be precise, unbalanced force.

Newton explained that if all the forces on an object balance out, its speed will be constant and its direction will not change, or it will not move if it is at rest. If the forces are not balanced the object's speed or direction will change.

It is the acceleration that makes roller coasters (Figure 2.60) such fun. Newton's first law of motion states that a moving object tends to stay moving. This resistance to change is called inertia. When the roller coaster speeds up, the back of the seat pushes you forward, accelerating you. When the roller coaster slows down, your body tries to keep going at its original speed. The harness in front of you pushes your body backward. These pushes and pulls on your body give you the thrills you enjoy.

1. What happens to the acceleration of the roller coaster if the force propelling it forwards increases?

2. Explain what would happen if the roller coaster had a negative acceleration and the passengers weren't wearing restraints.

Figure 2.44 Isaac Newton

Figure 2.45 A roller coaster

Figure 2.46 Forces on a ride

Looping the loop

Curves and loops on the ride cause the direction you are travelling in to change, so your velocity changes. Remember that a change in velocity is acceleration even if the speed remains constant. To change direction, there needs to be a force towards the centre of the circle that the curve is part of. This is an example of Newton's second law.

3 You feel the seat pushing you as you go round the loop. Suggest what would happen if there was no seat.

4 Why do we say that a train going round a loop is accelerating, even when its speed is constant?

5 Use this to explain the difference between speed and velocity.

6 Newton said that unless there is an unbalanced force, an object will continue in a straight line at a steady speed. Describe how this force is applied to the riders in the roller coaster.

Figure 2.47 A drop tower

Drop towers

Zumanjaro: Drop of Doom in America is the world's tallest drop tower at 125 m. Another example of a drop tower is shown in figure 2.47. After a brief pause at the top, you are released and fall under the pull of gravity. You are in free-fall for over 10 s, reaching speeds of over 140 km/h. The force is unbalanced and causes acceleration; the same thing (but much more gently) happens when you descend in a lift.

To slow the ride down and stop it, another unbalanced force is needed. This is provided by giant permanent magnets which provide an upward force.

7 If a free-fall ride accelerates at 10 m/s² and the loaded car has a mass of 2500 kg, what force is acting?

8 If the braking force at the end of the ride was half the size of the force of gravitational attraction, what acceleration would the riders experience?

9 A passenger on Zumanjaro was holding an open bottle of water. As the ride accelerated downwards he decided to tip the bottle upside down to make the water fall out. Explain what happened to the water.

DID YOU KNOW?

g-force is a way of comparing forces by measuring the acceleration they produce. A force of 1*g* causes acceleration the same as that of gravity (around 10 m/s²). Humans can tolerate greater *g*-forces horizontally than vertically; accelerating downwards rapidly forces blood into the brain and eyes; any more than 2*g* is dangerous.

Forces and energy in springs

Learning objectives:

- explain why you need two forces to stretch a spring
- describe the difference between elastic and inelastic deformation
- calculate extension, compression and energy transferred in stretching.

KEY WORDS

elastic deformation
plastic deformation
extension
compression
limit of proportionality
linear
non-linear
spring constant
energy transferred in stretching

Some skyscrapers are mounted on springs, to prevent them from shaking too much in an earthquake.

Forces on a spring

The spring in Figure 2.48 is being stretched by two forces. The weight of the mass is pulling the spring downwards. However, if this was the only force acting on the spring then it would accelerate towards the ground. The other force is from the bar, which is pulling the top of the spring upwards.

1 **What is the resultant force on the spring if it is at rest?**

2 **Determine the force at the top of the spring when the weight of the mass is 3 N.**

Elastic deformation occurs when the spring returns back to its original length when the forces are removed. A spring that is permanently altered has undergone **plastic deformation**.

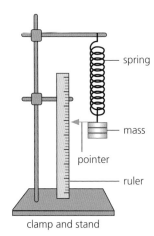

Figure 2.48 Forces stretching a spring

3 **What would happen to a bed mattress if its springs had undergone plastic deformation?**

The **extension** or **compression** of the spring is how much its length changes when the forces are applied. You measure extension when the spring is being stretched and compression when it is being squashed.

4 **A spring has an original length of 6.0 cm. It is then squashed to a length of 4.8 cm. Determine the compression of the spring.**

The relationship between force and extension

The graph in Figure 2.49 is a straight line up to the **limit of proportionality**. This shows that there is a **linear** relationship between the force and extension when the force applied is small.

Since the straight line goes through the origin, we can also say that force is directly proportional to the extension.

DID YOU KNOW?

Scientists have developed a material that can elastically deform to twenty times its original length without breaking.

You can calculate the force or the extension using the equation:

force = spring constant × extension

$F = ke$

where k, the spring constant, is measured in N/m and depends on the spring; e can be the extension or the compression and is measured in m.

Since $F = ke$, $k = F/e$ and the spring constant for an elastic material can be found from the gradient of the straight part of a force–extension graph. Note however that the graph in Figure 2.56 is plotted for extension against force, so the gradient of this graph is $1/k$.

5 A spring has an extension of 0.08 m when it is stretched by a force of 4 N. What is its spring constant?

6 A spring has a spring constant of 2000 N/m and is 10 cm long. What force is needed to compress the spring to a length of 4 cm?

Beyond the limit of proportionality, the line in Figure 2.49 begins to curve. The relationship between force and extension is now **non-linear**. For the first part of this curve, the spring may still return to its original shape if the force is removed. However, apply too much force and the spring will not return to its original shape. This is plastic deformation. If enough force is applied, the spring may even break.

Energy transferred in stretching

Doing work on the spring transfers energy into the **energy** store of the spring. The amount of work done equals the amount of energy stored. This energy can be transferred to other energy stores when the spring returns to its original length.

If the limit of proportionality is not exceeded then you can calculate the energy transferred in stretching from the equation:

energy transferred in stretching
= 0.5 × spring constant × (extension or compression)^2

$E_e = \frac{1}{2} ke^2$

Example:

A block is attached to a spring. The spring constant is 28 N/m and the total mass of the block and spring is 10 g. What is the maximum vertical height the block can reach after the spring is compressed by 5 cm then released? (g = 10 N/kg)

$E_e = \frac{1}{2} ke^2 = \frac{1}{2} \times 28 \times (0.05)^2 = 0.035$ J

Provided no energy is dissipated, the decrease in the energy transferred by stretching equals the increase in the gravitational potential energy store:

$E_p = mgh = 0.035$ J

$h = \dfrac{0.035}{(0.01 \times 10)} = 0.35$ m

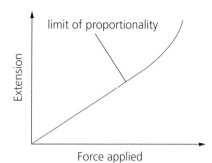

Figure 2.49 The relationship between force and extension for an elastic object, such as a spring

KEY INFORMATION

Formulae involving the spring constant only work if the limit of proportionality is not exceeded.

7 Calculate the energy transferred in stretching by a spring that has been stretched by 2 cm. The spring constant is 30 N/m.

8 A spring has a spring constant of 10 N/m. Determine its extension once 0.2 J of work is done stretching it. Assume the limit of proportionality is not exceeded.

9 A 10 g spring is stretched by 10 cm. It is then released and flies 1 m upwards before it starts to fall down again. Assuming all of the energy transfers to gravitational potential energy, estimate the spring constant of the spring. What else have you assumed in your calculation? (g = 10 N/kg)

PRACTICAL

Investigate the relationship between force and the extension of a spring

Learning objectives:

- interpret readings to show patterns and trends
- interpret graphs to form conclusions
- apply the equation for a straight line to the graph.

KEY WORD

extension
anomaly
mean
spring constant

A class of students have been making and testing springs. They have then investigated how these springs behave when loaded with a weight. They have carried out the experiment and gathered the data. Their next job is to see what it shows.

These pages are designed to help you think about aspects of the investigation rather than to guide you through it step by step.

Analysing the results

When analysing results look for patterns or similarities and see if these can be used to draw a conclusion.

Ellie investigated three springs and recorded her data in a table. The table shows the readings and the calculations.

Force (N)	Spring 1 extension (mm)				Spring 2 extension (mm)				Spring 3 extension (mm)			
	1st reading	2nd reading	3rd reading	Mean	1st reading	2nd reading	3rd reading	Mean	1st reading	2nd reading	3rd reading	Mean
10	8	9	7	8	3	3	4	3	4	4	4	4
20	20	13	12	15	6	7	6	6	8	9	10	9
30	20	19	30	23	10	10	11	10	14	13	12	13
40	34	30	32	32	13	13	13	13	16	16	16	16
50	35	45	40	40	16	17	17	17	22	22	20	21

1. What apparatus should be used to measure the force applied to the spring?

2. How should the extension of the spring be measured?

3. How did Ellie calculate the mean values?

4. Are there any anomalies?

5. Suggest whether these calculations are a good way of getting close to the true values of the extension.

DID YOU KNOW?

The relationship between the force on a spring and the extension it produces was first put forward by Robert Hooke in 1660. He was an inventor, a scientist and an architect. He invented the universal joint now used in the transmission systems of motor cars, the iris diaphragm used in cameras and was first to coin the word cell in biology. He designed many of the new buildings after the Great Fire of London.

Making sense of the graph

Darren's group have drawn a graph showing extension against the weight hung from the spring for one of their springs (Figure 2.57). They are now looking at the graph to see what conclusion they can draw.

6 What does the straight part of the graph show?

7 What happened in the curved part of the graph?

8 What conclusion could Darren draw from this graph?

9 At what weight should the experiment stop in order to be sure of preventing plastic deformation? Explain your answer.

Using the equation of a straight line

Katie's group have plotted the graphs from the results of their experiments for three springs on a graph (Figure 2.51). They know that any straight line graph can be described using the general formula $y = mx + c$ and they apply it to these lines.

With the first of these (A) they can see that:

- x is the force, which changes from 0 to 8
- y is the extension, which changes from 0 to 16
- c is the y-intercept, which is 0 as the line crosses the y-axis at (0,0)

Therefore $16 = (m \times 8) + 0$, so the gradient, $m = 2$

Since the intercept on Figure 2.51 is zero, the extension is directly proportional to the weight. Since:

force applied to a spring = spring constant × extension

extension = force applied to a spring/spring constant

so the gradient of the graph is 1/spring constant.

The spring constant can be found from 1/gradient, or 1/m.

10 Calculate the value of m for springs B and C.

11 Use the formula $k = F/e$ to calculate the spring constant for springs B and C. Explain which of the springs was the stiffest.

12 The spring constant can also be found by redrawing the graph so that extension is on the horizontal axis and force on the vertical axis. The spring constant is then the gradient of the line for each of the springs.

Try doing this and then check your answers against those for the previous question.

13 **a** Determine the area under line A in Figure 2.51. (Make sure the extension is in metres.)

b Calculate energy transferred by stretching in spring A when a force of 8 N is applied. $E_e = \frac{1}{2}ke^2$.

c Compare your answers to parts (a) and (b) and explain why this is the case.

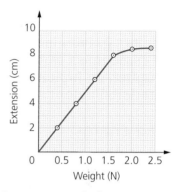

Figure 2.50 Results from Darren's group

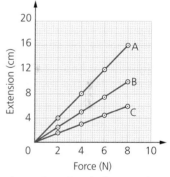

Figure 2.51 Results from Katie's group

REMEMBER!

The spring constant is always measured in N/m so it is important to make sure extension is measured in metres.

Potential energy

Learning objectives:

* consider what happens when a spring is stretched
* describe what is meant by gravitational potential energy
* calculate the energy stored by an object raised above ground level.

On Jupiter, gravity is three times stronger than on Earth. If the same mass was lifted to the same height on Earth and Jupiter, on Jupiter it would store three times the gravitational potential energy.

Stored energy

When a spring is stretched it stores energy. We call this potential energy. The stretched spring stores **energy transferred in stretching**. It stretches more if a greater force is applied, and returns to its original length when the force is removed.

Compressed springs are also used to store energy, for example, to keep batteries in position.

Figure 2.52 A stretched catapult stores energy transferred in stretching

1 Imagine slowly stretching a rubber band. Describe what you would feel as you stretch it more.

2 Suggest what happens to the amount of energy stored in the spring inside a the toy in Figure 2.53 as the key is turned.

Water stored behind a dam also stores energy. It is called **gravitational potential energy (GPE)**. The GPE stored by an object can be increased by moving it upwards. For example, you gain GPE by going up stairs.

3 An aircraft is flying horizontally at a height of **10 000 m**. Explain whether its gravitational potential energy is increasing, decreasing or remaining constant.

Figure 2.53 Turning the key twists a spring inside the toy. This stores energy which can be transferred to kinetic energy

Calculating changes in gravitational potential energy

Tom lifts a box. The amount of gravitational potential energy gained by the box depends on:

* the mass of the box, m, in kilograms, kg
* the height Tom raises the box, h, in metres, m.

We can calculate the amount of gravitational potential energy gained (E_p) using the equation:

$$E_p = mgh$$

Figure 2.54 The stored gravitational potential energy of water held behind a dam can be transferred to kinetic energy if the water is released

where m is measured in kg, g is the **gravitational field strength** in N/kg and h is measured in m.

The pull of gravity on the box (its weight) is calculated using

gravity force (weight) = mass × gravitational field strength

$$W = m \times g$$

The gravitational field strength is the pull of gravity on each kilogram. The value of g is 10 N/kg at the Earth's surface. Changes in E_p are measured in joules (J).

Zack gains gravitational potential energy when he walks up some stairs (Figure 2.55). The E_p Zack gains can be calculated using $E_p = mgh$ where h is the vertical height he raises her body.

Zack then walks on a level floor. He does not gain or lose any gravitational potential energy now because his height above the floor does not change.

4 **Lars is a weight lifter. He lifts a mass of 300 kg through a height of 2 m. Calculate the gravitational potential energy gained by the weight.**

5 **Sian picks up a ball from the floor and holds it 2 m above the ground. The ball has a mass of 60 g. Calculate the gravitational potential energy gained by the ball.**

Calculating energy transferred in stretching

The amount of energy stored in a spring can be increased by

- increasing the extension of the spring, e, in metres, m (as shown in Figure 2.56)
- increasing the spring constant, k, in newtons per metre, N/m

We can calculate the energy stored in a spring using the equation:

$$E_e = \frac{1}{2}ke^2$$

Example: Calculate the energy stored in a spring when it is extended by 6 cm. The spring constant is 150 N/m.

Answer: 6 cm = 0.06 m

$E_e = 0.5 \times 150 \text{ N/m} \times (0.06 \text{ m})^2 = 0.27 \text{ J}$

6 **Calculate the energy stored in a spring which has a spring constant of 300 N/m and is extended by 0.1 m.**

7 **A spring has a spring constant of 500 N/m. The original length of the spring is 20 cm. It is stretched to a length of 25 cm. Calculate the energy stored in the spring.**

8 **A spring stores 12 J when it is stretched by 16 cm. Calculate the spring constant.**

9 **A stretched spring has a total length of 20 cm and a spring constant of 200 N/m. It is storing 0.25 J. Determine the unstretched length of the spring.**

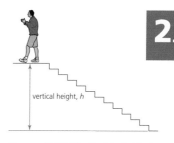

2.19

Figure 2.55 Vertical height, h

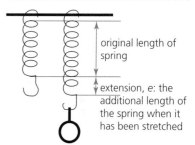

Figure 2.56 Extension of a spring

MATHS

Always put values into an equation using SI units (time in seconds, distance in metres etc.). If the values in the question are not in SI units, you have to change the values to SI units before starting the calculation.

REMEMBER!

Use the **vertical** height when finding the change in an object's height.

Heavy or massive?

Learning objectives:

- identify the correct units for mass and weight
- explain the difference between mass and weight
- understand how weight is an effect of gravitational fields.

KEY WORDS
....
mass
weight
gravitational
   field strength

Everyone knows that most things fall to the ground and that it's gravity that causes this to happen. This doesn't mean that gravity only acts downwards. It's a force of attraction between any two objects, such as you and the person you're sitting next to. However, you only notice it if at least one of the objects is massive.

Weight and mass?

Some people say they want to lose weight and they may keep weighing themselves. The scales are probably marked in kilograms (kg). Even if you never use scales, you'll know that you buy food such as sugar and flour by weight. The bags are marked in kilograms. In these examples weight is being confused with mass.

It's important, in science, to understand that mass and weight are not the same thing.

Mass is the amount of substance that is present in an object. It is measured in kilograms. **Weight** is the force acting on that mass, if it is in a gravitational field. As weight is a force; it is measured in newtons (N).

1 **An astronaut on the Moon feels much lighter than on Earth. Have they lost weight?**

2 **Denzil says that a weighing scale is actually a forcemeter. Is he right? Explain.**

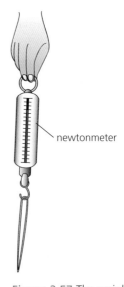
newtonmeter

Figure 2.57 The weight of an object can be measured using a **newtonmeter**.

Weight is a force

Gravity is a non-contact force. It is useful to think of it as a force field; anything (any matter) in a gravitational field will experience a force of attraction. All matter has a gravitational field that causes attraction. The strength of this gravitational field increases with increasing mass. It is much greater for massive objects. We are all in the Earth's gravitational field; it is attracting us towards the Earth.

Weight is the force acting on an object due to gravity. The weight of an object depends on the **gravitational field strength** at the point where the object is, and on the mass of the object. The weight of an object can be calculated using the equation:

weight = mass × gravitational field strength

$$W = mg$$

KEY INFORMATION
....
Remember that in science we measure mass in kilograms and weight in newtons. We use different units because they are different things, but there is a relationship between them.

Weight, W is measured in newtons, N (Figure 2.14), mass, m in kg and gravitational field strength, g in N/kg. On Earth g is taken to be 10 N/kg. g is also given as 10 m/s². The units are equivalent.

Example:

Calculate the weight on Earth of a 5 kg mass. Assume g = 10 N/kg.

$W = mg$

> $= 5 \text{ kg} \times 10 \text{ N/g}$
>
> $= 50 \text{ N}$

3 Write down the weight on Earth of objects having a mass of

a 7 kg

b 0.5 kg

c 400 g

4 A steel block weighs 30 N on Earth.

a What is its mass?

b The steel block is taken to Mars where it weighs 11.1 N. Calculate the gravitational field strength on Mars.

REMEMBER!

All objects falling to the surface of the Earth accelerate at the same rate. This is the acceleration of free fall, 10 m/s² near the surface of Earth.

Losing weight in space

Mass is a property of an object and is constant wherever you are. Weight, however, depends not only the mass but also the gravitational field strength. On the Moon, gravity (at the surface) is around a sixth of that on Earth, so everything weighs one sixth of what it does on Earth. Scales are forcemeters where the scale is given in kilograms. Standing on the scales in a lunar space station would give a reading one sixth of that on the Earth. Your mass is a constant but your weight is much less.

In deep space, well away from any stars or planets, you would be weightless. You would still have mass though, and if you wanted to move from one end of your spacecraft to the other, you would still need to apply a force.

5 Alex says that weighing scales should all carry a label saying 'calibrated for use on planet Earth only'. Is she right?

6 An astronaut in deep space (where there is no gravity) is at one end of her craft and wants to move to the other. She pushes against the inside of the craft with a force of 25 N and this causes her to accelerate at 0.5 m/s². What is her weight?

7 Describe a measuring instrument that could give a correct measurement of mass on the Earth and on the Moon without having to change any settings.

Check your progress

You should be able to:

Know that forces are vectors and have magnitude and direction →
Explain the difference between contact and non-contact forces →
Represent vector quantities by arrows

Understand that average speed = distance/time →
Know that acceleration is the rate at which speed changes →
Calculate acceleration from change in velocity/time taken

Explain the significance of the gradient of a distance–time graph →
Interpret a journey represented on a distance–time graph →
Determine the instantaneous speed from the tangent to a distance–time graph of an accelerating object

Explain the significance of the gradient of a velocity–time graph →
Interpret a journey represented on a velocity–time graph →
Determine total distance travelled from a velocity–time graph

Recall the equation for uniform motion →
Apply the equation for uniform motion →
Rearrange the equation for uniform motion

Draw a free-body diagram to represent forces acting on an object →
Calculate the resultant force acting on an object →
Determine the components of a force

Apply Newton's first law to a stationary object and an object moving in a straight line at a constant speed →
Link Newton's first law to the idea of a zero resultant force →
Explain what is meant by inertia

State Newton's second law and recall the equation $F = ma$ →
Use $F = ma$ to determine force, mass or acceleration →
Explain what is meant by inertial mass

Recognise that weight and mass are not the same →
Explain the difference between weight and mass →
Relate the ideas of weight and mass to Newton's second law

State Newton's third law →
Apply Newton's third law to simple equilibrium situations →
Explain how Newton's third law applies

Explain what is meant by momentum →
Relate ideas about forces and kinetic energy, and to rate of change of momentum →
Apply the principle of conservation of momentum to collisions

recognise that when a force moves an object along the line of action of the force, work is being done →
calculate the work done by a force from the size of the force and the distance moved →
use the equation for work done to solve problems, including changing the subject of the equation

state that various devices do work and, in doing so, transfer energy

Worked example

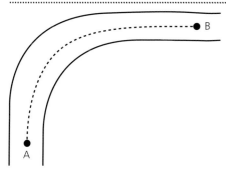

The diagram shows a car travelling round a bend at a constant speed of 20 m/s. It took the car 4.5 s to move from point A to B.

① Explain why the distance travelled by the car from A to B is greater than the car's displacement at B.

The car's displacement is the distance from A to B in a straight line. The car travelled a further distance as it was going round the curve.

This is correct. You should also note that distance is a scalar quantity but displacement is a vector quantity with size and direction.

② Calculate the distance the car travelled from A to B.

$v = \dfrac{s}{t}$ so $s = \dfrac{v}{t}$

$s = \dfrac{20}{4.5}$

$s = 4.44$ m

The student correctly remembered the equation $v = \dfrac{s}{t}$ but failed to rearrange it correctly as $s = v \times t$ to give the answer 90 m.

③ Explain why the car is accelerating as it travels round the bend at a constant speed.

Acceleration is a change in velocity and the car's velocity is changing as it goes round the bend.

Velocity is speed in a given direction. As the car goes round the corner, its speed stays the same but the direction is constantly changing, so its velocity is constantly changing which is acceleration.

End of chapter questions

Getting started

1 In what units are forces measured? `1 Mark`

2 Which one of these is not a force? `1 Mark`

    a weight   **b** air resistance   **c** mass   **d** upthrust

3 Give an example of a contact force and a non-contact force. `2 Marks`

4 What unit does the symbol Pa represent and what is it a measure of? `1 Mark`

5 Explain why a force is a vector quantity. `1 Mark`

6 Use the equation $s = vt$ to calculate the average speed of a car when it travels 100 m in 5 s. `1 Mark`

7 On Earth, what is the weight of a 50 kg boy? ($g = 9.8$ N/kg) `1 Mark`

8 Describe the motion represented by the graph below. `2 Marks`

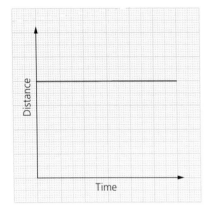

Going further

9 On a distance–time graph, what is represented by a straight line sloping upwards? `1 Mark`

10 Elise has a weight of 400 N and can clear a high jump of 2 m. Calculate how much work she does in raising her body up 2 m. `2 Marks`

11 An object moves in a circle at 2 m/s.

Choose the correct words. `1 Mark`

The speed of the object:

changes

remains constant

The velocity of the object:

changes

remains constant

12 How does the momentum of an 8 kg ball rolling at 1 m/s compare with that of a 16 kg ball rolling at 2 m/s?

`2 Marks`

13 A battery powered toy car is travelling along the floor. If the force applied by the motor is 10 N, friction of the moving parts opposing the motion is 3 N and air resistance 1 N, represent these on a free body diagram, calculate the resultant and describe the motion at that instant.

`4 Marks`

More challenging

14 A car is travelling at a constant speed of 20 m/s. Its mass is 1000 kg and the force of friction opposing the motion of the car is 1500 N.

Determine the size of the force that the engine is providing to drive the car.

`1 Mark`

15 Explain the meaning of limit of proportionality for a spring.

`2 Marks`

16 An apple falls 2 m from a tree branch to the ground.

`3 Marks`

  a If $g = 10 \text{ m/s}^2$ at what speed will it hit the ground?

  b Why is the speed it actually hits the ground likely to be less?

17 A car of 1500 kg hits a building at 20 m/s, coming to rest in 1 s

`4 Marks`

  a Calculate the force on the car.

  b The driver is wearing a seat beat which means that he stops travelling forward after 3 s. Use the concept of changing momentum to explain why this reduces the likelihood of injury.

Most demanding

18 What is Newton's third law?

`2 Marks`

19 A car of mass 1500 kg is travelling along a motorway at 25 m/s. Calculate the braking distance of the car if the brakes exert a force of 3000 N.

`2 Marks`

20 A snooker player hit a white ball with her cue. The white ball then collided with a stationary red ball. The player noticed that the white ball stopped after the collision. She also noticed that the red ball moved with the same velocity as the white ball had before the collision.

Explain the physics behind these observations and make a conclusion about the mass of the balls. Use sensible numerical values to illustrate your answer. Assume no friction acts during the collision.

`6 Marks`

`Total: 38 Marks`

ELECTRICITY AND MAGNETISM

IDEAS YOU HAVE MET BEFORE:

STATIC ELECTRICITY

- Electrical insulators can be charged by rubbing (friction).
- There are two kinds of electric charge – positive and negative.
- Like charges repel, unlike charges attract.

ELECTRIC CURRENT

- An electric current is due to a flow of charge.
- Resistors are used to control the current in circuits.
- Ohm's law is used to calculate resistance.

ENERGY

- Cells are sources of electricity.
- A battery is a number of cells joined together.
- Energy sources can be used to drive electrical generators to produce electricity.

PERMANENT MAGNETS

- Permanent magnets are made from nickel, cobalt and most steels.
- Iron is a magnetic material but loses its magnetism when the magnetising force is removed.
- Like poles repel and unlike poles attract.
- Repulsion is the only test for a magnet.

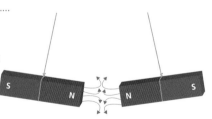

MAGNETIC EFFECT OF A CURRENT

- The wires carrying an electric current produce a magnetic field.
- The magnetic field made by the current in a wire is a circular shape around the wire.
- The magnetic field is increased if more turns are wound on the coil and/or the current in the wire is increased.

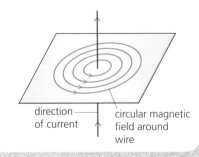

direction of current

circular magnetic field around wire

IN THIS CHAPTER YOU WILL FIND OUT ABOUT:

WHAT IS STATIC ELECTRICITY?

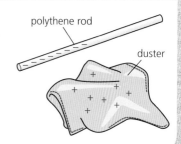

- Insulators become charged when they gain or lose electrons.
- Static electricity can give a person an electric shock and it may create a spark which could cause petrol vapour or natural gas to explode.

WHAT ARE THE KEY CONCEPTS IN ELECTRICITY?

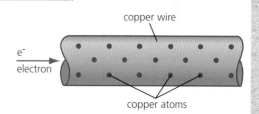

- Electric current is the rate of flow of charge through a conductor.
- Some electrical components resist the flow of electrons more than others so have greater resistance.
- Potential difference is a measure of the energy transferred per unit charge as charges move between two points in a circuit.

WHAT ARE THE CHARACTERISTICS OF SOME ELECTRICAL COMPONENTS?

- When electrical components are connected in parallel, there is more current passing through each component than when they are connected in series.
- A fixed resistor at constant temperature obeys Ohm's law, so the current through it is directly proportional to the potential difference across it.
- Diodes, thermistors and light-dependent resistors do not obey Ohm's law.

WHAT IS A MOTOR AND HOW DOES IT WORK?

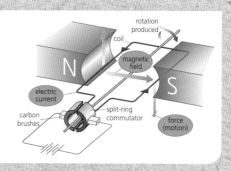

- Describe some uses of motors.
- Explain how a motor works.
- Explain how a commutator is used.

Static electricity

Learning objectives:

- describe how insulating materials can become charged
- know that there are two kinds of electric charge
- explain these observations in terms of electron transfer.

KEY WORDS

attract
conductor
electron
insulator
repel

Explosions can be caused by a spark from the discharge of static electricity.

Producing static electricity

Clouds become charged as small pieces of ice bump into each other. If enough charge builds up, a spark in the form of lightning jumps across the gap between the cloud and the ground and an electric current passes between the cloud and Earth (Figure 3.1) or between clouds.

Metals are good electrical **conductors.** Electric charges can move through them. But electric **insulators** such as glass, polythene or wood do not allow electric charges to move through them. Charge builds up. Many insulators can be charged by friction.

When a polythene rod is rubbed with a duster it becomes charged and can **attract** tiny pieces of paper (Figure 3.2).

Figure 3.1 Cloud-to-ground lightning

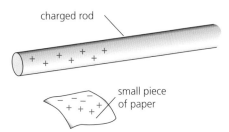

charged rod

small piece of paper

Figure 3.2 The charged rod attracts a small piece of paper by inducing a charge on the paper

Other materials can be charged by friction:

- When a balloon is rubbed on a sweater it becomes charged and sticks to a wall.
- Some dusting brushes are designed to become charged and attract dust.
- When hair is combed with a plastic comb both the comb and the hair become charged.

1 Name:

   a an insulator and

   b a conductor of electricity.

2 Explain why static charges do not build up on a conductor.

Two kinds of electric charge

There are two kinds of electric charge, positive and negative (Figure 3.3).

Like charges **repel**, unlike charges **attract**.

Forces of attraction and repulsion between charged objects are examples of non-contact forces.

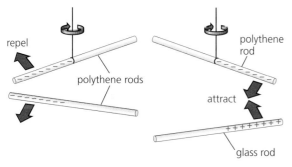

Figure 3.3 Like charges repel, unlike charges attract

3 Polythene, acetate and Perspex rods are charged with a duster. State whether these pairs of rods will attract or repel each other:

a a polythene rod and an acetate rod

b two Perspex rods

c a Perspex rod and a polythene rod

d an acetate rod and a Perspex rod.

4 A Van de Graaff generator produces a large electrostatic charge. Beth puts her hands on a Van de Graaff generator when it is switched off. When it is switched on she becomes charged (Figure 3.4). Explain why does her hair stand on end.

Figure 3.4 A Van de Graaff generator

Electron transfer

An atom consists of a small positively charged nucleus surrounded by negatively charged **electrons**. In a neutral atom there are equal numbers of positive and negative charges. All electrostatic effects are caused by the movement of electrons.

• If a polythene rod is rubbed with a duster, electrons **move from the duster to the polythene** making the polythene negatively charged.
• If an acetate rod is rubbed with a duster, electrons move **from the acetate to the duster** making the acetate rod positively charged.

5 When a polythene rod is charged by rubbing it with a duster what charge, if any, does the duster gain?

Electric charge and currents

Learning objectives:

- recall that an electric current is a rate of flow of electric charge
- recall that current has the same value at any point in a single closed loop
- recall and use the relationship between quantity of charge, current and time.

Sparking

The atoms and molecules of gases in the air contain positive and negative charges. Normally, air is an electrical insulator and does not conduct electricity. However, when there is a very strong electric field the atoms and molecules in the air break apart to form negative and positive ions. The charged ions experience forces of attraction and repulsion, and move around. This gives a **spark**.

Lightning is a very big spark. As a thundercloud charges up, a large difference in the size and sign of the charges builds up between the cloud and the Earth. When this difference is strong enough to ionise the air, the lightning strikes.

1. Can a spark occur between two charges which are in a vacuum? Explain your answer.

2. In a particular thunderstorm, a thundercloud causes lightning to the strike the ground at a rate of once every minute. The cloud then passes over a hill. Predict what happens to the rate of lightning strikes. Justify your answer.

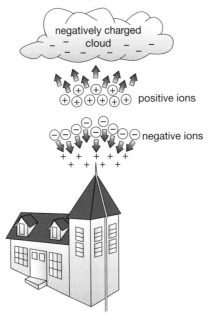

DID YOU KNOW?

To create a build up of charge that is strong enough to produce lightning, the potential difference between thunderclouds and the Earth can reach up to 35 million volts.

Figure 3.5 A lightning conductor is attached by a thick copper cable to a rod that is buried in the Earth below. When the air is ionised during a thunderstorm there is a path for current to travel into the ground rather than through the building itself.

Electric current and charge

Current is a rate of flow of electric charge. Electric charge is measured in **coulombs** (C). We now know that an electric current in a metal is actually a flow of electrons from negative to positive. The SI unit for electric current is the ampere (A). (You may see this abbreviated to 'amps'.)

electric charge (charge flow), Q = current, I × time, t.
(in C)   (in A)   (in s)

$$Q = It$$

Example: A wire carries a current of 1.2 A for 30 s. How much charge flows?

$Q = It = 1.2 × 30 = 36$ C

3 Calculate the current when 80 C of charge flows in 16 s.

4 A charge of 96 C flows in a wire carrying a current of 6 A. Calculate how long it takes for this amount of charge to flow.

DID YOU KNOW?

Japanese scientists have managed to achieve an electric current of 100 000 amperes – by far the highest to be generated in the world.

Current flow around a circuit

If we set up a circuit with a battery and three bulbs in series we can show it in a diagram like this:

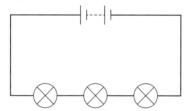

Figure 3.6

All the bulbs should light up and (as long as they are the same type) they should all be equally bright.

We could then find out how much current was flowing at each point in the circuit by putting an ammeter first at point A, then at B, etc. If we did this we would find out that it was the same current at all points.

5 If the reading at B was 0.3A, what would the reading be at point D?

6 If the battery started to run down and the bulbs got dimmer, the ammeter reading at A was now 0.2A, what would it be at D?

7 How could you summarise this idea in a single sentence?

Electric circuits and potential difference

Learning objectives:

- know circuit symbols
- recall that current (*I*) depends on resistance (*R*) and potential difference (*V*)
- explain how an electric current passes round a circuit.

KEY WORDS

parallel
potential
    difference (pd)
resistance
voltmeter

An electrostatic charge can build up in the air as a thunderstorm forms. The potential difference between a thundercloud and the ground can be up to 100 000 000 volts.

Electric circuits and symbols

In order for a current to flow, a complete circuit must be formed. Also, a source of energy is needed to drive the current. This source of energy can be a simple electrical cell, a battery of cells or a power supply connected to the mains electricity.

In a simple (series) circuit (see example in Figure 3.13, topic 3.4), the current that is measured at any point has the same value. This is because no electric charge that flows 'leaks' out of the circuit.

We can use this energy in a number of useful ways. Devices have been designed that can transfer energy to produce heat (electric bar heaters), light (lightbulbs and LEDs) and movement (electric motors). Each device is given its own symbol so that clear and complete circuits can be drawn. The symbols for the devices that you need to know about are shown in Figure 3.8.

1 Draw a simple circuit containing a cell and a variable resistor.

2 The symbol for a light-emitting diode (LED) is a diode with two short parallel lines pointing outwards, representing light. Use the same logic to suggest what 'LDR' stands for and what an LDR does.

Potential difference

Potential difference (pd) is the energy transferred per unit charge as charges move between two points in a circuit. It is measured in volts (V) using a **voltmeter**. A voltmeter is always connected across the component. We say the voltmeter is connected in **parallel** (Figure 3.9).

For an electric current to flow, there needs to be a complete loop and a source of potential difference.

Potential difference is sometimes referred to as voltage.

1 volt is the energy transferred when 1 coulomb of charge moves through a component. 1 V = 1 J/C. If a 12 V battery is used to light a lamp, each coulomb of charge going from the battery receives 12 J of energy.

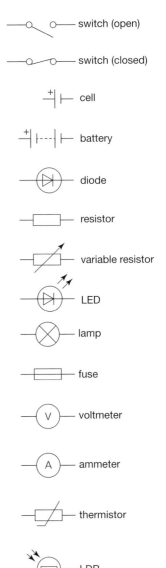

Figure 3.7 Circuit symbols

- switch (open)
- switch (closed)
- cell
- battery
- diode
- resistor
- variable resistor
- LED
- lamp
- fuse
- voltmeter
- ammeter
- thermistor
- LDR

3 Write two things that are needed for there to be an electric current.

4 A 6 V battery passes a current of 1 A through a lamp for 1 minute. Calculate how much energy is transferred from the battery to the lamp.

Current, resistance and potential difference

Electrons are 'pushed' around a circuit by a battery. They bump into the metal ions in the resistor. This makes the metal ions vibrate more so the resistor gets hotter. The increased vibrations of the ions held in their fixed lattice make it harder for the electrons to travel through the resistor, so its resistance increases (Figure 3.9).

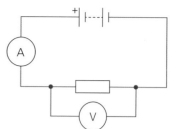

Figure 3.8 Measuring the pd across a resistor using a voltmeter

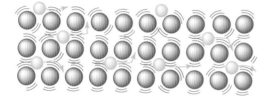

 metal ions in the resistor

electrons collide with the metal ions

Figure 3.9 The movement of electrons in a wire carrying a current

The filament in a lamp connected in a circuit becomes so hot it emits light.

Note that the net direction in which the electrons move is opposite to the direction of the conventional current. The conventional current direction, from positive to negative, was well established before scientists understood that the electrons actually moved from negative to positive. So they did not change it.

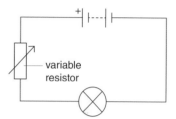

Figure 3.10 Circuit with variable resistor and lamp

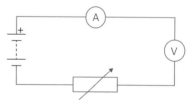

Figure 3.11

5 Why might the resistor in Figure 3.10 get warm?

6 The circuit shown in Figure 3.11 includes a variable resistor. Explain how the variable resistor can be used as a dimmer switch.

Current, *I*, **resistance**, *R* and potential difference, *V* are linked by the equation:

potential difference, *V* = current *I* × resistance, *R*

(in volts, V)   (in amperes, A) (in ohms, Ω)

$$V = IR$$

Example: Calculate the potential difference across a 5 Ω resistor when the current through it is 2A.

$$V = IR = 2 \times 5 = 10 \text{ V.}$$

7 Calculate the resistance of a car headlamp when the supply potential difference is 12 V and the current is 3 A.

8 Calculate the potential difference across a 6 Ω resistor when the current through it is 1.5 A.

Series and parallel circuits

Learning objectives:

- recognise series and parallel circuits
- describe the changes in the current and potential difference in series and parallel circuits.

All the electrical appliances in a home are connected in a parallel circuit. If they were connected in series you would need to switch on every single appliance in order to watch TV.

Lamps in series and parallel

In the **series circuit** in Figure 3.12, the lamps are connected next to each other and form a single loop with the battery and the switch. In the **parallel circuit,** both sides of the lamps are connected to each other – a little like the rungs of a ladder.

When they are shining, the lamps connected in parallel are brighter than lamps connected in series.

If an extra lamp is added to the series circuit, then all of the lamps in the circuit are even dimmer. If an extra lamp is added to the parallel circuit, the lamps are the same brightness as before.

1 None of the lamps in Figure 3.12 are currently shining. State what you would have to do to the circuits to make the lamps shine.

2 A third lamp is added to the series circuit. Describe what happens to the brightness of the two lamps that were already in the circuit.

3 Suggest what would happen if one bulb was unscrewed in each circuit.

Series circuit

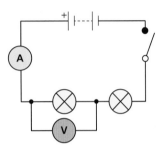

Parallel circuit

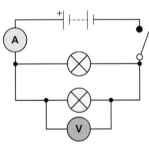

Figure 3.12 A series circuit and a parallel circuit

Resistors in series

In the series circuit in Figure 3.14 the current has to pass through *both* resistors, R_1 and R_2. There is nowhere else for it to go. This means that the readings on all of the ammeters are the same.

When components are connected in series, the same current flows through each component. The size of the current depends on the total resistance of the components.

For components in series, the total resistance is the sum of all of the resistances. The total resistance of the circuit in Figure 3.14 is $R_1 + R_2$.

The potential difference of the power supply is shared between the components. This means that the reading of voltmeter V_1 plus the reading of voltmeter V_2 would equal the potential difference of the battery.

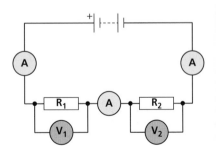

Figure 3.13 A series circuit

4 A motor, a lamp and a 12 V battery are connected in series. The resistance of the motor is 10 Ω and the resistance of the lamp is 20 Ω. The current through the lamp is 0.4 A.

a Determine the current through the motor.

b Calculate the total resistance of the circuit.

c If the potential difference across the motor is 4 V then what is the potential difference across the lamp?

d Suggest how the current would change if the lamp was replaced with a 50 Ω resistor.

Resistors in parallel

In the parallel circuit in Figure 3.14, the current can pass through either R_1 or R_2 in the circuit. This means that the reading on ammeter A_1 is equal to the sum of the readings on ammeters A_2 and A_3.

The potential difference of the power supply is the same as the potential difference across each component. So the reading of both voltmeters V_1 and V_2 would be the same and would equal the potential difference of the power supply.

Adding a resistor in series increases the total resistance because the electric charge has to pass through another component. Adding a resistor in parallel decreases the total resistance because you are providing an alternative path for the electric charge. The total resistance of a parallel circuit is always smaller than the smallest resistance of any component.

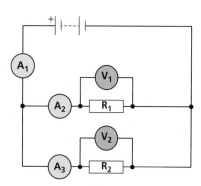

Figure 3.14 A parallel circuit

5 The 10 Ω motor, 20 Ω lamp and 12 V battery from Q4 are now connected in parallel. A current of 1.8 A passes through the battery and a current of 1.2 A passes through the motor.

a Determine the current through the lamp.

b Calculate is the potential difference across the motor.

c Explain whether the total resistance of this circuit is greater or smaller than 10 Ω.

d A further resistor is added in parallel to the motor and the lamp. Explain what happens to the size of the current passing through the battery.

> **DID YOU KNOW?**
> ....
> A current of 1 A means that more than 6 000 000 000 000 000 000 electrons pass each point every second. This is only a small fraction of the electrons in the wire!

Resistance

Learning objectives:

- set up a circuit to investigate resistance
- investigate the changing resistance of a filament lamp
- compare the properties of a resistor and filament lamp.

KEY WORDS

....

filament bulb

New light bulbs have been introduced to replace the filament bulb. The so-called 'energy saver' light bulb lasts longer and is more economical to use, but it has the disadvantage that it contains mercury, which is toxic.

Measuring resistance

The circuit shown in Figure 3.15 can be used to measure the resistance of a fixed resistor. As the variable resistor is changed, the readings on the ammeter and voltmeter are recorded. A graph of current (I) against potential difference (V) is plotted. A straight line through the origin shows that current is proportional to potential difference (Figure 3.16). Such resistors are ohmic – they obey Ohm's law. Their resistance is constant. The resistance is equal to 1/gradient of an I–V graph. Copper wire and all other metals give this shape of graph as long as the temperature does not change.

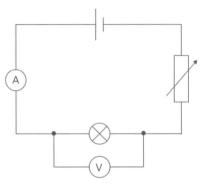

Figure 3.15 This circuit can be used to measure the resistance of a filament bulb

① **What does a straight line graph through the origin tell you about the quantities plotted?**

② **Which meter is connected in parallel, the ammeter or the voltmeter?**

The changing resistance of a filament lamp

If you switch on a light bulb using a dimmer switch, you will see that you can change the brightness of the bulb. This is because the higher the current, the higher the temperature of the filament. The hotter the bulb, the whiter and brighter the light from it becomes.

If the fixed resistor in Figure 3.15 is replaced by a **filament bulb** (Figure 3.17), the corresponding graph of current against potential difference is no longer a straight line. This is because the resistance of the filament bulb changes as its temperature changes. In Figure 3.18 the resistance is different for each potential difference and current value.

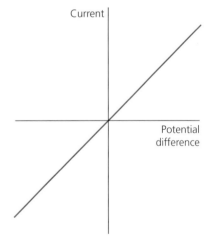

Figure 3.16 I–V graph for an ohmic conductor

When the filament in a bulb gets hot, two things happen. The free electrons move faster, and the metal ions in the filament vibrate more, taking up more space. As the atoms take up more space, the electrons collide with them more often, so the resistance and temperature of the bulb increase (Figure 3.17). This is why the resistance of a filament bulb increases with temperature.

The filament is made of tungsten as tungsten does not melt and evaporates very little at the typical filament bulb operating temperature of 2000 °C. An inert gas such as nitrogen or argon is usually included in the bulb to prevent the evaporation of the tungsten.

3 Explain how you know that the filament lamp is a non-ohmic conductor.

4 The filament in a bulb is made from tungsten. Tungsten, like other metals, obeys Ohm's law. Why is the *I–V* graph for a filament lamp not a straight line?

Comparing I–V graphs

A fixed resistor at constant temperature produces a straight line *I–V* graph (Figure 3.16), showing the resistance is constant. The value of the resistance is equal to the inverse of the gradient of the *I–V* graph.

The filament of a lamp is a heating element that gets so hot that it emits light. This huge temperature change means that the filament is non-ohmic – its resistance increases as the temperature increases. The *I–V* graph is a curve (Figure 3.18) – it is non-linear. The resistance of the bulb at different potential differences can only be found from instantaneous *I–V* values, not from the gradient.

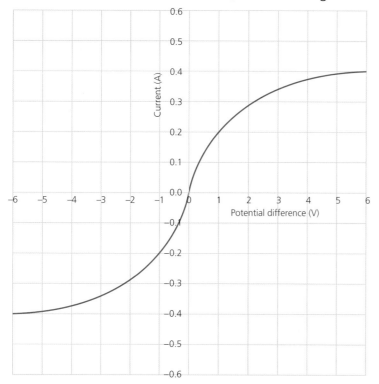

Figure 3.18 The changing slope of this graph shows that the resistance of the filament lamp increases as the current increases

5 **a** Calculate the resistance at 1 V and 6 V in Figure 3.18.

b Sketch a graph of resistance against time for the filament lamp immediately after it is switched on.

> **DID YOU KNOW?**
>
> The average light bulb has a lifetime of about 1000 hours. The tungsten used to make the filament evaporates at 2500 °C.

Figure 3.17 Coiled tungsten filament lamp

> **KEY INFORMATION**
>
> The resistance of a non-ohmic conductor is found from instantaneous values, not the gradient of the graph.

> **KEY INFORMATION**
>
> A graph of current against potential difference is called an *I–V* characteristic of the component.

PRACTICAL

Use circuit diagrams to set up and check appropriate circuits to investigate the factors affecting the resistance

KEY WORDS

potential
  difference
current
resistance

Learning objectives:

- use a circuit to determine resistance
- gather valid data to use in calculations
- apply the circuit to determine the resistance of different components.

We can use a circuit to determine the resistance of a component, as resistance can be calculated from measuring potential difference and current. We can then see how test other electrical components in a similar way.

> These pages are designed ❶ to help you think about aspects of the investigation rather than to guide you through it step by step.

Using a circuit to get useful data

The resistance of a component, such as a piece of wire, can be calculated using the formula:

resistance = potential difference ÷ current

$$R = \frac{V}{I}$$

If we set up a circuit with an ammeter and a voltmeter in it, we can record the data to calculate the resistance. The circuit we can use is shown in Figure 3.19. The rectangle represents the component being tested, such as a length of wire.

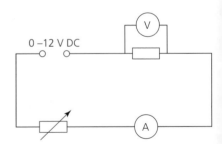

Figure 3.19 Circuit diagram for measuring potential difference across a component and the current passing through it

❶ **Explain what you would expect to happen to the current passing through the component as the potential difference across it is increased.**

❷ **Describe how the potential difference across the component is altered in the circuit shown.**

❸ **If the current passing through the component increases, describe what will happen to its temperature.**

Testing different components

If we replace the resistor in the circuit shown in Figure 3.19 with other components, we can carry out the same measurements and determine some of the behaviour of each component.

Figure 3.20 shows a number of components we can test in this way.

4 A lamp heats up and gives off more light as current in increased. Why is it important not to set the current too high?

5 A fuse is designed to allow current up to a certain value. Sketch a graph of current against potential for a fuse rated as 13 A maximum value. What happens if the current goes above 13 A?

6 Sketch a graph of resistance against light intensity for an LDR.

7 Suggest two types of circuit in which a thermistor might be useful.

8 The graph in Figure 3.21 shows current against potential difference for a diode. Interpret the graph and explain what it shows.

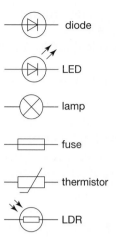

Figure 3.20 Circuit components that could be tested using the circuit in Figure 3.22

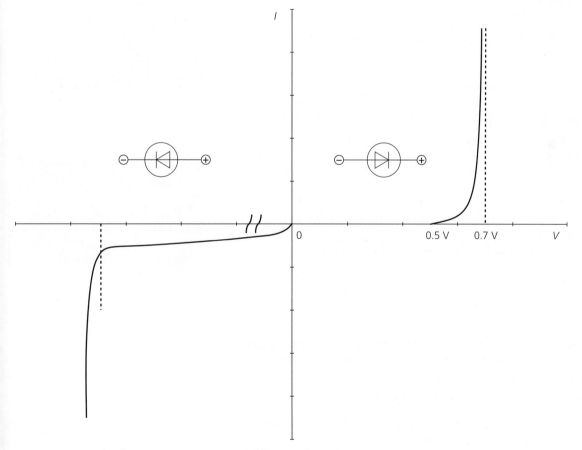

Figure 3.21 Graph of current against potential difference for a diode

Investigating circuits

Learning objectives:

* use series circuits to test components and make measurements
* carry out calculations on series circuits.

When a sports match is televised it can take 24 km of electrical cabling to connect up the TV cameras and the studio. If the equipment goes wrong, engineers need to check quickly that the cables are working. How can they do this?

Circuits for testing and measuring

You can use the circuit in Figure 3.22 to check if a component or an electrical cable conducts electricity easily. The buzzer should sound when the cable or the component is attached to the terminals.

1 Explain how the circuit in Figure 3.22 works.

The circuit in Figure 3.23 is used to investigate the resistance of a component. You connect the component between the terminals. This circuit can be used to investigate lamps and diodes as well as components that measure temperature and light intensity.

The **ammeter** measures the current passing through the component and the voltmeter measures the potential difference across the component. Ammeters are always connected in series with the component, and voltmeters are always connected in parallel. Voltmeters have a very high resistance, which means that only a very small current flows through a voltmeter. Ammeters have a very low resistance, which means that they do not have very much effect on the resistance of the circuit.

You can change the current by altering the resistance of the variable resistor. The resistance is usually altered by moving a slider or by turning a dial.

2 An electric heater is placed between the terminals of the circuit in Figure 3.23. The ammeter reading is 2 A and the voltmeter reading is 12 V.

   a Calculate the resistance of the heater.

   b Describe how you could alter the circuit so that a current of 1 A passes through the heater.

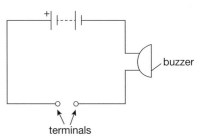

Figure 3.22 A circuit for testing components and cables

REMEMBER!

The resistance of a component equals the potential difference divided by the current.

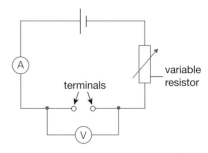

Figure 3.23 A circuit to measure the resistance of a component

Circuit calculations

These rules help you to calculate currents, potential differences and resistances in circuits.

For resistors in series, the total potential difference is the sum of the potential differences across the resistors and the current is the same through all of the resistors. The total resistance is the sum of the resistances of the resistors.

For resistors in parallel, the potential difference across each resistor is identical, but the total current is the sum of the currents that pass through each of the resistors.

3 A resistor, an ammeter and a voltmeter are connected in series with a 12 V power supply. The ammeter shows the current as 0 A. Suggest what is wrong with the circuit.

4 The potential difference across a resistor is 12 V and the current is 0.6 A. What is the value of its resistance?

5 A 5 Ω and a 7 Ω resistor are connected in series with a 6 V battery. Calculate the current in the circuit.

6 A 3 Ω and a 6 Ω resistor are connected in series with a 12 V battery. What is the potential difference across the 3 Ω resistor?

7 A 3 Ω and a 6 Ω resistor are connected in series with a battery. A current of 1 A passes through the 3 Ω resistor. Determine the potential difference of the battery.

8 A 4 Ω resistor is placed in series with another resistor and a 12 V battery. The potential difference across the 4 Ω resistor is 8 V. Determine the resistance of the other resistor.

Equivalent circuits

Sometimes you can simplify circuit calculations by replacing all the components in a circuit with a single resistor (Figure 3.24). The single resistor needs to have the **equivalent resistance** of the components in the circuit. You can then work out the current passing through the power supply.

9 A 12 V car battery is supplying a current of 60 A to the electric components in a car. The driver then switches on the sound system and a larger current passes through the battery. What happens to the equivalent resistance of the circuit?

10 A 12 Ω motor is connected in parallel with a 6 Ω lamp. Together these are connected in series with a 5 Ω resistor and a 9 V battery. The equivalent resistance of the motor, lamp and resistor is 9 Ω. Calculate the current passing through the battery.

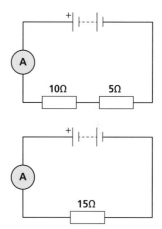

Figure 3.24 These circuits draw the same current from the battery

Control circuits

Learning objectives:

- use a thermistor and light-dependent resistor (LDR)
- investigate the properties of thermistors, LDRs and diodes.

KEY WORDS

diode
light-dependent
  resistor (LDR)
sensors
thermistor

LDRs are placed on top of street lights to turn them on when it gets dark.

Control circuits

Control circuits use components to detect changes. These components are called **sensors**.

A **thermistor** (Figure 3.25) is a temperature-dependent resistor. Its resistance changes a lot as temperature changes. At low temperatures its resistance is high. As the temperature increases its resistance decreases.

A **light-dependent resistor (LDR)** is a component whose resistance changes a lot as light intensity changes. When it is light the resistance of the LDR is low. When it is dark the resistance of the LDR is very high.

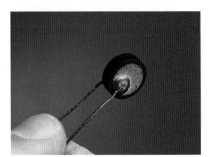

Figure 3.25 Thermistor

1 **What property of an LDR changes as the light level changes?**

2 **What happens when the temperature of a thermistor increases?**

The properties of thermistors

The resistance of a thermistor decreases as the temperature increases. Each thermistor has its own characteristics, but the resistance of a typical thermistor changes from 2000 Ω at –20 °C to 200 Ω at 20 °C.

A thermistor is made from a semi-conductor. A semi-conductor is neither a good conductor nor an insulator. When a semi-conductor is heated it can conduct more easily. This is because the rise in temperature releases more free electrons to carry the current. The higher the temperature the lower the resistance (Figure 3.26).

The resistance of a thermistor is highest when cold. It can be used to:

- turn on a heater when it gets cold, either in the house or in a greenhouse
- act as a fire alarm
- keep a fish tank from becoming too cold.

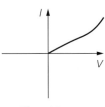

Thermistor

Figure 3.26 *I–V* graph for a thermistor

3. Explain how you know that a thermistor is not an ohmic conductor.

4. Explain how Figure 3.26 shows that a thermistor's resistance decreases when the temperature increases

The properties of light-dependent resistors

In bright sunlight an LDR has a resistance of about 100 Ω. When it is dark the resistance of the LDR becomes very large (Figure 3.27). It can be over 10 MΩ (10 000 000 Ω) in the dark.

An LDR connected in series with a battery and an ammeter can be used to make a simple light meter.

When it is bright the resistance of the LDR is low and the reading on the ammeter is high. When it is dark the resistance of the LDR is high and the reading on the ammeter is low.

This can be used by a cricket umpire to decide whether it is too dark to carry on playing safely.

5. Describe what happens to the current if you cover and uncover an LDR when a bright light is shining on it.

The properties of a diode

A **diode** is a component that only allows a current to flow in one direction – the direction in which the arrow points in the circuit symbol (Figure 3.28).

The current–potential difference characteristics for a diode (Figure 3.29) can be found using a circuit similar to the one used to draw the *I–V* graph for a filament lamp.

Most diodes start to conduct when the potential difference across them is about 0.6 V. The steep slope of the graph shows that current passes easily through the diode when it is conducting. With a negative potential difference, very little current flows.

6. Explain what the *I–V* graph for a diode tells you about the resistance of the diode when the potential difference is negative.

7. Explain why you often need another resistor to protect a diode in a circuit.

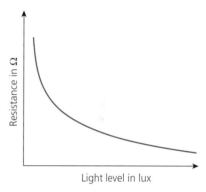

Figure 3.27 Change in resistance with light level in an LDR

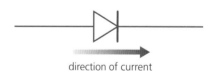

direction of current

Figure 3.28 The arrow on the diode symbol tells you which way the current passes through it.

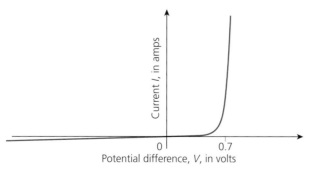

Figure 3.29 *I–V* graph for a diode

Power and energy transfers

Learning objectives:

- describe the energy transfers in different domestic appliances
- describe power as a rate of energy transfer
- calculate the energy transferred.

Much more energy is transferred when you heat a room than when you light a room.

Energy transfers

Electrical devices that we use every day are designed to transfer energy. All electrical appliances transfer energy. But different appliances transfer energy in different ways. They transfer energy from the a.c. mains supply or stores such as batteries to stores such as a motor or the energy stored by the hot water in a kettle.

1 State the energy transfers and stores when a kettle is used to heat water.

Figure 3.30 A hairdryer

Power and energy transferred

Consider a hairdryer (Figure 3.30). The hairdryer receives 1500 J of energy each second from the mains supply. It transfers 1500 J of energy per second from the mains supply to heat up the air and kinetic energy to move the air around.

The **power** is the amount of energy transferred each second. The units are joules per second, or watts (W). As the hairdryer transfers 1500 J each second, its power is 1500 W or 1.5 kW.

2 An electric drill (Figure 3.31) connected to the a.c. mains transfers 400 J every second.

   a Describe how the drill transfers energy and the stores it transfers energy to.
   b State the power of the drill.

Figure 3.31 An electric drill

The amount of energy transferred by an appliance depends on its power and the length of time it is used. We can use this equation to calculate the amount of energy transferred.

energy transferred   =   power   ×   time
   (in joules, J)   (in watts, W)   (in seconds, s)

$E = Pt$

Example:

Example:

The hairdryer in Figure 3.31 is used for 5 minutes. Calculate the total energy transferred by the hairdryer.

$E = Pt$

$\quad = 1500 \text{ W} \times (5 \times 60) \text{ s}$

$\quad = 450\ 000 \text{ J (or 450 kJ)}$

3 An electric oven with a power rating of 2.5 kW is switched on for 45 minutes.

Calculate the total energy transferred by the oven.

4 A hairdryer transfers 10 000 J of energy from the a.c. mains supply in 5 s. Calculate its power.

Charge and energy transferred

When charge flows in a circuit, electrical work is done. We can calculate the amount of energy transferred by electrical work using the equation:

energy transferred, E = charge, Q × potential difference, V

(in joules, J)   (in coulombs, C)   (in volts, V)

$E = QV$

Example:

A charge of 50 C flows through a device with a potential difference across the device of 12 V.

Calculate the total energy transferred.

$E = QV$

$\quad = 50 \text{ C} \times 12 \text{ V}$

$\quad = 600 \text{ J}$

5 A charge of 30 C flows through a TV which is connected to the mains supply of 230 V.

Calculate the total energy transferred.

6 A device transfers a total of 1800 J with a charge of 75 C.

Calculate the potential difference across the device.

7 A home appliance has a power of 1150 W and is switched on for 5 minutes.

  a Determine how much charge flows through the appliance.
  b Calculate the amount of charge that passes through a factory appliance when the same amount of energy is transferred.

DID YOU KNOW?

Homes and offices use electricity at 230 V, but hospitals and schools receive it at 11 000 V. Large factories receive it at 33 000 V.

Calculating power

Learning objectives:

- calculate power
- use power equations to solve problems
- consider power ratings and changes in stored energy.

KEY WORD

power
energy transfer
charge
potential difference

We use the word power a lot – 'a powerful idea' or 'a powerful piece of music'. However, in science, we use it in a very specific way – as a measure of how quickly energy is transferred. Unlike ideas or music, this power can be calculated.

Calculating power

The power transfer in any component is related to the potential difference across it and the current passing through it. We can calculate power using the equation:

power, P = potential difference, V × current, I

(in watts, W)   (in volts, V)   (in amps, A)

$P = VI$

When a current passes through a resistor, such as a kettle element, it has a heating effect. Work is done by the electrons which is transferred to thermal energy in the element.

As $V = IR$, so $P = (IR) \times I = I^2R$

So the power transfer is also given by the equation:

power = (current)^2 × resistance

(in watts, W)   (in amps, A)^2 (in ohms, Ω)

$P = I^2R$

① An electric heater takes a current of 4 A when connected to a 230 V supply.

  a Calculate its power.

  b Calculate its resistance.

② A lamp has a power of 36 W when connected to a 12 V supply.

  a Calculate the current through the lamp.

  b Calculate the resistance of the lamp.

Heating up

We can use equations for power and energy transfer to solve problems.

Example: Jo boils a kettle of water to make a cup of tea (Figure 3.32). The kettle has a power rating of 2.4 kW.

The mains supply is 230 V. Calculate:

a the current in the kettle element

b the resistance of the kettle element.

Answer:

a $P = VI$

Rearrange the equation to make I the subject:

$I = P \div V$ = 2400 W $\div$ 230 V = 10.4 A

b Resistance of element, $R = P \div I^2$ = 2400 $\div$ (10.4)^2 = 22.2 Ω

Figure 3.32 An electric kettle

Example:

An electric kettle connected to the 230 V mains supply draws a current of 10 A. It contains 2 kg of water. Calculate the rise in temperature of the water when the kettle is switched on for 1 minute.

The specific heat capacity of water is 4200 J/kg °C

Power of kettle, $P = V I = 230$ V $\times$ 10 A = 2300 W

Energy transferred in 1 minute (60 s) = Pt

= 2300 W $\times$ 60 s = 138 000 J

If we assume all this energy is given to the 2 kg of water in the kettle we can calculate the rise in temperature, $\Delta\theta$.

Energy transferred to water = $mc\,\Delta\theta$

138 000 J = 2 kg $\times$ 4200 J/kg °C $\times$ $\Delta\theta$

$\Delta\theta$ = 138 000 ÷ (2 $\times$ 4200) = 4.5 °C

3 In the example above it was assumed that all the energy transferred by the electric current is transferred into energy stored by the water. Suggest what other stores the energy might be transferred to.

4 Al has an outdoor swimming pool. It is 15 m long, 10 m wide and 2 m deep. The density of water is 1000 kg/m³.

 a Calculate the mass of water in the pool.

 b Al wants to warm the water from 17 °C to 22 °C. Calculate how much energy is transferred.

 c The power of the heater is 2 kW. Calculate how long it takes to raise the temperature of the water.

Figure 3.33 Energy is transferred between stores as this car moves

Changes in stored energy

A more powerful appliance can transfer energy more quickly.

A **battery-operated toy car** (Figure 3.33) with a power rating of 5 W transfers 5 J every second. Energy is transferred from the store of energy in the battery to the store of kinetic energy in the toy car. Although the total amount of energy is conserved, the decrease in the energy store of the battery does not equal the increase in the energy store of the car. The toy does work against friction, so the energy that is dissipated is transferred to the thermal energy store of the surroundings.

An **electric cooker** (Figure 3.34) with a power rating of 2 kW transfers 2 kJ every second. The energy transferred by the electric current increases the thermal energy stored in the food, the saucepan and the surroundings.

5 Describe how different stores of energy change when these appliances are in use.

 a A microwave oven with a power rating of 800 W.

 b A vacuum cleaner with a power rating of 1.6 kW.

Figure 3.34 Cooking involves energy being transferred from one store to another

Investigating series and parallel circuits

Learning objectives:

- use a circuit to determine resistance
- gather valid data to use in calculations
- apply the circuit to determine the resistance of combinations of components.

KEY WORDS

potential
   difference
current
resistance
series
parallel

We can use a circuit to determine the resistance of a component, as resistance can be calculated from measuring potential difference and current. We can then see how the resistance is affected by factors such as the length of a wire or when several components are combined.

Length of a wire and its resistance

When the component being tested is a length of wire, we can find out how the resistance changes when the length is altered. For each length of wire, we can record the potential difference across the wire and current passing through it and use them to calculate the resistance. We can then plot a graph of resistance against length of the wire to show how changing the length of the wire affects the resistance.

One of the factors that can affect the accuracy of the results is temperature. As more current passes through the wire it gets hotter and this alters the resistance. It is important to avoid increasing the thermal energy stored by the wire.

These pages are designed to help you think about aspects of the investigation rather than to guide you through it step by step.

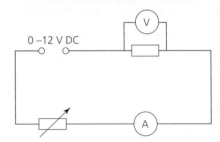

Figure 3.35 Circuit diagram for measuring potential difference across a component and the current passing through it

REMEMBER!

The greater the resistance, the higher the potential difference is needed to make a certain current pass.

1 In this experiment, state what readings would be taken and what calculations would be done.

2 a Predict what effect the length of a wire will have on its resistance.

  b Sketch a graph showing your prediction.

3 Suggest a good way of stopping the heating effect of the current affecting the results too much.

Investigating combinations of components

We can also join components together and see what the combined resistance is. We can connect them in series, as shown in Figure 3.36. We can then measure the potential difference across it and the current passing through and calculate the combined resistance of the resistors in series.

Figure 3.36 Resistors in series

We can also do this with components in parallel, as shown in Figure 3.37. This will enable us to investigate what the combined resistance of the resistors in parallel is.

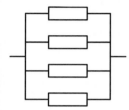

Figure 3.37 Resistors in parallel

4 **a** Draw circuit diagrams to show how measurements could be taken to calculate the resistance of two components in series and in parallel.

b For both series and parallel combinations, predict what you would expect the combined resistance to be, compared with the resistance of the individual components.

A student connected two resistors in turn to the circuit in Figure 3.23. The first resistor produced a current of 0.10 A and a pd of 6.0 V. The second resistor produced a current of 0.20 A and a pd of 3.0 V. When the student connected the resistors in series, they produced a current of 0.05 A and a pd of 3.9 V.

5 **a** Explain why the result for the resistors in series was unexpected

b Suggest a reason for the unexpected result

DID YOU KNOW?

The formula $V = IR$ is also known as Ohm's law. This is not strictly correct as the formula applies to any component, whereas Ohm's law only applies to certain components, and then only if the temperature is kept constant.

KEY CONCEPT

What's the difference between potential difference and current?

Learning objectives:

- understand and be able to apply the concepts of current and potential difference
- use these concepts to explain various situations.

KEY WORDS

charge
current
energy transfer
potential
  difference
power
resistance

When we're exploring and using electrical circuits it's useful to be able to measure things. This enables us to explain why electricity is sometimes really safe and sometimes lethally dangerous. It isn't simply a case of saying that 'there's more electricity in one than the other'. You may well have seen a Van de Graaff generator being used. This produces sparks that will jump across several centimetres of air, yet science teachers will sometimes demonstrate how they can make people's hair stand on end.

Potential difference and current

To understand what is going on, we need to think about two quantities, **potential difference** and **current**. These are not the same; understanding the difference will help make sense of a lot of things to do with circuits.

Current is a flow of **charge**. If you rub a balloon on a woollen jumper it becomes charged. The charge stays in the balloon (which is why it's called static – it doesn't move). As soon as it moves – we have a current. If you set up a simple circuit with battery, wires and a bulb, the bulb lights because there is a current in the circuit. Current is a flow of electrons moving through the wires. Current is measured in amperes (A).

Potential difference is the work done in moving that charge. It is an indication of how much energy is transferred to a unit charge when charge moves between two points, such as between the terminals of a battery. Potential difference is measured in volts (V). Potential difference is often referred to as voltage and both terms can be used, but the appropriate scientific term is potential difference. A 1.5 V battery does not transfer much energy to each unit of charge. In Figure 3.45, if you touch the two terminals you won't feel anything. A 12 V battery (such as that used in a car) transfers more energy to each unit of charge and the mains electricity supply (230 V) transfers much more energy to each unit charge.

Figure 3.38 A 1.5 V battery

1. If you pull a nylon jumper over your head in a darkened room you can sometimes feel something crackling and see sparks. What is happening?

2. Trucks have electrical systems that run on 24 V. How could you produce this using two car batteries?

The difference between potential difference and current

Potential difference is the energy transferred per coulomb of charge between two points. Current is the flow of electrical charge. The size of the electric current is the rate of flow of electrical charge.

Figure 3.39 A torch

The bulb in the torch shown in Figure 3.39 is designed to use 4.5 V and carry 750 mA of current. The energy transferred by the current is enough to make the bulb glow, but not so hard that the bulb would blow (break).

The electrical heater shown in Figure 3.40 is designed to use mains voltage (230 V) and carry 8 A. Each coulomb of charge is carrying more energy and there is also more electrical charge flowing per second.

When lightning strikes, both the potential difference and current are huge. A thunderstorm can generate a potential difference of up to 500 000 V and the current from lightning can reach thousands of amps.

Figure 3.40 An electric heater

So why can someone touch the charged dome of a Van de Graaff generator and not be in danger? The potential difference is high (even a small generator designed for schools can produce up to 100 000 V) but the discharge current is tiny, usually only a few milliamps. The high potential difference produces the spectacular effects but the low current means it's safe.

Why are potential difference and current important ideas?

Electrical **power** shows how quickly energy is being transferred; it is calculated from potential difference times current: $P = VI$. Increasing either V or I means more power.

Resistance shows how hard the current is being opposed. A greater resistance means that there is less current (if the potential difference is the same). Sometimes we want a high current to pass through a component, such as the heating element in an electric oven (Figure 3.41). An electric oven can have a power rating of about 4 kW and operate at up to 30 A. On other occasions we want the current to be very small, such as for a light bulb. The electric oven and light bulb both operate from the mains, but the light bulb has a much higher resistance. Resistance is calculated from potential difference divided by current: $R = V/I$.

③ Is it true to say that the highest potential differences are always the most dangerous?

④ Why do electricians sometimes say the 'It's the volts that jolts but the current that kills.'

⑤ What is the power rating of a bulb working on the mains voltage of 230 V and drawing a current of 0.05 A?

⑥ What would the resistance of this bulb be?

Figure 3.41 An electric oven

MATHS SKILLS

Using algebra in electric circuit calculations

Learning objectives:

* Solve algebraic equations including using appropriate substitutions, numerical values and units
* Change the subject of an equation
* Use the symbols =, <, <<, >>, >, ∝, ~

There are several equations we can use when calculating quantities for electric circuits. Before trying to calculate a quantity, note down which quantities are already known and choose the appropriate equation that will give you the quantity you need. Sometimes you will need to rearrange an equation or use two equations together.

Current, charge and time

Remember that the amount of charge passing a point in an amount of time is the current multiplied by that time. The equation is

$Q = It$

Example: A current of 2.4 A flows for 20 seconds. What total amount of charge passes a point in this circuit?

Substituting the values of current and time into the equation $Q = It$ gives $Q = 48$ C.

1 A current of 4.5 A flows for one minute. Calculate the amount of charge that flows past a point in the circuit.

Example: Determine the current in a circuit if a charge of 120 C flows past a point over a time of 2 minutes.

Rearrange the equation $Q = It$ to make I the subject of the equation.

Divide both sides by t and swap the sides over:

$$I = \frac{Q}{t}$$

Substitute $Q = 120$ C and $t = 120$ s (always convert times into the SI unit, the second).

$$I = \frac{120}{120} = 1.0 \text{ A}$$

2 Calculate the current when a charge of 35 C flows past a point in 14 s.

Potential difference and resistance

Remember that the resistance of a component is defined by the equation resistance = potential difference/current

$$R = \frac{V}{I}$$

3 What is the resistance of a component if the potential difference across it is 12.5 V and the current measured is 2.5 A?

4 Rearrange the resistance equation to make the current its subject.

5 Determine the current if a potential difference of 12 V is applied across a resistance of 200 Ω.

Combining equations

Sometimes we need to combine two equations to produce the quantity we need. One way of solving this type of problem is first to substitute the values in one equation, to tell us one quantity. Then substitute this new quantity in the second equation to get the answer we need.

Another way to solve this type of problem is to combine the equations before substituting the known values.

Example: How much charge flows through a resistor of 200 Ω in a time of 180 seconds if there is a potential difference of 5 V across it?

State the equation for resistance:

$$R = \frac{V}{I}$$

Rearrange this equation to make the current the subject:

$$I = \frac{V}{R}$$

State the equation relating charge and current:

$$Q = It$$

Substitute $I = V/R$ in the second equation:

$$Q = \frac{Vt}{R}$$

Substitute the known values to find the answer:

$$Q = \frac{(5 \times 180)}{200} = 4.5 \text{ C}$$

6 The equation for power produced by an electrical supply is $P = VI$. Power is also related to the work done by the equation $E = Pt$. Use these equations to determine the work done by an electrical supply rated as 12 V if a current of 2.0 A flows for 5 minutes.

7 Suggest other equations you could use to obtain the answer to question 6.

> **KEY INFORMATION**
>
> You will sometimes see different symbols used in place of the equals sign '='. These include:
> greater than: >
> much greater than: >>
> less than: <
> much less than: <<
> proportional to: $\propto$
> of the order of: ~

MATHS SKILLS

Using formulae and understanding graphs

Learning objectives:

- recognise how algebraic equations define the relationships between variables
- solve simple algebraic equations by substituting numerical values
- describe relationships expressed in graphical form.

KEY WORDS

algebraic equation
direct proportion
linear relationship
constant of
   proportionality

Mathematics helps you to express abstract concepts and ideas in a more concrete and helpful way.

Algebraic equations and relationships

Algebraic equations show relationships between variables, which are represented as letters. For example, the relationship between potential difference (V), current (I) and resistance (R):

$V = IR$, where:

V = potential difference in volts, V

I = current in amps, A

R = resistance in ohms, Ω

From the equation, you can see that if the resistance R is constant, the bigger the potential difference V between two points in a circuit, the bigger the current I. The current through a conductor between two points is **directly proportional** to the potential difference across the two points. This is written mathematically as:

$V \propto I$, where the symbol $\propto$ means 'proportional to'.

1 **a** Calculate the potential difference across a component of resistance 100 Ω when the current is 10 A.

   b Calculate the potential difference across a component of resistance 3 kΩ when the current is 5 A.

2 Show how you would rearrange the equation $V = IR$ to calculate the resistance R of a component.

Power and energy transfer in circuits

The equation for power is:

power = potential difference × current

REMEMBER!

To express very large quantities, use larger multiples or smaller submultiples of the base unit. For example, 1000 Ω is usually written as 1 kΩ, and 2500 Ω can be written as 2.5 kΩ. Here, 'k' means kilo, which is 10^3 or 1000. But remember – in calculations, always use the base unit (in this example, ohms): 1000 Ω and 2500 Ω.

and the algebraic equation is:

$P = VI$, where:

P is power in watts, W

V is potential difference in volts, V

I is current in amps, A

The same relationship can also be expressed by substituting IR for V, as $V = IR$. The expression becomes:

$P = (IR) \times I$

which can be written as $P = I^2R$.

③ Calculate the power of a motor supplied with a potential difference of 230 V and a current of 5 A.

④ How would you rearrange the equation to calculate the current I when you are given the potential difference V and the power P?

⑤ Calculate the power of a motor supplied with a current of 5 A if the resistance is 1000 Ω.

Describing relationships expressed in graphical form

Figure 3.42 shows that there is a **linear relationship** between potential difference and current through an ohmic conductor at constant temperature – the graph is a straight line. Because the straight line goes through the origin, we can also say that current is directly proportional to the potential difference, $V \propto I$.

We can insert a **constant of proportionality** (k) to describe the relationship between V and I:

$V = kI$

In Figure 3.42, the reciprocal of the slope or gradient of the line (1/gradient) is equal to the constant of proportionality, which in this graph is the resistance in the circuit, R. The straight line indicates that the resistance is constant (it does not change).

The relationship between potential difference and current flowing through a filament lamp is different (Figure 3.50). Initially, at low values of V and I, the gradient is straight, but then it quickly becomes a curve. This indicates that the gradient is changing, which means that the resistance is changing.

The resistance of a filament lamp increases as the temperature of its filament increases. As a result, the current flowing through a filament lamp is not directly proportional to the potential difference across it.

⑥ What does the slope of a straight-line graph indicate?

⑦ Looking at a graph, how would you know if the relationship is not directly proportional?

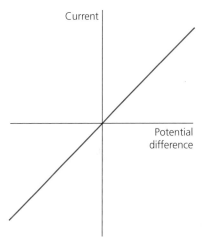

Figure 3.42 I–V graph for an ohmic conductor

KEY INFORMATION

Note also that the values of potential difference and current can also be negative, so the line stretches back into the negative quadrant.

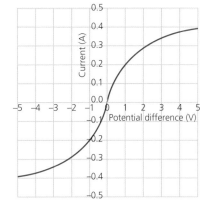

Figure 3.43 I–V graph for a filament lamp

Magnetism and magnetic forces

Learning objectives:

- explain what is meant by the poles of a magnet
- plot the magnetic field around a bar magnet
- describe magnetic materials and induced magnetism.

KEY WORDS

poles
repel
attract
magnetic field
induced magnet
permanent magnet

A maglev (magnetic levitation) train has no wheels. It uses the fact that like poles repel so that it hovers above its track. The maglev train in Shanghai can carry passengers 30 km to the airport in 7 minutes and 20 seconds (Figure 3.44).

The poles of a magnet

The **poles** of a magnet are the places where the magnetic forces are strongest. When a bar magnet is suspended by a thread, it will settle with one end pointing north. This end is called the north-seeking pole, or north pole.

Figure 3.44 A maglev train in Shanghai

When the ends of two bar magnets are brought near each other, two north poles or two south poles **repel** each other but a south pole and a north pole **attract** each other (Figure 3.45). These are examples of non-contact forces.

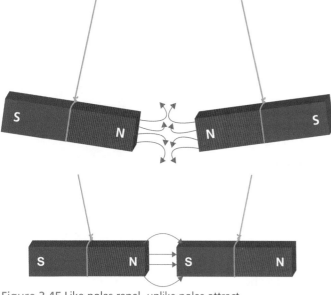

Figure 3.45 Like poles repel, unlike poles attract.

KEY INFORMATION

Magnetic field lines always start at a north pole and finish at a south pole. The lines show the direction of the magnetic field.

1 **What happens when the south poles of two magnets are brought together?**

Magnetic fields

A **magnetic field** is the region around a magnet where a force acts on another magnet or on a magnetic material. The direction of a magnetic field is the direction of the force on a north pole placed at a point in the field.

You can use a plotting compass to reveal the magnetic field of a magnet (Figure 3.46). Put the magnet on a piece of paper and draw round it. Place the plotting compass near the north pole of the magnet. Draw a dot by the head of the arrow on the compass. Move the compass so that the tail of the pointer is by the dot you have just drawn. Draw another dot by the head of the arrow.

Repeat moving the compass and drawing a dot by the head of the arrow until you have gone all the way round to the south pole. Draw a smooth curve to join all your points.

Repeat for slightly different starting points near to the north pole of the magnet.

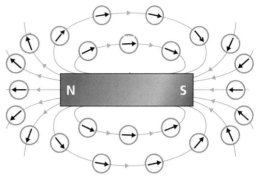

Figure 3.46 The needle of a plotting compass shows the magnetic field around a bar magnet.

2 Explain why you need to put the plotting compass in several different places near the north pole of the magnet when using it to plot the magnetic field.

Induced magnetism and magnetic materials

Iron, some steels, nickel and cobalt are magnetic materials. They can all be magnetised. Iron only makes a temporary magnet. It loses its magnetism as soon as the magnetising force is removed.

A permanent magnet produces its own magnetic field. An **induced magnet** is a material that becomes a magnet when it is placed in a magnetic field. When removed from the magnetic field it loses most or all of its magnetism quickly. Iron is an example of this type of magnetic material. **Permanent magnets** are made from nickel, cobalt and some types of steel.

The force between a magnet and a magnetic material is always attractive.

Steel pins or iron tacks are attracted to a magnet (Figure 3.47). Each pin or tack becomes a small magnet because of induced magnetism. If you carefully separate the magnet from the steel pins and tacks, the steel pins remain magnetised but the iron tacks lose their magnetism and are no longer attracted to each other.

You can test whether a material is a magnet by bringing another magnet close to it.

> **KEY INFORMATION**
>
> Magnetic field lines never meet or cross.

Figure 3.47 Magnets attract some metals such as iron and steel.

3 Explain why the pins and tacks behave as described.

4 Explain what forces of attraction and repulsion can take place between the pins and tacks once they have been removed from the magnet (Figure 3.47).

5 Suggest how you know whether an object is a magnet when you bring another magnet close to it.

6 Suggest how the behaviour of a magnetic compass is related to evidence that the core of the Earth must be magnetic.

Compasses and magnetic fields

Learning objectives:

- describe the Earth's magnetic field
- describe the magnetic effect of a current.

KEY WORDS

Earth's magnetic field

Objects like steel girders in bridges are often found to be slightly magnetised by induction from the Earth's magnetism, particularly if the structure is hammered or shaken by vibrations.

Magnetic compass

A compass contains a small bar magnet. One end is a north pole and one end is a south pole. The south pole of a compass needle is attracted to a magnetic north pole. This is how we use a compass to plot the magnetic field of another magnet (Figure 3.46 in section 3.1).

1 **Draw a labelled diagram to show how a compass needle will behave when placed near**

a **a north pole**

b **a south pole.**

The Earth's magnetic field

The fact that a compass needle points north is evidence that the Earth has a magnetic field. The Earth behaves as if there is a bar magnet inside it. (Such a magnet cannot really exist because the centre of the Earth is too hot.) The odd thing is that the south pole of this imaginary magnet is in the northern hemisphere near the Earth's geographic north pole (Figure 3.48). The geographic north pole is a magnetic south pole. The end of the compass that points towards geographic north is called a north-seeking pole.

DID YOU KNOW?

At the Earth's centre is a solid inner core surrounded by a fluid outer core, which is hottest next to the inner core. Hot molten iron rises within the outer core, then cools and sinks. These movements create an electric current, which, combined with the rotation of the Earth, are thought to produce the Earth's magnetic field.

DID YOU KNOW?

The magnetic poles move around over time, and the Earth's magnetic field has reversed direction many times in the Earth's history. These flips are becoming more frequent. Many millions of years ago, the field reversed direction every 5 million years, but now it reverses approximately every 200 000 years.

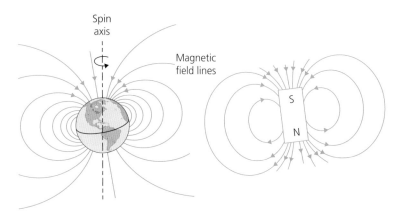

Figure 3.48 The Earth's magnetic and geographic poles do not exactly coincide.

The closer the field lines are together, the higher the strength of the magnetic field. Figure 3.48 shows that the Earth's magnetic field is strongest at the poles.

2 What is the polarity of the end of the imaginary bar magnet inside the Earth that is nearest the geographic south pole?

3 Explain why the north pole of a compass is often called the north-seeking pole.

The magnetic effect of a current

When a current flows in a wire, the current creates a magnetic field around the wire. This effect can be investigated using a plotting compass placed at different points around the wire (Figure 3.49).

DID YOU KNOW?

When Hans Christian Oersted discovered that electricity produced magnetism, scientists started to look for the reverse effect. In 1831, Michael Faraday discovered how to make electricity using magnetism.

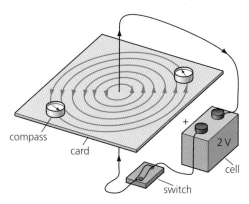

Figure 3.49 The magnetic field around a current-carrying wire is circular.

The strength of the magnetic field decreases with distance from the wire. Further from the wire, the field lines would get further apart. The strength of the magnetic field also depends on the current through the wire. The higher the current, the stronger the magnetic field.

If the current direction is reversed, the direction of the magnetic field is reversed. The direction of the magnetic field is given by the right-hand grip rule (Figure 3.50).

To work out the direction of the magnetic field, grip the wire in your right hand so that your thumb points in the current direction. Then your fingers point around the wire in the direction of the magnetic field.

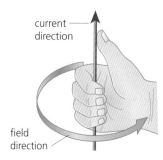

Figure 3.50 The right-hand grip rule

4 A wire goes into the plane of a page. Draw a diagram to show the magnetic field and its direction around the wire.

5 Copy Figure 3.49 and sketch a diagram to show how the magnetic field pattern would change if the current in the wire was increased.

6 Explain why a compass placed towards the edge of the card in Figure 3.49 might not point along the field line as expected.

Magnetic effects

Learning objectives:

- draw the magnetic field around a conducting wire and a solenoid
- describe the force on a wire in a magnetic field.

KEY WORDS

Fleming's left-hand rule
solenoid
motor effect

Electricity and magnetism are very closely connected. By combining the two, we can create much more powerful magnets or electromagnets.

Magnetic field of a loop of wire

You have seen how a current flowing through a wire creates a magnetic field around it. The magnetic field becomes more complicated when the wire becomes a loop. The field lines are squashed together in the middle of the loop.

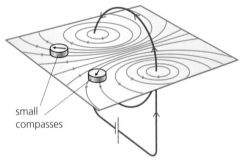

Figure 3.51 The magnetic field in the centre of a loop is stronger than outside the loop.

1 The direction of the current in the wire in Figure 3.51 is reversed. What is the direction of the magnetic field now?

The magnetic field in a solenoid

A **solenoid** is a long straight coil of wire. When a current is passed through a solenoid the magnetic field of all the coils combines to produce a magnetic field like that of a bar magnet (Figure 3.52).

The polarity of the solenoid can be worked out by looking at the end of the solenoid and seeing which way the current passes (Figure 3.53).

2 Sadie looks at the end of a solenoid and notes that the current is in a clockwise direction. What is the magnetic pole at that end of the solenoid?

3 Suggest two things that you can do to make the magnetic field stronger.

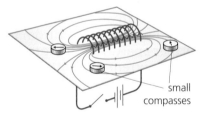

Figure 3.52 The magnetic field around a solenoid is similar to that of a bar magnet.

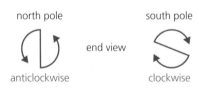

Figure 3.53 North and south poles of a coil of wire.

The kicking wire

When a straight wire with a current passing through it is placed between the poles of a magnet the two magnetic fields combine, making the resultant magnetic field stronger in one area and weaker in another area. This produces a force on the wire which makes the wire move (Figure 3.54). This is called the **motor effect**. The direction of the force and the motion is perpendicular to both the magnetic field and the current.

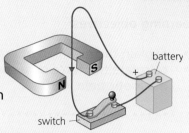

Figure 3.54

Fleming's left-hand rule (Figure 3.55) allows us to work out the relative directions of the current, magnetic field and motion of the wire.

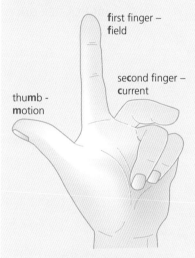

first finger – field

second finger – current

thumb - motion

Figure 3.55 Fleming's left-hand rule.

REMEMBER!

The right-hand grip rule and Fleming's left-hand rule use different hands. Be careful not to muddle them up.

KEY INFORMATION

Conventional current is from positive to negative terminal of a battery. This is the *opposite* direction to the direction of electron flow.

Hold your thumb and first two fingers of your left hand at right angles to each other.

Point your first finger in the direction of the magnetic field (from north to south).

Point your second finger in the direction of the current. This is what is known as conventional current – flowing from positive to negative.

Your thumb then shows the direction of motion of the wire.

You can increase the force on the wire by increasing:

- the strength of the magnetic field
- the current passing through the wire
- the length of the wire that is in the magnetic field.

4 A wire is placed between the poles of a magnet. When the current is switched on the wire moves to the left.

  a Which way does the wire move when the current direction is reversed?

  b Which way does the wire move when the poles of the magnet are reversed?

5 Explain how you could decrease the force on the wire.

6 Which way will the wire move when the switch is pressed in Figure 3.54?

Calculating the force on a conductor

KEY WORDS

tesla (T)
magnetic flux
    density

Learning objectives:

- explain the meaning of magnetic flux density, B
- calculate the force on a current-carrying conductor in a magnetic field.

The stronger the force on a current-carrying conductor, the more powerful the motor.

HIGHER TIER ONLY

Magnetic flux density, B

The spacing of the magnetic field lines in Figure 3.56 tells us how strong the magnetic field is. Where the lines are closer together, the field is stronger. The magnetic field inside the coil is much stronger than the magnetic field outside the coil.

The strength of a magnetic field is called the **magnetic flux density**.

1 **Explain how the strength of the magnetic field varies inside the solenoid.**

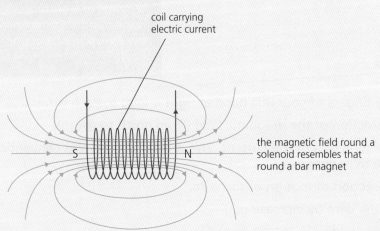

coil carrying
electric current

the magnetic field round a
solenoid resembles that
round a bar magnet

Figure 3.56 Magnetic flux density tells us about the strength of a magnetic field.

Force on a wire

The size of the force, F, in N on a wire carrying a current at right angles to a magnetic field is proportional to

- the current, I, in A
- the length of wire in the field, L, in m.

So F is proportional to IL. The force is given by the equation *force on a conductor (at right angles to a magnetic field) carrying a current (N) = magnetic flux density (T) × current (A) × length (m)*
$F = BIL$

where B is the magnetic flux density. Its unit is the **tesla** (T).

Example:

A wire carrying a current of 10 A passes at right angles through a magnetic field of 0.15 T. Calculate the force acting on a wire of length 0.2 m.

$F = BIL$

$B = 0.15$ T, $I = 10$ A, $L = 0.20$ m

$F = 0.15 \times 10 \times 0.20 = 0.30$ N

2. What happens to the force on a wire carrying a current when:

   a the current in the wire doubles?

   b the current in the wire and the length of wire in the magnetic field both double?

3. Calculate the force on each wire. The wire is perpendicular to the magnetic field.

   a Length of wire is 2 m, current is 0.5 A and the magnetic flux density is 0.05 T.

   b Current in the wire is 2 A, length of the wire is 50 cm and the magnetic flux density is 0.1 T.

4. A wire lies at right angles to a uniform magnetic field of magnetic flux density 0.02 T. 0.3 m of the wire is inside the length of the magnetic field. If the force on this length of wire due to the current in it is 0.03 N downwards, what are the magnitude and direction of the current in the wire?

5. A wire is perpendicular to a magnetic field and has a force on it of 0.05 N. 0.25 m of wire is inside the the magnetic field. Calculate the magnetic flux density when the current in the wire is 3 A.

6. Will there be a force acting on a wire carrying a current of 2 A running parallel to a magnetic field? Explain your answer.

7. A metal wire is lying near the equator perpendicular to the Earth's magnetic field. Length of the wire = 2.0 m, weight of wire = 0.30 N, Earth's magnetic flux density B = 0.00003 T

   a Calculate the current needed to lift the wire off the ground.

   b Explain whether the wire could be lifted if it was placed near one of Earth's magnetic poles.

> **REMEMBER!**
>
> Make sure you use the correct units when substituting in the equation $F = BIL$. If the values in the question are not in tesla, amps and metres, you have to change the values to the correct units before starting the calculation.

Electric motors

Learning objectives:

- list equipment that uses motors
- describe how motors work
- describe how to change the speed and direction of rotation of a motor
- explain how a dynamo generates direct current.

KEY WORDS

Fleming's
  left-hand rule
split-ring
  commutator
dynamo

Every part of a car where you press a button to move something requires a motor.

HIGHER TIER ONLY

Using motors

Electric motors have many uses around the home. Any electrical machine that has moving parts is likely to have a motor. For example, an electric lawn mower, a food processor and an electric drill (Figure 3.18) all contain electric motors.

1 **Give three more examples of equipment that contains an electric motor.**

Figure 3.57 Electric motors are used in many appliances such as this drill.

How motors work

When a current passes through a coil placed between the poles of a magnet there is a force on each side of the coil. **Fleming's left-hand rule** shows that the forces on each side of the coil are in opposite directions, so the coil will move. One side of the coil moves up and the other side moves down. This makes the coil start to spin.

A direct current (d.c.) motor has a **split-ring commutator** that rotates with the coil between two carbon brushes (Figure 3.58). The commutator allows the motor to continue to spin without reversing direction every time it gets to the vertical position.

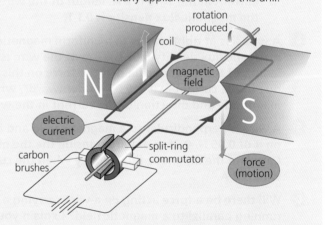

Figure 3.58 The circuit for a d.c. motor.

You can use Fleming's left-hand rule to work out the direction of the force. On the left-hand side of the coil in Figure 3.58, the direction of the current is towards the commutator and the field is to the right. So the force is upwards. On the right-hand side of the coil, as the current is in the opposite direction, away from the commutator, the force will also be in the opposite direction, which is downwards. So the coil spins clockwise. When the coil is vertical, the circuit is broken and no current flows. Since the coil is moving, there is enough momentum for the coil to carry on rotating a little further. The side of the coil that was on the left is now on the right, and in contact with the other carbon brush. The direction of the current in the coil then reverses and the force on the other side of the coil is now upwards so the motor continues to spin in the same direction.

Practical motors have curved pole pieces. This produces a radial field (Figure 3.20).

The coil is always at right angles to the magnetic field. This increases the force and keeps it constant as the coil turns.

The direction the motor turns can be reversed by reversing the current or reversing the direction of the magnetic field.

2 Why does the coil start to spin in Figure 3.58?

3 Explain how a split-ring commutator works.

4 For the rectangular coil in Figure 3.58, only two of the sides experience a force. Why does no force act on the other two sides?

5 How can you increase the induced potential difference?

6 Comment on the similarities between the design of a d.c. motor and a dynamo.

> **KEY INFORMATION**
> ....
> In an electric motor, the force on a conductor is at right angles to the magnetic field and to the current. For each side of the coil, Fleming's left-hand rule represents the relative orientation of the force, the current in the conductor and the magnetic field.

> **KEY INFORMATION**
> ....
> The factors that affect the size of the force on each side of the coil of wire are:
> * the number of turns on the coil
> * the size of the current
> * the strength of the magnetic field.

The dynamo

Figure 3.59 shows a **dynamo**. It is used to generate a direct current by moving the coil in a magnetic field. As the coil turns it cuts the magnetic field lines. Doing this induces a potential difference between the ends of the coil. This causes an induced current to pass through the coil and through the circuit the coil is a part of.

The split-ring commutator rotates with the coil and maintains a complete circuit with the external circuit. However, each half turn the sides of the coil connect to the opposite side of the circuit. So although the direction of the induced potential difference between the ends of the coil reverses when the coil cuts through field lines in the opposite direction, the direction of the current induced in the circuit does not change.

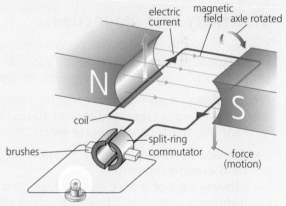

Figure 3.59 A d.c. dynamo

KEY CONCEPT

The link between electricity and magnetism

Learning objectives:

- explore how electricity and magnetism are connected.

In 1820, Hans Christian Oersted was demonstrating an experiment with batteries and electric current in a circuit. He noticed that every time he switched the batteries on and off, the needle in a compass that was lying on the bench beside his work deflected from magnetic north. This was when he realised that there was a direct relationship between electricity and magnetism.

HIGHER TIER ONLY

Electricity *and magnetism*

Electricity has to do with the properties and movement of electrically charged particles. Magnetism involves the properties of magnets and magnetic materials.

Electricity and magnetism are interrelated. Movement of electrical charges creates **magnetic fields**, while changes in magnetic fields can generate electricity.

- Current flowing through a circuit creates a magnetic field around the wire.
- Moving part of a wire circuit through a magnetic field **induces** a potential difference across the wire and that potential difference begins to drive electrons round the circuit.

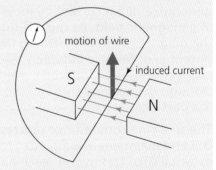

Figure 3.60 One of Faraday's experiments showed that moving a wire through a magnetic field would generate an induced current in the wire.

1. Name a device where an electric current is used to produce a magnetic field.

2. Name a device where an electric current and a magnetic field produce motion.

Explaining the motor effect

Imagine you bring a current-carrying conductor, which has a magnetic field around it, and put it into a magnetic field. The magnetic field around the conductor interacts with the magnetic field of the magnet. The combination of the magnetic fields creates an instantaneous force between the magnet and the conductor. This is the underlying principle behind the electric motor.

Figure 3.61 A modern electric motor in a disc drive

4. **Describe in your own words the underlying principle of the electric motor.**

5. **A wire carrying a current is placed between the poles of a U-shaped magnet (Figure 3.62). Describe how the direction of the resulting magnetic force on the wire can be found.**

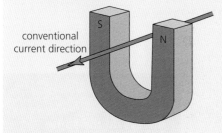

conventional current direction

Figure 3.62

MATHS SKILLS

Rearranging equations

Learning objectives:

- change the subject of a equation
- explain how the potential differences in two circuits linked by a transformer depend on the ratio of the numbers of turns.

KEY WORDS

rearrange an equation
subject of an equation
substitute
transformer equation

Equations are used throughout Physics. Calculating the value of a from the equation $a = b \times c$ when you know b and c is straightforward. It becomes more difficult when you want to work out the values of b or c. You need to rearrange the equation.

HIGHER TIER ONLY

Force on a conductor

The force on a conductor carrying a current is $F = BIL$ where the force (F) is in newtons, N, the magnetic flux density (B) is the strength of the magnetic field, in tesla, T, the current (I) flowing through the conductor is in *amps*, A and the length (L) of the conductor is in metres, m.

To work out the force when you know B, I and L, **substitute** the values into the equation.
To work out one of B, I or L you need to **rearrange** the equation. You can rearrange the equation and substitute the values or substitute the values and rearrange the equation.

Example:

Calculate the magnetic field strength when a force of 0.02 N is produced on a conductor that is 50 m long, carrying a current of 5 A.

Method 1: substitute the values and rearrange the equation to make B the **subject**:

$F = BIL$

$0.02 \text{ N} = B \times 5 \text{ A} \times 50 \text{ m}$

Rearrange the equation: divide both sides by 5 A × 50 m:

$$B = \frac{0.02 \text{ N}}{(5 \text{ A} \times 50 \text{ m})}$$

$$= 8 \times 10^{-5} \text{ T}$$

MATHS

Always do the **same** operation to both sides of the equation.

Remember the unit in your answer.

Method 2: rearrange the equation and substitute the values:

$F = BIL$

Rearrange the equation: divide both sides by IL:

$B = F / IL$

Substitute the values into the rearranged equation:

$$B = \frac{0.02\,\text{N}}{(5\,\text{A} \times 50\,\text{m})}$$

$$= 8 \times 10^{-5}\,\text{T}$$

1. Calculate the force on a conductor that is 25 m long carrying 3 A in a magnetic field of strength 3×10^{-5} T.

2. a Calculate the current in a coil of wire 250 m long with a magnetic field of strength 1.0×10^{-4} T, when the force is 0.125 N. Work out the answer using both methods in the example.

   b Which method did you find easier?

3. Calculate the length of conductor when a current of 2.5 A experiences a force of 0.05 N in a magnetic field of flux density 3×10^{-5} T. Use your preferred method.

Check your progress

You should be able to:

Describe how insulating materials can become charged	→ Recall that like charges repel and unlike charges attract	→ Explain how a person can get an electric shock
Recall that an electric current is a flow of electrical charge and is measured in amperes (A)	→ Remember that charge is measured in coulombs (C) and recall and use the equation $Q = It$	→ Explain the concept that current is the rate of flow of charge. Rearrange and apply the equation $Q = It$
Recognise and use electric circuit symbols in circuit diagrams	→ Draw and recognise series and parallel circuits. Compare the brightness of lamps connected in series and parallel	→ Recall that the current in a series circuit is always the same and that the total current in a parallel circuit is the sum of the currents through each branch
Recall that the current through a component depends on the resistance of the component and the potential difference across it	→ Recall and apply the equation $V = I R$ and for series circuit $R_{total} = R_1 + R_2$	→ Explain the effect of adding more resistors to series and parallel circuits
State the main properties of a diode, thermistor and light-dependent resistor (LDR)	→ Describe the behaviour of a thermistor and LDR in terms of changes to their resistance	→ Describe applications of diodes, thermistors and LDRs and explain their uses
Draw I–V graphs for a filament lamps	→ Explain the properties of components using I–V graphs	→ Use I–V graphs to determine if the characteristics of components are ohmic or non-ohmic
Recall that cells and batteries produce low-voltage direct current	→ Recall that domestic supply in the UK is 230 V a.c. and 50 Hz	→ Explain the difference between direct and alternating potential difference
Understand that electrical appliances transfer energy	→ Recall and use the equation energy transferred $E = Pt$	→ Recall and apply the equation energy transferred $E = QV$
Recall that power is measured in watts (W) and 1 kW = 1000 W	→ Recall and use the equation $P = V \times I$	→ Recall and apply the equation $P = I^2R$
Plot the magnetic field around a bar magnet	→ Recognise that the magnetic field is the region around a magnet where a force acts on another magnet or on a magnetic material	→ Explain how the behaviour of a magnetic compass is related to evidence that the core of the Earth must be magnetic
State how the strength of an electromagnet can be increased	→ Draw the magnetic field around a conducting wire and a solenoid	→ Explain how electromagnets are used in devices
State that a force acts on a current-carrying conductor in a magnetic field	→ Describe the motor effect that applies to a current-carrying conductor in a magnetic field	→ Explain how the direction of the force on the conductor can be identified using Fleming's left-hand rule
State that magnetic flux density is measured in tesla (T)	→ Explain what the size of a force on a conductor depends on	→ Use the equation $F = BIL$ to calculate the force on a conductor

Worked example

The diagram below shows a circuit used to investigate the resistance of a piece of thin wire.

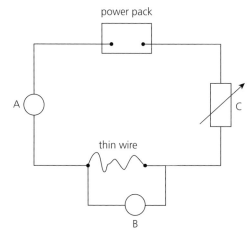

① **Name the three components in the circuit labeled A, B and C.**

  A is an ammeter, B is a voltmeter and C is a thermistor.

  > A and B are correct, but C is a variable resistor.

② **Give the purpose of component C.**

  To regulate the temperature.

  > Component C is used to change the potential difference across the test material.

③ **The student recorded the potential difference across the thin wire and the current passing through it. She plotted her results on a graph. Explain which variable she should plot on each axis.**

  She should plot potential difference on the x-axis and current on the y-axis.

  > This is correct, but the explanation has not been given. Potential difference is plotted on the x-axis because it is the independent variable, and current is plotted on the y-axis because it is the dependent variable.

④ **The student increased the potential difference to 12 V. Explain what you think would have happened.**

  The wire gets very hot.

  > The wire gets hot because of the large current passing through it. Large currents transfer lots of energy.

⑤ **Explain how you would expect the graph to look if the wire had been replaced by a filament lamp.**

  The same

  > The line would initially be straight but then curve with a shallower gradient as the temperature of the filament increases.

End of chapter questions

Getting started

1 Draw the circuit symbol for a voltmeter. `1 Mark`

2 State whether the ammeter should be connected in series or parallel when measuring an electric current. `1 Mark`

3 Calculate the current when 100 C of charge flows in 20 s. `2 Marks`

4 Where is the magnetic field around a bar magnet strongest?

A Near the poles　　　　B Along the side

C Above the magnet　　　D Well away from the magnet `1 Mark`

5 Which of these will not strengthen the magnetic field created by a current through a wire? `1 Mark`

A Shape the wire into a coil　　B Stripping the plastic insulation off the wire

C Increasing the potential difference　　D Using a thicker wire

6 Give two differences between a permanent magnet and an induced magnet. `2 Marks`

7 What happens when two like poles are brought near to each other? `1 Mark`

A They attract　　B There is no interaction

C They repel　　D It isn't possible as they are at opposite ends of the same magnet.

8 Jemima has made an electromagnet using a coil of wire and a power supply. Which of these will not indicate how strong the magnetic field is?

A Seeing from how far away the coil will attract a paper clip

B Seeing how many paper clips it will attract

C Seeing what potential difference the power supply is set to

D Seeing from how far away it can affect a plotting compass `1 Mark`

9 An electric doorbell has an electromagnet in it. This is to: `2 Marks`

A Make the doorbell heavier　　　　B Make the doorbell louder

C Attract the striker to hit the gong　　D Use more electricity `1 Mark`

Going further

10 There are two small iron bars on the bench. One is magnetised and the other is not. Explain how you could identify which is which. `2 Marks`

11 Draw the circuit symbol for a thermistor. `1 Mark`

12 Two balloons are hung down next to each other by cotton threads. Describe what will happen if both balloons are positively charged. `1 Mark`

13 Suggest what will happen to the brightness of the lamps and the current in a series circuit if an additional lamp is added. `2 Marks`

14 A 2 kW kettle is attached to a 230 V mains supply. Calculate the current through the kettle.

`2 Marks`

15 Describe how you can make an electromagnet as strong as possible.

`2 Marks`

More challenging

16 A student was investigating how the magnetic force on a length of wire depends on its length. Explain how the student can make this a fair test.

`2 Marks`

17 What happens to the resistance of an LDR when the light level is decreased?

`1 Mark`

18 Draw a circuit diagram of a circuit you could use to find the resistance of a short piece of nichrome wire.

`2 Marks`

19 Calculate the current through a lamp of resistance 8 Ω when connected to a 12 V battery.

`2 Marks`

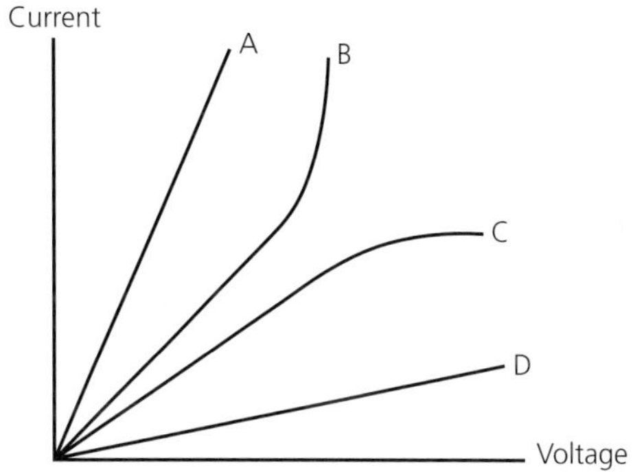

20 The current–voltage characteristics for four components, A–D, were investigated and the results drawn on the graph above. Which component was a filament lamp and which was a high-valued resistor?

`2 Marks`

21 Which one of these does the size of the force in the motor effect not depend upon?

A The strength of the magnetic field
B How hard the person pushes the wire

C The size of the current   D The length of the wire

`1 Mark`

Most demanding

22 Give power as an equation in terms of current and resistance.

`1 Mark`

23 Explain the effect of adding resistors in series and in parallel on the total resistance of a circuit.

`3 Marks`

24 Calculate the energy transferred in 1 minute by a 60 W light bulb connected to a 230 V mains supply.

`2 Marks`

25 Four appliances were switched on for various times. Incomplete information about each and how long they were on for is shown in the table below. Which appliance transferred the most energy in the time given and how much energy was transferred?

`4 Marks`

Appliance	Power rating (W)	Current (A)	Voltage (V)	Time left on (s)
Kettle	3000	12		20
Microwave	920		230	60
Torch		5	12	200
Food mixer		6	230	50

`Total: 43 Marks`

WAVES AND RADIOACTIVITY

LIGHT WAVES AND WATER WAVES HAVE SOME THINGS IN COMMON

- All waves carry energy from one place to another.
- When waves hit an object they may be absorbed by it, transmitted or reflected back.
- Waves may change direction (refract) at the point where two different materials meet.

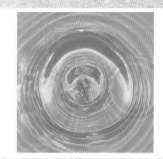

DESCRIBING WAVES

- Frequencies of waves are measured in hertz (Hz).
- Waves travel at different speeds in different materials.
- Sound waves are longitudinal.
- Ripples on the surface of water are transverse.

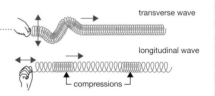

VISIBLE LIGHT

- Sunlight (white light) is made up of a mixture of many different colours.
- Each colour of light has a different frequency.
- Light waves can travel through a vacuum.

AN ATOM CONTAINS PROTONS, NEUTRONS AND ELECTRONS

- The atoms of an element have the same number of protons.
- Atoms of different elements have different masses.
- All the atoms of an element have the same chemical properties.

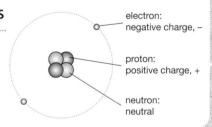

CHEMICAL EQUATIONS SUMMARISE WHAT HAPPENS IN A CHEMICAL REACTION

- The atom is the smallest particle that can take part in a chemical reaction.
- Each element is represented by a symbol of up to 3 letters, starting with a capital letter.
- There is always the same number of each type of atom before and after a chemical reaction.

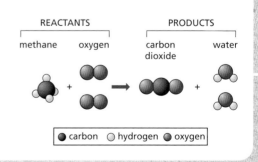

IN THIS CHAPTER YOU WILL FIND OUT ABOUT:

IN WHAT WAYS DO OTHER ELECTROMAGNETIC WAVES BEHAVE LIKE LIGHT?

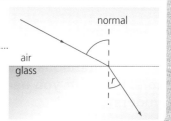

- All electromagnetic waves are transverse waves that transfer energy.
- All electromagnetic waves can be reflected and refracted at a boundary between two different media.

WHAT CHARACTERISTICS OF WAVES CAN BE MEASURED?

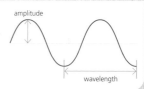

- We can measure the speed, wavelength and frequency of waves.
- We can calculate one of these three properties using the other two.

ARE THERE ANY WAVES BEYOND THE VISIBLE SPECTRUM?

- The visible spectrum is only a small part of a much wider spectrum called the electromagnetic spectrum.
- Gamma rays, X-rays and ultraviolet rays have the highest frequencies (smallest wavelengths) and transfer the most energy.

ARE ALL THE ATOMS IN AN ELEMENT EXACTLY THE SAME?

hydrogen-1 nucleus
(1 proton)

- The number of protons in the nucleus is called the atomic number and this defines an element.
- Isotopes are atoms of the same element with different numbers of neutrons and so have a different atomic mass.
- A radioisotope has nuclei that are unstable and undergo radioactive decay.

hydrogen-2 (deuterium) nucleus
(1 proton plus 1 neutron)

CAN EQUATIONS BE USED TO REPRESENT NUCLEAR REACTIONS?

$$^{238}_{92}\text{U} \rightarrow {}^{234}_{90}\text{Th} + {}^{4}_{2}\text{He}$$

alpha particle

- Atoms can be represented by their atomic symbols with their atomic number and mass number.
- There is always the same number of each type of subatomic particle before and after a nuclear reaction.

Describing waves

Learning objectives:

- describe wave motion
- define wavelength and frequency
- apply the relationship between wavelength, frequency and wave velocity.

Light and sound are both waves, but in a thunderstorm, you see lightning before you hear thunder. Light is almost instantaneous but sound travels at about 330 m/s. How can you use this to estimate how far away a thunderstorm is?

Wavelength, amplitude and frequency

Wavelength (λ) is the distance from a point on one wave to the equivalent point on the adjacent wave. Wavelength is measured in metres (m).

The **amplitude** of a wave is the maximum displacement of a point on a wave away from its undisturbed position.

Frequency (f) is the number of complete waves passing a point in 1 second. It is measured in **hertz (Hz).** A frequency of 5 Hz means there are five complete waves passing a point in 1 second. Frequencies are also given in kilohertz (kHz) and megahertz (MHz).

1000 Hz = 1 kHz

1000 kHz = 1 MHz

Time period (T) is the time to complete one wavelength.

Time period is the reciprocal or inverse of frequency.

Frequency is the number of complete waves passing a point in one second. $T = \dfrac{1}{f}$.

For example: When the frequency of a wave is 5 Hz there are 5 waves passing a point each second. The time for one wave to pass is $\dfrac{1}{5}$ s or 0.2 s.

The period, $T = \dfrac{1}{f}$

$\qquad = \dfrac{1}{5}$

$\qquad = 0.2$ s

> **REMEMBER!**
>
> Displacement includes both the distance an object moves and the direction.

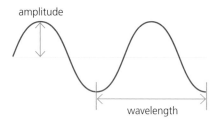

Figure 4.1 Amplitude and wavelength of a wave

> **DID YOU KNOW?**
>
> Sea waves carry a lot of kinetic energy (Figure 4.2). In 2014 severe storms destroyed part of the sea wall and the railway line at Dawlish in Devon.

Figure 4.2 These waves carry a lot of kinetic energy.

1 A wave has a frequency of 2 Hz. How many waves pass a point in 1 second?

2 Suggest how the amount of energy transferred by a wave changes as the amplitude increases.

3 Work out the frequencies of waves with time periods of

　a 0.1 s

　b 0.25 s.

The wave equation

A wave transfers energy. The wave speed (also called the wave velocity) is the speed that the wave transfers energy, or the speed the wave moves at.

All waves obey the **wave equation**:

wave speed (velocity) = frequency × wavelength

$$v = f\lambda$$

where the wave speed v is in metres per second (m/s), the frequency f is in hertz (Hz) and the wavelength λ is in metres (m).

If we know two of these three variables we can calculate the third using the wave equation.

Example:

A radio station produces waves of frequency 200 kHz and wavelength 1500 m.

　a Calculate the speed of radio waves.

　b Another station produces radio waves with a frequency of 600 kHz. What is their wavelength? Assume that the speed of the wave does not change.

a $v = f\lambda$ = 200 000 Hz × 1500 m

　　= 300 000 000 m/s

　　= 3×10^8 m/s

b wavelength, $\lambda = \dfrac{v}{f}$

　$= \dfrac{300\ 000\ 000 \text{ m/s}}{600\ 000 \text{ Hz}}$

　= 500 m

4 A wave has a frequency of 2 Hz and a wavelength of 10 cm. What is the speed of the wave?

5 When the frequency of a wave doubles, what happens to its wavelength?

6 The frequency of a wave triples and its wavelength doubles. What has happened to its speed?

REMEMBER!

Always check that you put values into the wave equation using SI units (e.g. wavelengths in metres, frequency in hertz). If the values in the question are **not** in SI units, you first have to convert them.

DID YOU KNOW?

The light that we can see has a wavelength of about $\dfrac{1}{2000}$ of a millimetre!

Transverse and longitudinal waves

Learning objectives:

- compare the motion of transverse and longitudinal waves
- explain why water waves are transverse waves
- explain why sound waves are longitudinal waves.

KEY WORDS

transverse wave
longitudinal wave
compression
rarefaction

Why wouldn't anyone hear you if you screamed in space?

Transverse and longitudinal waves

Transverse and **longitudinal** waves can be produced on a Slinky spring.

In a transverse wave on a spring the vibrations of the particles are at right angles to the direction of the energy transfer (Figure 4.3). If the particles move up and down vertically, the energy carried in the wave is transferred horizontally, away from the energy source creating the wave. The wave moves but the spring oscillates about a fixed position.

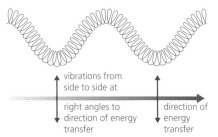

vibrations from side to side at

right angles to direction of energy transfer

direction of energy transfer

Figure 4.3 A transverse wave on a Slinky spring

① **Make a sketch of a transverse wave to explain what is meant by the terms a amplitude and b wavelength.**

Ripples on water are transverse waves (Figure 4.4). The wave looks as if it is moving outwards but the water particles actually move up and down.

A cork floating in water bobs up and down on a water wave. It only has vertical motion and it is not carried along by the wave.

② **What evidence do you have that suggests water waves are transverse waves?**

③ **Alex says, 'The particles in a transverse wave do move because waves carry items over the sea.' Suggest reasons for why he is wrong.**

In a longitudinal wave the vibrations of the particles are parallel to the direction of energy transfer (Figure 4.5). Longitudinal waves show areas of **compression** and **rarefaction**. A compression is when the waves bunch up. A rarefaction is when they spread out. If the particles move from side to side horizontally, the energy carried in the wave moves along the same horizontal direction, away from the energy source.

Sound waves in air are longitudinal waves.

④ **When the oscillations are at right angles to the direction of energy transfer, then the wave is a ____ wave.**

A longitudinal   **B** sound   **C** standing   **D** transverse

Figure 4.4 If the water moved outwards it would leave a hole in the centre

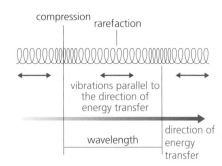

compression   rarefaction

vibrations parallel to the direction of energy transfer

wavelength

direction of energy transfer

Figure 4.5 A longitudinal wave on a Slinky spring

⑤ Describe a method you could use to measure the amplitude of a longitudinal wave on a Slinky spring.

Sound waves

All sound is produced by vibrating particles. The vibrations are along the direction of the energy transfer. The particles bunch up and spread out. This sets up a pressure wave with compressions and rarefactions.

Sound waves are longitudinal. However, a microphone (Figure 4.6) connected to a cathode ray oscilloscope (CRO) can be used to display sound waves on graphs of potential difference against time, so they look like transverse waves. It makes it easier for us to see and measure the frequency of sound waves.

Figure 4.7 shows two sound waves. They have the same amplitude but one wave has twice the frequency of the other wave. The frequency is found from the time for one complete cycle of the wave.

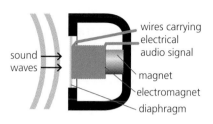

Figure 4.6 A sound wave reaching a microphone makes the diaphragm vibrate.

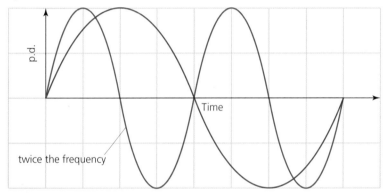

Figure 4.7 High and low frequency waves displayed on a CRO

⑥ Which wave in Figure 4.7 has the highest frequency?

⑦ Adjacent compressions in a sound wave are 15 cm apart. What is the wavelength of the sound?

> **KEY INFORMATION**
>
> A medium (plural media) is a material through which a wave travels.

Medium	Speed of sound (m/s)
air	330
water	1500
steel	5000

> **KEY INFORMATION**
>
> Sound waves cannot travel in a vacuum because longitudinal waves travel by passing the vibrations from one particle to another.

Measuring wave speeds

Learning objectives:

- explain how the speed of sound in air can be measured
- explain how the speed of water ripples can be measured
- describe the use of echo sounding.

KEY WORDS

echo
echo sounding

Mice can sing like birds, but usually at such high frequencies (up to 70 000 Hz) we don't hear them.

Measuring the speed of sound in air

Zoe and Darren measured the speed of sound in air. Sound reflects off a wall in a similar way to light reflecting off a mirror. The reflected sound is called an **echo**.

Zoe stood 50 m away from a large wall. She clapped and listened to the echo (Figure 4.8).

Zoe tried to clap each time she heard an echo while Darren timed 100 of her claps with a stop clock. He timed 100 claps in 40 s.

The time between claps is $\dfrac{40}{100}$ = 0.4 s

During the time from one clap to the next the sound had time to go to the wall and back, a distance of 100 m.

$$\text{Speed} = \frac{\text{distance}}{\text{time}}$$
$$= \frac{100\,\text{m}}{0.4\,\text{s}}$$
$$= 250\,\text{m/s}$$

① Jo and Sam also measured the speed of sound in air using the same method. They counted 50 claps in 23 s. Jo also stood 50 m from the wall.
What value did they get for the speed of sound?

② Suggest why this method is not likely to produce an accurate value for the speed of sound in air.

The speed of water waves

The speed of a water wave can be found by measuring the time it takes for a water wave to travel a measured distance. For example, make a splash at one end of a 25 m swimming pool and measure, with a stop clock, the time it takes the wave to travel to the other end.

DID YOU KNOW?

For ripples on a water surface or sound waves in air, it is the wave and *not* the water or air itself that travels.

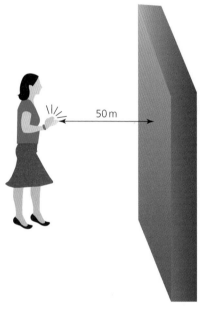

Figure 4.8 Zoe tried to clap each time she heard an echo

③ **a** Is this method an accurate way of measuring the wave speed? Explain why.

b Explain how you could improve the accuracy.

④ The crest of an ocean wave moves a distance of 20 m in 10 s. Calculate the speed of the ocean wave.

Echo sounding

Many animals, such as cats and dogs, can hear sounds of a higher frequency than humans. Bats emit pulses of sound between 30 Hz and 100 000 Hz. and they find their way around by listening to the echoes. This is echo location. We cannot hear such high frequencies.

Ships use high frequency sound waves to find the depth of the seabed or to locate a shoal of fish (Figure 4.9). This is **echo sounding**.

Figure 4.9 Ships use echo-sounding to find the depth of the seabed

Example: A ship sends out a sound wave and receives an echo after 1 second. The speed of sound in water is 1500 m/s. How deep is the water?

Time for sound to reach the seabed = 0.5 s.

$$\text{speed} = \frac{\text{distance}}{\text{time}}$$

distance = speed × time

$\qquad$ = 1500 m/s × 0.5 s

$\qquad$ = 750 m

REMEMBER!

In echo sounding remember the wave goes 'there and back', so make sure you use the correct distance in calculations.

5 Ships also use echo sounding to detect shoals of fish. The echo from the shoal of fish in Figure 4.10 is received after 0.1 s.

   a How far below the boat is the shoal of fish?

   b In Figure 4.10 the reflected pulse lasts longer than the emitted pulse. Suggest a reason for this.

Figure 4.10 Detecting fish using echo sounding

6 A ship is 220 m from a large cliff when it sounds its foghorn.

   a When the echo is heard on the ship, how far has the sound travelled? (The speed of sound in air is 330 m/s.)

   b How long is it before the echo is heard?

7 Explain why the pulse of sound needs to be very short for accurate echo location.

Measuring the wavelength, frequency and speed of waves in a ripple tank and waves in a solid

Learning objectives:

- develop techniques for making observations of waves
- select suitable apparatus to measure frequency and wavelength
- use data to answer questions.

> **These pages are designed to help you think about aspects of the investigation rather than to guide you through it step by step.**

Frequency and wavelength of waves in a ripple tank

We can use a set of equipment called a ripple tank to explore waves. By careful observation and measurement we can measure and calculate the wavelength and frequency of the waves and then work out their speed. A strobe light can be used to 'freeze' the movement of the waves for making certain measurements.

1. **A motor is attached to the wooden rod. What does this do?**
2. **What are the units of**
   a wavelength?
   b frequency?
3. **Suggest what equipment you could use to measure the wavelength, and how you should set it up.**
4. **When measuring the wavelength, you might measure the length of ten waves on the screen or table and then divide by ten. Explain why this is done.**
5. **Louise is looking at a certain point on the screen and counting how many waves pass that point in ten seconds. How can she then calculate the frequency of the waves?**

Speed of waves in a ripple tank

Sahil's group are comparing two ways of working out the speed of the waves as they travel through the water. One of these is by using speed equals distance/time and the other is by using speed equals frequency times wavelength.

6. **Explain how the group could measure the speed of the waves using the equation speed = distance/time.**

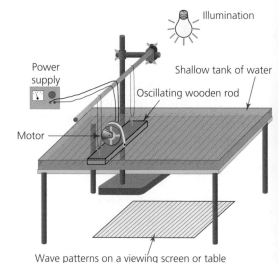

Figure 4.11 Ripple tank used for observing waves in water

Figure 4.12 Shadows of waves travelling across a ripple tank. The wavelength is the distance between two dark patches, which are the peaks (crests) of the waves.

7 Now explain how the group could calculate the speed of the waves using the equation speed = frequency × wavelength.

8 Why do scientists sometimes try to use two different methods to answer a question?

Speed of waves on a stretched string

We can use an electric motor to vibrate a stretched string or elastic cord (Figure 4.13). The motor transfers energy continuously to the string. This produces transverse waves that travel along the string, just like when you shake a rope up and down. Changing the vibration frequency changes the wavelength of the waves. The speed of the wave travelling along the string stays the same – it depends on how heavy the string is and how tightly it is stretched.

By changing the frequency of vibration, it is possible to produce a stable wave pattern. You can then count the number of wavelengths along the string and work out their speed. The frequency will be the frequency of the power supply.

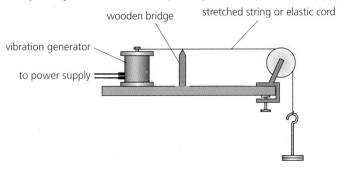

Figure 4.13 Setting up waves on a stretching string

9 Suggest what equipment you could use to measure the wavelength, and how you should set it up.

10 Give two reasons why it would be difficult to obtain measurements with a normal stop clock which you operate by pressing a start/stop button.

11 What difficulties are there in measuring the wavelength accurately in this experiment?

12 By changing the frequency of the vibration generator or changing the length of string allowed to vibrate (moving the wooden bridge in Figure 4.13) it is possible to increase the number of 'loops' seen in the vibrating string.

How could you use this effect to verify the speed of the waves on the string?

> **REMEMBER!**
>
> If you have a set of readings, don't simply average all the results but look at them first to see if there are any anomalies. These should be eliminated before finding the average or they will influence the outcome.

DID YOU KNOW?

It may seem strange that you are calculating a wave speed along the string when the string is moving up and down and has some points that don't move at all. In this special situation there are two waves travelling in opposite directions along the string (the wave created at the vibrating end and a wave reflected at the other end). These two waves meet and actually pass through each other!

MATHS SKILLS

Using and rearranging equations

Learning objectives:

* select and apply the equations $T = \frac{1}{f}$ and $v = f\lambda$
* substitute numerical values into equations using appropriate units
* change the subject of an equation.

KEY WORDS

proportional
rearrange an equation
subject of an equation
substitute

The names of units are often taken from the name of the scientist who first worked in that particular field of physics. The unit of frequency is the hertz (Hz) after the German physicist Heinrich Hertz.

Period and frequency

Remember, frequency, f, is the number of waves passing a point each second. The unit of frequency is the hertz (Hz), which means cycles per second. The time period, T, is measured in seconds (s).

Period and frequency are linked by the equation:

$$T = \frac{1}{f}$$

Example: A wave has a frequency of 5 Hz. What is its period?

Substituting 5 Hz into the equation $T = \frac{1}{f}$ gives $T = \frac{1}{5}$ s. When there are 5 cycles of a wave in 1 second, then one cycle, or the period T, is $\frac{1}{5}$ s or 0.2 s.

① **Work out the period of a wave when the frequency is:**

    a 100 Hz   **b** 1000 Hz   **c** 15 000 Hz.

Example: Calculate the frequency when the period is 4 seconds. Use the equation $T = \frac{1}{f}$.

Rearrange it to make f the **subject of the equation**.

Multiply both sides by f: $Tf = 1$

Divide both sides by T: $f = \frac{1}{T}$

Substitute $T = 4$ s into the rearranged equation.

    $f = \frac{1}{4}s = 0.25$ Hz

② **Work out the frequency of a wave with period:**

    a 5 s   **b** 10 s   **c** 150 s.

KEY INFORMATION

You do not need to remember the equations on this page as they will be on the equation sheet. But you need to know when and how to use each equation. You also need to be able to rearrange an equation. Rearranging an equation means making another variable the subject of the equation. The subject of the equation is on its own, usually on the left-hand side.

Speed, frequency and wavelength

You can calculate the speed at which wave moves using the equation:

$$speed = \frac{distance}{time}$$

The unit of distance is the metre (m). The unit of time is the second (s). So the unit of wave speed is metres per second (m/s).

Wavelength is the distance from a point on one wave to the equivalent point on the adjacent wave, such as between two adjacent crests. The symbol for wavelength is λ and the unit is the metre (m).

The wave equation links wave speed, frequency and wavelength:

wave speed = frequency × wavelength

$$v = f\lambda$$

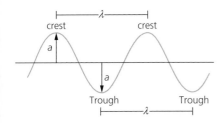

Figure 4.14 Wavelength of a transverse wave

3 Use the equation $v = f\lambda$ to work out the speed of a wave with:

   a frequency 100 Hz and wavelength 2 m

   b frequency 100 Hz and wavelength 2 cm

   c frequency 100 Hz and wavelength 2 mm.

4 Rearrange the wave equation to make frequency the subject.

5 Work out the frequency of a wave with

   a wavelength 0.5 m and speed 25 m/s

   b wavelength 0.05 m and speed 250 m/s

   c wavelength 0.005 m and speed 2500 m/s.

6 **a** Rearrange the wave equation to calculate the wavelength given the speed and the frequency.

   b Calculate the wavelength of a sound wave in air with frequency 500 Hz and speed 330 m/s.

> **REMEMBER!**
>
> When you rearrange an equation, always do the same operation (such as multiplication or division) to both sides. For example, if you divide one side of the equation by the variable λ, you must divide both sides of the equation by λ.

KEY CONCEPT

Transferring energy or information by waves

Learning objectives:

- to understand that all waves have common properties
- to understand how waves can be used to carry information
- to understand various applications of energy transfer by different types of electromagnetic waves.

KEY WORDS

energy
transfer
vibration
amplitude
absorb

All waves transfer energy or information from one place to another. Water waves at the seaside transfer energy when they hit the shore to move sand and shingle up the beach. Radio waves transfer picture and sound information from the transmitter to your television set at home.

A wave is a regular vibration that carries energy. Ripples on the surface of a pond, sound in air, ultrasound, visible light, X-rays and infrared rays are all types of wave. In water, the surface just moves up and down, but the energy is carried outwards from the source. A Mexican wave in a stadium is caused by spectators just standing up and sitting down but the wave travels all round the stadium (Figure 4.15).

Figure 4.15 A Mexican wave

Why not look on YouTube at the world record of a Mexican wave?

Common properties of waves

No matter what their speed, wavelength or frequency, waves transfer energy. When we watch a firework display, sound waves travel slowly compared with light waves but they still transfer energy from the explosion to our eardrums. We see the flash of the explosion when light waves transfer energy to sensors in our eyes.

Amplitude measures the maximum displacement of the wave above or below its rest point. The larger the amplitude of a water wave, the more energy it can transfer. An earthquake underwater can create a tsunami with waves 30 m high. This huge amplitude wave could transfer enough energy to power the whole of the UK for a year.

1 Why do you hear the sound of thunder after you see the flash of lightning?

2 Draw a diagram to show two transverse waves with different amplitudes.

3 What would you notice if the amplitude of a sound wave increased?

Using waves to transmit information

Since waves can carry energy, we use them to transmit information by varying the amount of energy carried by the wave. This can be done by simply switching the wave source on and off to create a pulsed code, as in Morse code by light, or by varying the frequency or amplitude of the wave.

Visible and infrared light is used to send internet data and telephone calls down fibre optic cables (Figure 4.16). Information that has been transformed into binary code is sent as pulses of light to be converted into digital signals read by computers or converted into sound in telephones. The use of fibre optic cables and light waves enables vast amounts of information to be sent over far greater distances than with copper wires.

4   **What are the advantages of fibre optic cables over copper wires?**

Electromagnetic waves

Each different part of the electromagnetic spectrum is used to transfer energy.

- Microwaves can transfer data to mobile phones.
- An electric fire transfers energy to our bodies by infrared waves warming us up.
- Some energy from the Sun is transferred by ultraviolet rays.
- Not all energy from an X-ray machine is transferred. Some is absorbed by the body when an X-ray image is produced.
- Energy from radioactive sources can be transferred by gamma rays.

Mobile phones use microwaves that are similar to the waves that are used in microwave ovens (Figure 4.17). However, strict limits are applied to the amount of energy a mobile phone can transfer. In the UK it is illegal to sell phones that transfer more than 2 J of energy per second (2 W). This energy is transmitted in all directions not just into your brain. Typically your phone transfers about 5000 times less energy to your brain than a microwave oven would.

5   **For each of the examples of electromagnetic waves in the list above, suggest one piece of evidence that shows the energy transferred by the wave can be either absorbed or reflected.**

6   **If energy is being transmitted away from the Sun then why isn't the Sun continually cooling down?**

DID YOU KNOW

Optical fibres transmit data at 200000 km/s, which is the speed of light in glass. Many telephone conversations and computer data travel long distances through optical fibre cables with little energy loss by absorption in the glass.

Figure 4.16 Light coming out of a fibre optic cable

Figure 4.17 Do mobile phones cook your brain?

The electromagnetic spectrum

Learning objectives:

- recall the similarities and differences between transverse and longitudinal waves
- recognise that electromagnetic waves are transverse waves
- describe the main groupings and wavelength ranges of the electromagnetic spectrum.

All electromagnetic radiation (including visible light) travels the 149 million kilometres from the Sun to the Earth in about 8 minutes.

Transverse and longitudinal waves

As you saw earlier, there are two types of waves: **transverse** and **longitudinal**. In a transverse wave the vibrations are at right angles to the direction of energy transfer and in a longitudinal wave they are parallel to the direction of energy transfer (Figure 4.18).

Ripples on water (Figure 4.19) and a rope or Slinky moved from side to side are transverse waves.

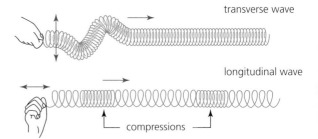

Figure 4.18 Comparing transverse and longitudinal waves

1 Explain what is meant by

   a the amplitude and

   b the wavelength of a wave.

2 Give an example of a longitudinal wave.

Electromagnetic waves

We know light is a wave because it has the same properties as other waves: it can be reflected and refracted.

White light is a mixture of waves with different wavelengths which we see as different colours. These colours can be separated into what we call the **visible spectrum**. When scientists investigate the visible spectrum they can detect invisible waves on both sides, showing that the visible spectrum is really part of a much wider spectrum, which we call the **electromagnetic spectrum**.

All the waves in the electromagnetic spectrum are transverse waves with many properties in common with visible light.

Just like other waves, all **electromagnetic waves** transfer energy from one point to another. In electromagnetic waves, electromagnetic fluctuations occur at right angles to the direction in which energy is being transferred by the wave.

Figure 4.19 Water waves are transverse: although it looks as if the water particles move outwards they actually move up and down.

Some waves have to travel through a material.
Sound waves can travel through air, liquids and solids but not a vacuum. Water ripples travel along the surface of water.

Electromagnetic waves are different from other waves because they do not need a material. They can travel through a vacuum. This is a special property of electromagnetic waves, which enables light and infrared waves to reach us from the Sun. All electromagnetic waves travel at the same speed in a vacuum, 3.0×10^8 m/s.

3 What are the similarities and differences between transverse and longitudinal waves?

4 Explain how waves in the electromagnetic spectrum are different from other waves.

5 What properties do all electromagnetic waves have in common?

The electromagnetic spectrum

Figure 4.20 shows that electromagnetic waves span a wide, continuous range of wavelengths and frequencies.

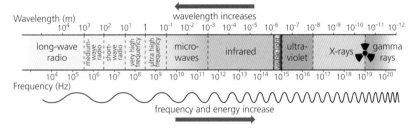

Figure 4.20 The wavelengths and frequencies of waves in the electromagnetic spectrum

The groups of waves in the electromagnetic spectrum are :

- radio, TV and microwaves: above 10^5m to 10^{-3} m
- infrared: 10^{-3} to 10^{-7} m
- visible (red to violet): 10^{-7} m
- ultraviolet: 10^{-7} to 10^{-8} m
- X-ray: 10^{-8} to 10^{-10} m
- gamma ray: 10^{-10} to less than 10^{-12} m.

The shorter the wavelength of the electromagnetic wave, the further it can travel through other materials. The higher the frequency of a wave, the more energy it can transfer to another object when the radiation is absorbed.

6 Which grouping in the electromagnetic spectrum has the highest frequency?

7 Ultraviolet light used in a sunbed has a wavelength of 3.5×10^{-7} m. Calculate the frequency of this light.

8 Calculate the frequency of an electromagnetic wave with a wavelength of 20 cm. Use standard form for your answer.

9 Suggest why ultraviolet waves are more dangerous than radio waves.

REMEMBER!

Remember the order of electromagnetic wave groupings.

KEY INFORMATION

The shorter the wavelength (the higher the frequency) of an electromagnetic wave the more dangerous the radiation.

KEY INFORMATION

All electromagnetic waves travel at the same speed in a vacuum, 3.0×10^8 m/s.

Gamma rays and X-rays

Learning objectives:

- list the properties of gamma rays and X-rays
- recall examples of the practical uses of X-rays and gamma rays
- compare gamma rays and X-rays.

KEY WORDS

radiation dose
X-ray
gamma ray
tracer

X-ray machines called pedoscopes were introduced in the 1930s in shoe shops in the UK. They enabled parents and children to see how well shoes fitted. They were very popular with children, who loved to watch their bones move as they wriggled their toes. Unfortunately people using these machines did not realise how dangerous X-rays can be, and some shoe shop assistants might have developed cancer because of using them.

Gamma rays

Gamma rays have the shortest wavelengths and transfer the most energy of all the waves in the electromagnetic spectrum. This means they can be harmful to living cells. Gamma rays are used to kill cancer cells or reduce the size of a tumour (radiotherapy). However, the **radiation dose** from a single treatment is usually low in comparison with the level of background radiation. Radiation dose is measured in sieverts (Sv) and millisieverts (mSv).

Gamma rays are also used in medical imaging. Technetium-99m is a radioactive isotope that emits gamma rays. It is used as a radioactive **tracer**. A gamma camera monitors where gamma rays are emitted from in the body, to produce a moving image that shows how organs are functioning (Figure 4.21).

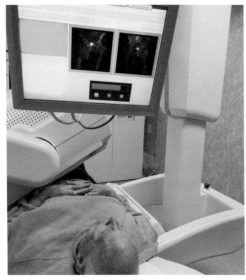

Figure 4.21 This patient is having a scan using a gamma tracer and gamma camera.

X-rays

X-rays pass through soft tissues in the body but will be absorbed by bone. X-ray images can be used to check for broken bones (Figure 4.22).

X-rays are also used in computerised tomography (CT) scans. Multiple images are taken at many different angles to build up a detailed picture of inside a patient's body (Figure 4.23).

In addition to medical imaging for diagnosis, X-rays are used in radiotherapy to treat cancer.

HIGHER TIER ONLY

3 Should X-rays used in radiotherapy have longer or shorter wavelengths than those used for medical diagnosis? Explain your answer.

4 Suggest why gamma rays are not used for medical imaging in the same way as X-rays.

Comparing gamma rays and X-rays

Gamma rays and X-rays have very similar ranges of wavelengths and frequencies, and so have very similar effects. Their high frequencies mean they carry the most energy and are the most penetrating forms of electromagnetic radiation, so therefore they can also be the most dangerous to human body tissue when the radiation is absorbed.

Both gamma rays and X-rays are highly ionising radiation. This is how they damage and destroy cancer cells. Large doses of ionising radiation can cause the mutation of genes in cells, which can cause cells to become cancerous.

The key difference between gamma rays and X-rays is how they are produced. Gamma rays are emitted from the nucleus of an unstable atom during radioactive decay. This is a random process. X-rays are generated by an X-ray machine when high-speed electrons collide with metals and lose energy.

5 Describe the similarities and differences between gamma rays and X-rays.

6 Explain why an X-ray source needs an electric power supply but a gamma source does not.

7 Why must great care be taken when using X-rays and gamma rays?

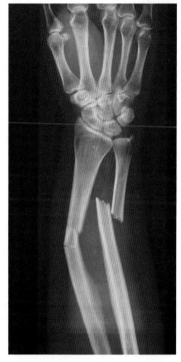

Figure 4.22 This X-ray shows a broken ulna in the wrist.

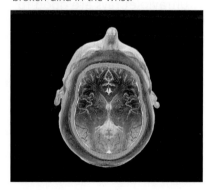

Figure 4.23 A CT scan can give good pictures of soft tissue regions but exposes a patient to a much higher radiation dose than a single X-ray.

KEY INFORMATION

Like all electromagnetic waves, gamma rays and X-rays travel at the same velocity in both a vacuum and air, but at slower speeds when they travel in a material.

Ultraviolet and infrared radiation

Learning objectives:

- describe the properties of ultraviolet and infrared radiation
- describe some uses and hazards of ultraviolet radiation
- describe some uses of infrared radiation.

KEY WORDS

infrared radiation
ultraviolet radiation

Some of the dyes in inks are only visible under ultraviolet light. These are used in security pens used to mark valuable equipment such as computers and bicycles. Many banknotes have a special feature which is only visible under ultraviolet light.

Ultraviolet radiation and its uses

Ultraviolet rays have shorter wavelengths than violet light. They are emitted from very hot objects (4000 °C or more) such as the Sun.

One use of ultraviolet is in fluorescent lighting. This type of light is more energy-efficient than traditional filament light bulbs and this technology is used in compact fluorescent light bulbs.

Our skin absorbs ultraviolet light from sunlight. Small doses of ultraviolet rays are good for us, as this produces vitamin D in our skin. A sun tan (from sunlight or a sunbed) is a natural darkening of the skin to protect itself from too much ultraviolet radiation.

Figure 4.24 Some of the ink used in Euro banknotes is only visible in UV light.

1 State three uses of ultraviolet radiation.

2 Describe how ultraviolet radiation can be used to mark a TV.

3 Suggest why many shops have an ultraviolet lamp by the till.

4 John says that ultraviolet light has a purple colour. Explain whether John is correct.

The hazards of ultraviolet radiation

Ultraviolet light has a higher frequency than visible light and transfers more energy when it is absorbed by skin. Too much sunlight or use of sunbeds causes premature aging of the skin, such as wrinkles and dark pigmentation spots. Large doses of ultraviolet rays can be harmful to our eyes and may also cause skin cancer, especially in people with fair skin.

Sun-screens can reduce the risks of sunburn and skin cancer (Figure 4.25).

Figure 4.25 Sun-screens contain substances that absorb or reflect some of the Sun's ultraviolet radiation.

5. Explain why small doses of ultraviolet rays can be good for you but large doses can be harmful.

6. Suggest why skiers might be at a greater risk of sunburn than people on the beach.

Infrared radiation

Infrared radiation is next to red light on the electromagnetic spectrum, and has longer wavelengths than red light. Anything that is warmer than its surroundings emits energy by giving out infrared radiation. You cannot see infrared radiation but you can feel the infrared radiation given out by hot things such as a fire, a heater or an oven.

The traditional way of cooking is by using infrared radiation. However, infrared radiation only heats the surface of food. The radiation is not transmitted very far into food. Meat that appears to be cooked may be raw on the inside (Figure 4.26).

Energy from infrared radiation is absorbed by the particles on the surface of the food. They vibrate more and energy can then be transferred slowly by conduction to the food below the surface.

7. Why is the chicken in Figure 4.26 still undercooked in the middle when it appears to be fully cooked on the outside?

8. What energy transfer processes heats the centre of the food?

Remote controls for electronic devices such as TVs and radios work by emitting an infrared signal. The remotely controlled device won't work if an object is between it and the control because the infrared signal is absorbed. Infrared beams can also be used for security alarms.

Thermal imaging cameras (Figure 4.27) detect low levels of infrared radiation from warm objects.

9. Suggest two ways that infrared sensors can be used in a burglar alarm.

10. Suggest one way a TV remote control could still work when not pointed directly at the TV set.

DID YOU KNOW?

Halogen hobs work by using ring-shaped halogen lamps beneath a glass cooktop. Although you see a bright red light, the glowing filament in the lamp radiates mostly infrared radiation.

Figure 4.26 This chicken is undercooked in the middle

Figure 4.27 A thermal imaging camera detects infrared radiation given off by an object or person.

Microwaves

Learning objectives:

- list some properties of microwaves
- describe how microwaves are used for communications.

KEY WORDS

microwaves

Mobile phones use microwaves. A mobile phone today can have more computing power than the first computers used to land man on the Moon.

Properties of microwaves

Microwaves are radio waves with short wavelengths. The wavelengths of microwaves vary between 1 mm and 30 cm. Microwaves used for communication have a longer wavelength than those used for cooking. This means that there is less energy associated with mobile phones than with microwave ovens (Figure 4.28).

KEY INFORMATION

Remember, the higher the frequency of electromagnetic waves the more energy associated with the radiation.

Figure 4.28

1. List two uses of microwaves.
2. Suggest what use is likely to be made of microwaves with a wavelength of 25 cm.

Cooking with microwaves

Microwave ovens do not use a flame or heated metal to cook food. They use microwaves instead. Microwave ovens cook food faster and are less expensive to run than conventional ovens.

Microwaves penetrate about 1 cm into the outer layers of food before being absorbed. The energy transferred by the microwaves makes water (Figure 4.29) or fat molecules in the outer layers of food vibrate more (Figure 4.30). Energy is then transferred from the vibrating water or fat molecules to the centre of the food by conduction.

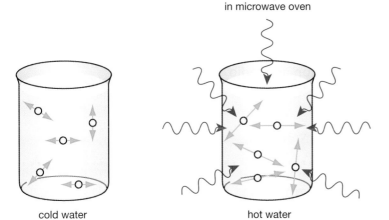

microwaves produced
in microwave oven

cold water

hot water

Figure 4.29 Microwaves cook food by making
the water or fat molecules vibrate more.

DID YOU KNOW?

The inside walls of
microwave ovens must
be made of metal. Metal
reflects microwaves so the
microwaves are trapped
inside. This is important to
make sure we do not cook
ourselves. The door of a
microwave oven is made
from special glass that
also reflects microwave
radiation.

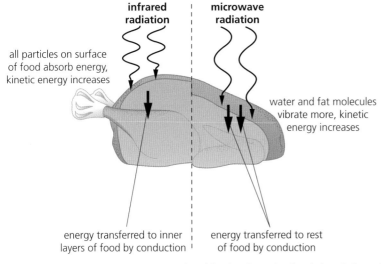

infrared
radiation

microwave
radiation

all particles on surface
of food absorb energy,
kinetic energy increases

water and fat molecules
vibrate more, kinetic
energy increases

energy transferred to inner
layers of food by conduction

energy transferred to rest
of food by conduction

Figure 4.30 Microwaves are transmitted further into the food than infrared
radiation before being absorbed.

3. **Explain the differences between the ways a microwave oven
and a conventional oven cook food.**

4. **Suggest two advantages of using a microwave oven instead of
an infrared oven.**

5. **Explain what would happen if you tried to make toast in a
microwave oven.**

Radio and microwave communication

Learning objectives:

- describe how radio waves are used for television and radio communications
- describe how microwaves are used in satellite communications
- describe the reflection and refraction of radio waves.

Bluetooth is a wireless technology for exchanging data over short distances using microwaves.

Using radio waves for communication

A system using electromagnetic waves to communicate must contain a **transmitter** to send a signal and a **receiver** to receive it. Terrestrial radio and TV signals are sent by **radio waves**. The radio waves travel through the air at the speed of light. The path between transmitter and receiver usually has to be a straight line with no large obstructions such as hills and large buildings, so the transmitters are placed on towers that may be hundreds of metres tall (Figure 4.31).

1 Describe the properties of radio waves that make them useful for radio communication.

2 A radio wave has a wavelength of 100 m. What is its frequency?

HIGHER TIER ONLY

Radio waves can be produced by oscillations in electrical circuits. When a current flows through a wire it creates an electric field around the wire. When the current changes, the electric field changes. The changing current produces radio waves. This is how radio transmitters work.

Radio waves can induce oscillations in an electrical circuit, with the same frequency as the radio wave itself.

3 Suggest how a radio receiver works.

4 Some radios do not need a power supply (even a clockwork one). Suggest where they might get the energy from that they need to produce the sound.

Figure 4.31 A radio transmitter

Using microwaves for communication

Microwaves are used to transmit mobile phone signals. Microwave transmitters or base stations are placed on high buildings or masts to give better line of sight communication over large distances. Although most microwave signals are sent directly, some are sent from a transmitter to a receiver via a satellite (Figure 4.32). Microwave satellite communications are used for satellite phones and for satellite TV.

5 Suggest why satellite dishes are placed on the walls or roofs of houses.

6 Suggest why aerials for mobile phone signals are placed close together in towns and cities.

HIGHER TIER ONLY

Reflection and refraction of radio signals

Like all other electromagnetic waves, radio waves can be reflected and refracted. Radio waves are refracted in the upper layers of the atmosphere, called the ionosphere. The amount of refraction depends on the frequency of the wave.

Waves with a long wavelength and low frequency undergo most refraction in the ionosphere. Figure 4.32 shows how radio waves are refracted in the ionosphere so the wave returns to the Earth's surface. Microwaves with shorter wavelengths are not refracted or reflected and pass straight through the ionosphere. This is why microwaves, not radio waves, are used for satellite communication.

7 State what happens to some radio waves in the ionosphere.

8 A radio station broadcasts with a frequency of 103.4 MHz from the transmitter in Figure 4.33. Explain why a radio at point X will not receive the signal.

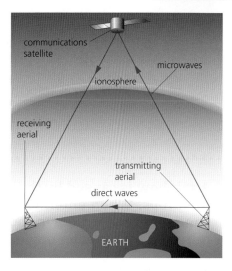

Figure 4.32 Direct and satellite microwave communication

DID YOU KNOW?

Using a satellite for communication delays a signal by less than 0.3 s.

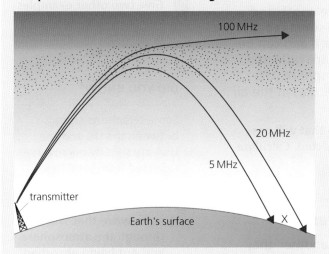

Figure 4.33 Waves of different frequencies are refracted by different amounts when entering the ionosphere.

Reflection, refraction and wave fronts

Learning objectives:

- explain reflection and refraction and how these may vary with wavelength
- use wave front diagrams to explain refraction in terms of the difference in velocity of the waves in different substances.

KEY WORDS

reflection
transmission
absorption
refraction
ray diagram
wave front

A rainbow is caused by the refraction of sunlight by raindrops. When entering a raindrop, blue light in sunlight is slowed down more than red light, so is refracted by a greater angle.

HIGHER TIER ONLY

Reflection of electromagnetic waves

Studying how visible light behaves is relatively easy because we can see what happens. This then enables us to predict, check and understand how other electromagnetic waves behave.

All waves, including all electromagnetic waves, can be **reflected**, **transmitted** or **absorbed**.

One way of keeping things warm is to use aluminium foil to reflect the infrared radiation emitted by a warm object back towards the object. Figure 4.34 illustrates how this can be done. It can also be used to keep objects cool.

The proportion of a wave's energy that is reflected, transmitted or absorbed depends on its wavelength and on the medium it enters. For example, while some radio waves from stars pass through the atmosphere and can be detected on Earth, some radio wavelengths are reflected back into space from the Earth's upper atmosphere (the ionosphere). At other wavelengths, gas molecules in the air absorb incoming radio waves.

3. **10 MHz is the lowest frequency radio wave that will pass through the ionosphere without being reflected. Calculate the wavelength of these waves.**

Refraction of electromagnetic waves

When light waves travel from one medium into another, they change speed and may change direction (Figure 4.35). This is called **refraction**.

aluminium foil

Figure 4.34 Putting aluminum foil behind a radiator means the foil will reflect infrared radiation back into the room.

1. Explain how using aluminium foil behind a radiator could reduce the household energy bill.

2. Give two other examples where infrared radiation is reflected to keep things warm or cool.

DID YOU KNOW?

Some telephone signals between the UK and the USA are sent by microwaves reflected from satellites.

4. The shortest wavelength radio wave that will pass through the atmosphere without being absorbed is 100 m. Calculate the frequency of these waves.

All electromagnetic waves can be refracted when they enter a medium in which the wave velocity is different. The shorter the wavelength, the more the wave is refracted.

Different substances refract the same wavelength in different ways. For example, radio waves travel in a straight line from the transmitter, but are refracted in the lower layer of the atmosphere. The amount of refraction can be affected by differences in atmospheric temperature and pressure.

6 Suggest why radio signals can sometimes travel further between two points on the Earth as atmospheric conditions change.

Explaining refraction

A **wave front** is a line that joins all the points on a wave which are moving up and down together at the same time. The wavefront is at right angles to the direction the wave is travelling. We can see what happens when waves are refracted by looking at plane water waves in a ripple tank (Figure 4.36).

When a wave strikes a boundary at an angle, one part of the wave reaches the boundary before the rest of the wave. This part changes speed first. In Figure 4.36 the left-hand parts of the wave fronts get closer together, because waves travel slower in shallower water. The wave front changes direction. The wave is refracted towards the normal.

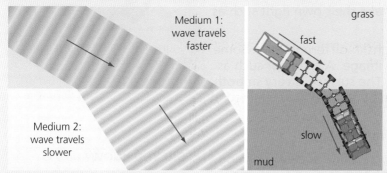

Figure 4.37 The way that waves refract when going from a higher speed medium to a lower speed medium is similar to what happens when a car drives at an angle into mud. The wheels that reach the mud first slow down first so the car changes direction.

7 Look at Figure 4.36.

a What happens to the wavefronts in Figure 4.36 when the water waves move from deep to shallow water?

b Do the waves travel faster in deep or shallow water? Explain your answer.

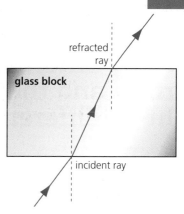

Figure 4.35 Light is refracted towards the normal when it travels from air to glass, and away from the normal when it travels from glass to air.

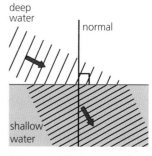

Figure 4.36 Water waves with a plane (straight) wave front travelling from deep to shallow water

KEY INFORMATION

The wave fronts get closer together because speed = frequency × wavelength and the frequency of the waves (which depends on the source of the waves) is constant. If the speed decreases, the wavelength must also decrease.

PRACTICAL

Investigate the reflection of light by different types of surface and the refraction of light by different substances

Learning objectives:

* make and record observations of how light is reflected and transmitted at different surfaces
* measure angles and discuss the method, apparatus and uncertainty in measurements
* draw conclusions from experimental results.

Waves can be reflected, transmitted or absorbed at the boundary between two different materials.

Reflection at different surfaces

Lots of objects reflect light. When you look around the room, most of the objects you can see are visible because they reflect light (the exceptions are ones that make their own light such as the Sun and light bulbs).

However, different objects reflect light in different ways. Some objects reflect light so as to form an image. A reflector such as a mirror forms a **specular reflection**. The surface is very smooth and all the light rays coming from one direction are reflected at the same angle.

Other objects, though, work in a different way.

You cannot see a reflection in a rough surface such as clothing or paper. At a rough surface, the light rays coming from one direction are reflected at many different angles. This is **diffuse reflection**.

Figure 4.38 Reflection in a mirror – an image is formed

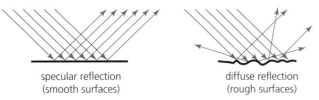

specular reflection
(smooth surfaces)

diffuse reflection
(rough surfaces)

Figure 4.39 Specular and diffuse reflection

1. Give three examples of objects that produce diffuse reflection.

2. Explain why it might be dangerous for bicycle reflectors to use specular reflectors.

DID YOU KNOW?

Retroreflectors used on bicycles and safety clothing are good at reflecting light but you can't see an image in them. All the light coming from one direction is reflected back in the same direction.

Figure 4.40

Measuring angles

Clearly, angles are important when it comes to reflection. Gemma and her group were asked to find out how the angle that light approached a mirror at would affect the angle it was reflected at. They wanted to see if there was a pattern in the results.

3 Suggest what equipment they could use, how they should set it up and what measurements to take.

4 When they are measuring the angles of the rays, where should they measure them from?

5 What difficulties are there in measuring angles accurately with this apparatus? What could you do to reduce the uncertainty in the results?

6 How would you process data from the experiment, to see if there is a relationship that links the incident ray to the reflected ray?

7 Gemma thinks that these results only apply to specular reflections – is she right?

> **REMEMBER!**
>
> When measuring the angles of light rays, remember to measure them from the normal, the line drawn at right angles to the surface where the ray meets the other medium.
> Remember the reflective surface of the mirror is the silvering behind the glass not at the front.

Exploring refraction

If a light ray hits another transparent medium, such as glass or water, it may travel through. Alex's group is investigating this; they used a prism and a single ray of light. Figure 4.41 shows what they found from their experiment. They were also interested in seeing what happened when the light left the prism and went back into air.

8 What conclusion can they form from this about what happens to the light when it:

   a enters the prism?

   b leaves the prism?

9 What should they notice about the direction of the light leaving the block compared with the direction of the light entering the block?

10 Do you think they would get similar results no matter what angle the light approached the block at?

11 What do you think might happen if the light then passes through a second inverted prism?

12 What do you think would happen if the prism was rectangular rather than triangular?

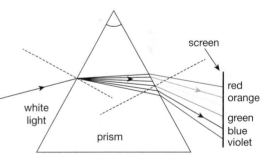

Figure 4.41 Dispersion is the separation of light into its constituent colors.

Atomic structure

Learning objectives:

- describe the structure of the atom
- use symbols to represent particles
- describe ionisation.

Radium is one of the most powerful radioactive substances known. It emits one million times more radiation than uranium.

The structure of the atom

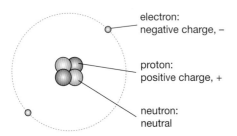

electron:
negative charge, −

proton:
positive charge, +

neutron:
neutral

Figure 4.42 An atom contains protons, neutrons and electrons

An atom contains protons, neutrons and electrons (Figure 4.42). The protons and neutrons are at the centre of the atom and form the atom's nucleus. Protons and neutrons are also called **nucleons**. The electrons are arranged at different distances from the nucleus (different **energy levels**).

Neutrons are neutral – they have no charge. Protons have a positive electric charge and electrons have a negative electric charge of the same size. There are the same number of electrons and protons in an atom. This means that atoms have no overall electrical charge because the charges cancel out.

1 A radium atom has 88 protons and 226 neutrons. How many electrons does it have?

2 A uranium atom has 92 electrons and 238 nucleons. Determine how many protons and how many neutrons it has.

The number of protons in the atom determines what element it is. All atoms with six protons, for example, are carbon atoms. Atoms of the same element can have a different number of neutrons though. This means that elements can exist as different **isotopes**. Isotopes of an element have the same number of protons in them but different numbers of neutrons.

3 Two atoms are from the same element but they form different isotopes. Compare the numbers of electrons, protons and neutrons in the two atoms.

Using symbols to represent atoms

The number of nucleons in the atom is the **mass number (A)**. The number of protons in the atom defines the element and is called the **atomic number** Z.

mass number ——— $^{238}_{92}$U $^{234}_{90}$Th
atomic number ———

Figure 4.43: We represent an atom or nucleus with the element symbol, mass number and atomic number

So, for ^A_ZX, where

A = mass number (or nucleon number)

Z = atomic number (or proton number)

X = chemical symbol for the element

Z is the number of protons in the nucleus, so the number of neutrons is (A – Z).

For example, $^{14}_{6}$C has a mass number of 14 and an atomic number of 6. So it has 14 nucleons and 6 protons. The number of neutrons in the nucleus is 14 – 6 = 8 neutrons.

When an atom gains or loses electrons it becomes **ionised** – it has become charged. The atom has become an ion and can be positively or negatively charged. As we shall see in topic 4.16, ionisation can occur when ionising radiation from radioactive decay knocks one or more outer electrons out of the atoms the radiation passes through.

4 How many protons and neutrons are in the nucleus of an atom of:

   a $^{14}_{7}$N

   b $^{235}_{92}$U ?

5 Explain how ionising radiation can turn some atoms into positive ions and some into negative ions.

Electrons and energy levels

Electrons occupy the space around the nucleus at specific distances or **energy levels**. An individual electron can change energy levels (move closer to or further from the nucleus) only if the atom absorbs or emits electromagnetic radiation (Figure 4.44).

The wavelength of the electromagnetic radiation is determined by the difference in energy between the two electron energy levels. A wide range of wavelengths can be emitted or absorbed, from gamma rays through X-rays, ultraviolet, visible light and infrared radiation. Each element has a unique pattern of energy levels, so the wavelengths emitted or absorbed can be used to identify elements.

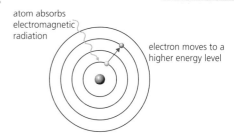

atom absorbs electromagnetic radiation

electron moves to a higher energy level

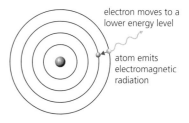

electron moves to a lower energy level

atom emits electromagnetic radiation

Figure 4.44

KEY INFORMATION

You can calculate the number of neutrons by taking the proton number away from the mass number.

DID YOU KNOW?

The Sun's visible spectrum has dark lines crossing it at certain wavelengths. These are absorption lines caused when atoms in the Sun's gaseous atmosphere absorb electromagnetic radiation coming from the Sun's interior. These lines led to the discovery of an unknown element in the Sun's atmosphere in 1870. It was named helium after the Greek sun god, Helios.

Radioactive decay

Learning objectives:

- describe radioactive decay
- describe the types of nuclear radiation
- understand the processes of alpha decay and beta decay.

Henri Becquerel discovered radioactivity by accident in 1896. When he left some uranium salts next to a wrapped photographic plate he found that the plate had become 'fogged'. He realised that some invisible radiation must be coming from the uranium.

Radioactive decay

Most nuclei are stable but some are not. An unstable nucleus undergoes radioactive decay to become more stable. It emits radiation as it decays. An atom with an unstable nucleus is called a **radioisotope**.

The **activity** of a radioisotope is the number of nuclear decays each second. The activity is measured in **becquerels** (Bq) or counts per second. 1 Bq = 1 count per second.

Radioactivity is a **random** process. It is not possible to predict when a nucleus will decay. If we increase or decrease the temperature of the nucleus, we still cannot predict when it will decay. Radioactive decays is independent of physical changes such as changes in temperature.

1. **The activity of a radioactive source is 150 Bq. How many counts would be recorded in 20 s?**

2. **What can you say about the nuclei of all elements larger than lead-208?**

3. **Explain what random means with regard to radioactive decay.**

Radioactive decay produces **nuclear radiation – radiation** emitted from the nucleus. The nuclear radiation emitted may be an alpha particle, beta particle, gamma ray or a neutron. **Neutron radiation** is the release of a high-speed neutron from the nucleus, either from the nucleus of a radioactive atom or as the result of nuclear fission.

Alpha decay

In alpha decay, an **alpha particle** is emitted from the nucleus (Figure 4.45). An alpha particle is a helium nucleus. It has 2 protons and 2 neutrons.

When an alpha particle is emitted from a nucleus:

- The nucleus has two fewer protons (p), so the atomic number (Z, the proton number) decreases by two.
- The nucleus also has two fewer neutrons, so the mass number (A, the nucleon number) decreases by four.
- A new element is formed.

KEY INFORMATION

Lead-208 means that the relative atomic mass = 208. It is the same as $^{208}_{82}$Pb.

DID YOU KNOW?

The largest stable nucleus is lead-208. When the atoms from larger nuclei decay they often eventually turn into lead. This is why lead is often found near radioactive rocks.

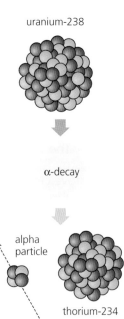

uranium-238

α-decay

alpha particle

thorium-234

Figure 4.45 Uranium splits into thorium and an alpha particle during alpha decay.

Beta decay

In beta decay one of the neutrons in the nucleus decays into a proton and an electron. This electron is emitted from the nucleus and is called a **beta particle**.

When a beta particle is emitted from a nucleus:

- The nucleus has one more proton (p), so the atomic number (Z, the proton number) increases by one.
- The nucleus has one less neutron (n), but the mass number (A, the nucleon number) is unchanged.
- A new element is formed.

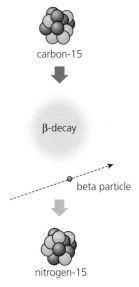

carbon-15

β-decay

beta particle

nitrogen-15

Figure 4.46 The carbon nucleus emits a beta particle and turns into nitrogen in beta decay.

4 In Figure 4.46, what are the differences between the nitrogen nucleus and the carbon nucleus?

5 What happens to a nucleus when **a** an alpha particle and **b** a beta particle is emitted?

Gamma decay

In gamma decay, **gamma rays** are emitted from a nucleus. These are very high-energy electromagnetic waves. They have no charge and no mass. The wavelength of the gamma rays emitted depends on the particular configuration of the radioactive nucleus and the particular change that takes place as it decays.

The emission of a gamma ray does not cause the mass or the charge of the nucleus to change.

6 When a nucleus undergoes radioactive decay, the mass number is unchanged but the atomic number has increased by 1. What type of decay is it?

7 Suggest why gamma decay often happens immediately after alpha or beta decay.

Nuclear equations

Learning objectives:

- understand nuclear equations
- write balanced nuclear equations.

KEY WORDS

alpha decay
beta decay
nuclear equation

Uranium-238 undergoes a series of 14 radioactive decays to become lead-206. The series contains both alpha and beta decays.

Nuclear equations

Chemical equations show what happens in a chemical reaction. The number of atoms on each side has to be the same – the equation has to be balanced.

Nuclear equations show what happens when there are changes in the nucleus. They show the number of nucleons and charge. As with chemical equations, they have to be balanced. The number of nucleons and charge has to be the same on both sides of the equation.

1 What do chemical and nuclear equations have in common?

2 What is a key difference between chemical and nuclear equations?

Nuclear equations for alpha decay

Alpha decay and **beta decay** can be shown as nuclear equations. Figure 4.47 shows the **nuclear equation** for the alpha decay of uranium-238.

$$^{238}_{92}\text{U} \xrightarrow{\alpha\text{-decay}} {}^{4}_{2}\text{He} + {}^{234}_{90}\text{Th}$$

Figure 4.47 The equation for the alpha decay of uranium-238

The mass numbers add up to the same number on both sides of the equation (238 = 234 + 4). This means that mass is conserved.

The atomic numbers also add up to the same on both sides of the equation (92 = 90 + 2), so the number of protons also is conserved. We can also say that the charge has been conserved.

When you write nuclear equations, make sure that the mass numbers and atomic numbers balance on both sides of the equation.

3 Copy and complete these nuclear equations for alpha decay.

a $^{226}_{\underline{}}\text{Ra} \rightarrow {}_{86}\text{Rn} + {}^{4}_{2}\text{He}$

b $^{219}_{86}\text{Rn} \rightarrow {}_{\underline{}}\text{Po} + {}_{\underline{}}\text{He}$

DID YOU KNOW?

Smoke alarms contain a small amount of americium-241 which decays by emitting an alpha particle. It becomes neptunium-237.

$^{23}_{11}$Na sodium	$^{24}_{12}$Mg magnesium											$^{27}_{13}$Al aluminium	$^{28}_{14}$Si silicon	$^{31}_{15}$P phosphorus	$^{32}_{16}$S sulfur	$^{35}_{17}$Cl chlorine	$^{40}_{18}$Ar argon
$^{39}_{19}$K potassium	$^{40}_{20}$Ca calcium	$^{45}_{21}$Sc scandium	$^{48}_{22}$Ti titanium	$^{51}_{23}$V vanadium	$^{52}_{24}$Cr chromium	$^{55}_{25}$Mn manganese	$^{56}_{26}$Fe iron	$^{59}_{27}$Co cobalt	$^{59}_{28}$Ni nickel	$^{64}_{29}$Cu copper	$^{65}_{30}$Zn zinc	$^{70}_{31}$Ga gallium	$^{73}_{32}$Ge germanium	$^{75}_{33}$As arsenic	$^{79}_{34}$Se selenium	$^{80}_{35}$Br bromine	$^{84}_{36}$Kr krypton
$^{85}_{37}$Rb rubidium	$^{88}_{38}$Sr strontium	$^{89}_{39}$Y yttrium	$^{91}_{40}$Zr zirconium	$^{93}_{41}$Nb niobium	$^{96}_{42}$Mo molybdenum	$^{99}_{43}$Tc technetium	$^{101}_{44}$Ru ruthenium	$^{103}_{45}$Rh rhodium	$^{106}_{46}$Pd palladium	$^{108}_{47}$Ag silver	$^{112}_{48}$Cd cadmium	$^{115}_{49}$In indium	$^{119}_{50}$Sn tin	$^{122}_{51}$Sb antimony	$^{128}_{52}$Te tellurium	$^{127}_{53}$I iodine	$^{131}_{54}$Xe xenon
$^{133}_{55}$Cs caesium	$^{137}_{56}$Ba barium	$^{139}_{57}$La lanthanum	$^{178}_{72}$Hf hafnium	$^{181}_{73}$Ta tantalum	$^{184}_{74}$W tungsten	$^{186}_{75}$Re rhenium	$^{190}_{76}$Os osmium	$^{192}_{77}$Ir iridium	$^{195}_{78}$Pt platinum	$^{197}_{79}$Au gold	$^{201}_{80}$Hg mercury	$^{204}_{81}$Tl thallium	$^{207}_{82}$Pb lead	$^{209}_{83}$Bi bismuth	$^{210}_{84}$Po polonium	$^{210}_{85}$At astatine	$^{222}_{86}$Rn radon
$^{223}_{87}$Fr francium	$^{226}_{88}$Ra radium	$^{227}_{89}$Ac actinium															

Figure 4.48 Part of the periodic table showing the most common isotopes

Nuclear equations for beta decay

In beta decay, a neutron changes into a proton and an electron.

$$^{1}_{0}n \rightarrow {}^{1}_{1}p + {}^{0}_{-1}e$$

The atomic number can also be thought of as the charge on the particle. This means that the atomic number for an electron is –1. The equation shows that the charge on both sides of the equation is 0, so charge is conserved.

Figure 4.49 demonstrates how the mass number is conserved (15 = 0 + 15) during beta decay. Figure 4.49 also shows that the charge is conserved (6 = 7 – 1) during beta decay.

4 **Copy and complete these equations for beta decay.**

   a $^{90}_{\_}Sr \rightarrow {}^{\_}_{39}Y + {}^{0}_{-1}e$ **b** $^{\_}_{15}P \rightarrow {}^{32}_{\_}S + {}^{0}_{-1}e$

5 **When radioactive sodium-24 decays, magnesium-24 is formed. One particle is emitted.**

   a copy and complete the equation.

      $^{\_}_{\_}Na \rightarrow {}^{\_}_{\_}Mg + \_\_$

   b What is the name of this particle?

6 **This equation represents the decay of thorium-232.**

   $^{232}_{90}Th \rightarrow {}^{A}_{Z}X + {}^{4}_{2}He$

   a What type of radiation is emitted?

   b What are the values of A and Z?

7 **Write a word equation and symbol equation for each radioactive decay:**

   a platinum-190, which emits an alpha particle

   b rhenium-187, which emits an alpha particle

   c copper-66, which emits a beta particle

   d nickel-66, which emits a beta particle

   e rhodium-105 which decays to palladium-105

   f osmium-186 which decays to tungsten-182.

REMEMBER!

Isotopes of the same element can have different mass numbers but they all have the same atomic number. The periodic table (Figure 4.48) shows the elements in order of atomic structure.

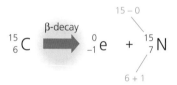

Figure 4.49 The equation for the beta decay of carbon-15

KEY INFORMATION

Radioactive decay by emitting a gamma ray causes no change in mass number or atomic number.

Radioactive half-life

KEY WORDS

....

half-life

Learning objectives:

- explain what is meant by radioactive half-life
- calculate half-life
- choose the best radioisotope for a task.

Radioisotopes are often used as medical tracers to monitor a biological process in the body. The half-life of the tracer has to be considered to minimise the patient's exposure to ionising radiation.

Half-life

We cannot predict when the nucleus of one particular atom will decay. It could be next week or not for a million years. Radioactive decay is a random process. If there is a very large number of atoms, some of them will decay each second. We plot a graph of activity against time and draw a curve of best fit. We can then use this curve to find when the activity has halved (Figure 4.50). The **half-life** of a radioisotope is the average time it takes for half the nuclei present to decay, or the time it takes for the count rate to fall to half its initial level. We use half-life because we cannot predict the time it will take for all the atoms to decay.

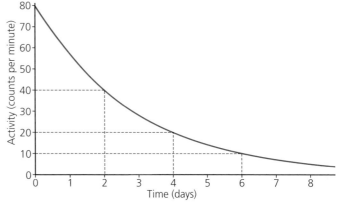

Figure 4.50 The time it takes for the activity to halve is constant

The activity of a radioactive substance gets less and less as time goes on. The graph line in Figure 4.50 gets closer and closer to the time axis but never reaches it because the activity halves each half-life.

1. **Explain why you can't predict when a particular atom will decay.**

2. **Explain what is meant by 'half-life'.**

3. **What will the activity in Figure 4.50 be after:**
   a 2 days?   **b** 4 days?   **c** 6 days?   **d** 8 days?

KEY INFORMATION

....

When you draw a curve of best fit on a graph of activity against time for a radioisotope, not all of the points will be on the curve. Some will be above the curve and and some will be below the curve because of the random nature of radioactive decay.

HIGHER TIER ONLY

Calculating half-life

To calculate the half-life of a radioisotope, plot a graph of activity against time, as shown in Figure 4.51. The background count should be subtracted from each reading before the graph is plotted. Plot the points and then draw a smooth curve of best fit through the points. Then find several values for the half-life from the graph by finding the time for the activity in counts per minute to fall from 80 to 40, 60 to 30, 40 to 20 and so on. You should calculate the average of the values you have found. The time for the activity to halve may not be exactly the same each time. Any differences will be due to the random nature of radioactive decay.

3 Calculate the half-life of the radioisotope shown in Figure 4.51.

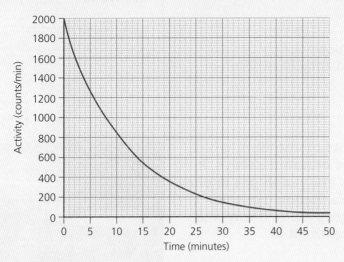

Figure 4.51

4 The table shows the activity of a radioactive sample over time.

   a Draw a graph of activity against time.

   b Draw a best-fit curve through the points.

   c Calculate the half-life by looking at time for the activity to halve at three different points on your curve. Calculate the average.

5 The activity of a radioactive sample took 4 hours to decrease from 100 Bq to 25 Bq. Calculate its half-life.

Time in minutes	Activity in Bq
0	100
0.5	76
1.0	51
1.5	40
2.0	26
2.5	18
3.0	12
3.5	10
4.0	8

Choosing the best radioisotope for a task

For some applications such as a smoke alarm, a radioisotope with a long half-life is most suitable so that the rate of decay does not decrease significantly. Some radioisotopes are used as tracers, using the radiation they emit to trace the path of a substance the radioisope is attached to.

Radioisotopes can be used as environmental tracers (such as detecting a leak in a pipe) or medical tracers. For these applications, a short half-life is best. This means that the activity will decrease to a level similar to the background count fairly quickly because the time taken for half the radioactive nuclei to decay is very short.

DID YOU KNOW?

The half-lives of different radioactive isotopes vary from a fraction of a second to millions of years.

Background radiation

Learning objectives:

- recall sources of background radiation
- describe how different types of radiation have different ionising power.

KEY WORDS

background radiation

Granite rocks contain small amounts of uranium, which is radioactive. When this isotope of uranium decays, it goes through a sequence of decays and radon gas is one of the radioisotopes in the sequence. Radon can seep into houses (Figure 4.52). It undergoes alpha decay and is a health risk because you can breathe it in.

Figure 4.52 Granite houses in Cornwall

Background radiation

Background radiation is ionising radiation that is around us all the time.

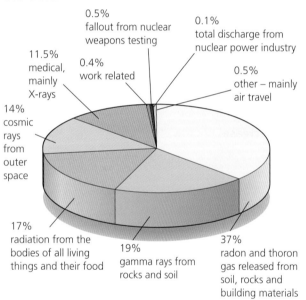

0.5% fallout from nuclear weapons testing

0.1% total discharge from nuclear power industry

11.5% medical, mainly X-rays

0.4% work related

0.5% other – mainly air travel

14% cosmic rays from outer space

17% radiation from the bodies of all living things and their food

19% gamma rays from rocks and soil

37% radon and thoron gas released from soil, rocks and building materials

Figure 4.53 The sources of background radiation

Figure 4.53 shows that background radiation comes from:

- natural sources such as rocks, especially granite, and cosmic rays from space
- human sources such as medical applications and a small amount from the fallout from nuclear weapons testing and nuclear accidents.

The level of background radiation varies from place to place and from day to day. The radiation dose received may be affected by your occupation and where you live but it is low level and does not cause harm.

DID YOU KNOW?

Most background radiation comes from natural sources such as rocks and soil. You are naturally radioactive – you emit low levels of radioactivity from the radioisotopes in your body.

Background radiation from human activity includes:

- waste products from hospitals
- waste products from nuclear power stations and other industries
- manufactured radioisotopes.

Radiation dose is measured in sieverts (Sv).

1. Use the pie chart in Figure 4.53 to list the sources of background radiation in order, starting with the highest.

2. What percentage of background radiation comes from natural sources?

3. Suggest why background radiation varies
   a in different areas and **b** at different times.

Penetration of different types of radiation

The three types of nuclear radiation have different penetrating powers and abilities to ionise particles they hit. Figure 4.54 shows the penetrating power of the three types of ionising radiation. Gamma rays are the most penetrating, able to penetrate through several metres of concrete or several centimetres of lead, but they are the least ionising. Beta particles can travel a few metres in air and can be stopped by aluminium about 3 mm thick. Alpha particles are the least penetrating, and can be stopped by a few centimetres of air or a few sheets of paper, but are the most ionising.

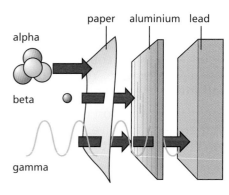

Figure 4.54 The three forms of nuclear radiation have very different penetrating powers

It is considered safe to use alpha emitters in smoke detectors because they are easily stopped by the air. Therefore, alpha sources are the safest to use outside the body.

However, inside the body, the situation is reversed. Alpha particles have the largest mass and the highest charge, so they have the highest ionising power. They can be thought of as the radioactive equivalent to cannon balls with their huge charge and mass. If you breathe in or swallow an alpha emitter, all of the alpha particles are absorbed by your body. Beta particles do less damage and gamma rays the least because they are the least ionising.

4. Describe the penetrating and ionising powers of beta particles.

5. Which type of radiation can penetrate a few centimetres of aluminium?

6. Explain why radon gas is considered to be a significant hazard.

7. Suggest how the amount of radiation to which pilots and cabin crew in aeroplanes are exposed differs from the average person. Justify your answer.

> **REMEMBER!**
>
> Alpha particles causes most ionisation.

MATHS SKILLS

Using ratios and proportional reasoning

KEY WORDS

scale
value
curve of best fit

Learning objectives:

- draw a curve of best fit to calculate radioactive half-life
- calculate the net decline.

When you draw a graph of activity for a radioisotope against time, the points do not fit a smooth curve – you have to draw a curve of best fit.

Working out the half-life of a radioisotope usually involves drawing a graph and using the graph to calculate the half-life.

Figure 4.55 shows counts per minute against time for a certain radioactive isotope. You can use the graph to work out the half-life of the isotope.

Look for numbers on the vertical scale that are easy to halve. For example, you can halve 40 easily to get 20 .

From the 40 on the vertical axis, draw a line across to the graph. Then draw a line down to the time axis. So the count at 2 days is 40 counts/minute.

Now repeat this for 20 counts/minute. The time is 4 days.

It takes 4 – 2 = 2 days for the activity to reduce by half from 40 to 20 counts/ minute.

So the half-life is 2 days.

You should always repeat for a second step, just to check. Choose another value that can be halved easily, e.g. 20. Repeating the process gives the same answer, 2 days.

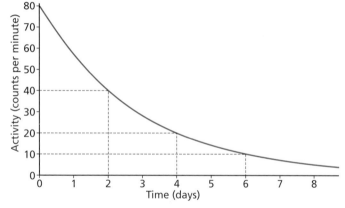

Figure 4.55

Drawing a curve of best fit

When plotting experimental values, you need to draw a curve of best fit (Figure 4.56).

The curve should have approximately equal numbers of points above it and below it – it does not go through all the points. The curve should also be smooth, as shown in Figure 4.56.

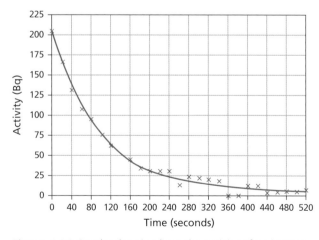

Figure 4.56 Graphs showing how the activity of an isotope changes over time

1 Calculate the half-life for the source shown in Figure 4.56.

  Work out three values for the half-life.

  Calculate the average of the values.

2 **a** From the data in the table, plot a graph of activity against time.

Time/minutes	0	10	20	30	40	50	60	70	80	90
Activity/Bq	96	78	62	54	40	32	26	21	15	14

  b Calculate the half-life.

Half-life calculations

A radioactive isotope has a count rate of 160 Bq and has a half-life of 2 hours. What is the count rate after 6 hours?

Every 2 hours the count will halve (i.e. one half-life). 6 hours means three half-lives. 2 + 2 + 2 = 6.

Starting with 160 Bq at time 0,

after 1 half-life, activity = 80 Bq;

after 2 half-lives, activity = 40 Bq;

after 3 half-lives, activity = 20 Bq.

The count rate after 6 hours will be 20 counts/second.

This can also be expressed as a ratio: $\dfrac{20}{160} = \dfrac{1}{8}$

After 6 hours the count rate will have reduced to $\frac{1}{8}$ of the original.

This is called the net decline.

3 Sodium-24 has a half-life of 15 hours. A sample of sodium-24 has an activity of 640 Bq.

  a Calculate the activity after 60 hours.

  b Calculate the net decline.

4 Iodine-131 has a half-life of 8 days. A sample of iodine-131 has an activity of 1800 counts per second.

  a Calculate the count rate after 32 days.

  b Calculate the net decline in the activity of the sample.

5 The activity of a sample decreases to 1/16th of its original value over 24 hours.

  Calculate the half-life of the sample.

6 A sample of pure Polonium-210 decays into lead-206 with a half-life of 138 days. Calculate how long it would take for the sample to contain three times as much lead as polonium.

Hazards and uses of radiation

Learning objectives:

- describe radioactive contamination
- give examples of how radioactive tracers can be used.

KEY WORDS

hazard
radioactive contamination
tracer

Many of the servicemen who watched the first nuclear explosion in the Arizona desert then went on to develop cancers. Their bodies were contaminated by radioactivity.

Radioactive contamination

Radioactive contamination is the unwanted presence of materials containing radioactive atoms. They can be on surfaces or within solids, liquids and gases, including in the human body and on the skin.

Radioactive materials in the environment, whether natural or artificial, can expose people to risks. Radioactive materials are marked with a **hazard** symbol (Figure 4.57).

Contamination occurs when people swallow or breathe in radioactive materials. Radioactive materials can also enter the body through an open wound or be absorbed through the skin. Some radioisotopes may be absorbed by specific organs, where it is possible they could cause cancer or mutations of genes.

1 What is radioactive contamination?

2 Why is contamination a hazard?

The type and amount of radiation emitted affect the level of hazard.

The most unstable nuclei have the shortest half-lives. However, they can give out a lot of radiation in a very short time. Unstable nuclei with long half-lives may give out much smaller amounts of radiation, but this will build up over a long period of time.

DID YOU KNOW?

If nuclear radiation enters the body it can cause serious problems if it is absorbed. The severity of the problems depends on the properties of the contamination and the half-life of the decaying substances. This is why it is important to minimise the amount of nuclear radiation getting into the body.

Radiation

Figure 4.57 Radioactive sources are marked with this hazard symbol.

How the type of radiation affects the level of contamination

The level of contamination is affected by two things: the penetrating power of the radiation and its ionising power. These are very different and have contrasting effects.

3 State the least hazardous form of radiation when the contamination is inside the body.

4 Explain why contamination by an alpha particle emitter is much more dangerous if it gets inside the body.

REMEMBER!

Alpha particles have the most ionising power but the least penetrating power. Gamma rays are the most penetrating but have the weakest ionising power.

Using medical tracers

A medical **tracer** is a radioisotope that is put into the body, either by injecting it or eating it. The tracer can be used to:

- monitor the functioning of internal organs
- check for a blockage in a patient's blood vessel (Figure 4.58).

When using radioisotope tracers, a background count should be taken several times first, in the absence of the radioisotope, and an average background count should be calculated. This value is then subtracted from readings obtained with the radioisotope.

4 **a** Why is it important to take a background count?

b Why should you take several readings of the background count?

The tracer needs to produce nuclear radiation that can pass from inside the body to the outside so it can be detected. It also needs to be weakly ionising so that it does not do too much damage to the body.

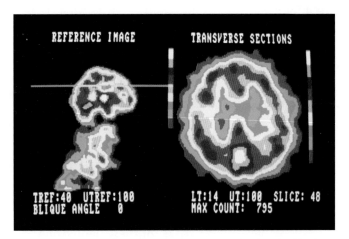

Figure 4.58 Image from a gamma tracer in a brain. The black area shows where the brain tissue has died because a blood vessel is blocked.

Tracers move around the body in the patient's blood. As the tracer emits radiation, we can monitor where the blood flows to. Therefore blockages in the blood flow can be detected.

Once the patient has been monitored, the tracer is no longer needed. If the tracer remained in the body it would continue to damage the cells without being of any use. Therefore it is important that we use tracers with a short half-life.

5 Suggest how a tracer could be used to check for a blockage in a patient's blood vessel.

DID YOU KNOW?

People who have been diagnosed using medical tracers remain radioactive for several days. They have to avoid too much contact with young children and pregnant women. Nuclear radiation is particularly dangerous to bodies that are growing rapidly, such as an unborn baby.

Irradiation

Learning objectives:

- explain what is meant by irradiation
- understand the distinction between contamination and irradiation
- appreciate the importance of communication between scientists.

Some foods are irradiated, which kills microorganisms living on them. The foods can then be kept much longer before they go off.

Irradiation

Irradiation is where an object is exposed to nuclear radiation. The exposure can originate from various sources, including natural sources and background radiation. Figure 4.59 summarises some of the ways we are irradiated each day.

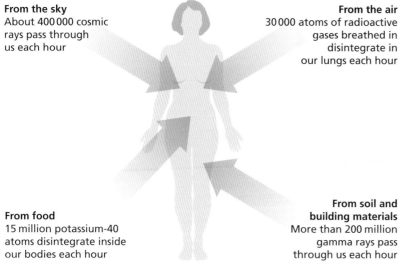

From the sky
About 400 000 cosmic rays pass through us each hour

From the air
30 000 atoms of radioactive gases breathed in disintegrate in our lungs each hour

From food
15 million potassium-40 atoms disintegrate inside our bodies each hour

From soil and building materials
More than 200 million gamma rays pass through us each hour

Figure 4.59 Each day our bodies are irradiated from different sources.

DID YOU KNOW?

Low levels of irradiation have little effect on the health of humans. However, if people are exposed to high levels of irradiation it is important to consider the radiation risks for these people and their descendants.

Some things are irradiated with X-rays or gamma rays for therapeutic purposes or to sterilise food. Gamma rays are sometimes used in hospitals to sterilise food for seriously ill patients. Irradiation is also used by some supermarkets to kill bacteria on fresh food so that the food stays fresh for longer.

Nuclear radiation causes ionisation. The cells in our bodies can also be changed by radiation. DNA can be changed by nuclear radiation. This is called **mutation**. Sometimes when a cell mutates it divides in an uncontrollable way. This can lead to cancer.

1. Describe what is meant by irradiation.

2. Compare the level of irradiation we receive from food with the irradiation from the air.

Effects of irradiation

Damage to a person's cells is called damage *by* irradiation. Figure 4.60 shows the effects, which are cell death, accurate repair or misrepair causing mutation of genes.

Suitable precautions must be taken to protect against any hazard the radioactive source used in the process of irradiation may present.

3 **List the three possible effects of irradiation on human body cells in order of increasing harm.**

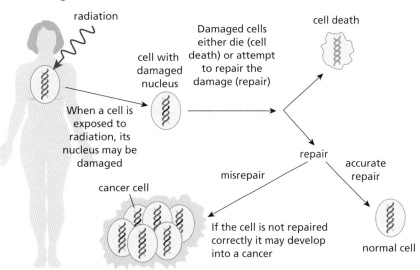

Figure 4.60 The three possible effects of irradiation on body cells

Natural and artificial sources of radiation include radioactive contamination and nuclear industry wastes. Risks for people who work with nuclear radiation and become irradiated and their descendants must be considered. The calculation of these risks is used to define the tolerance levels of both an irradiation and contamination of drinking water and food products.

4 **Why could irradiation have an effect on somebody's grandchildren?**

5 **Explain the difference between irradiation and contamination.**

> **KEY INFORMATION**
>
> **An irradiated object does not become radioactive.**

Publishing scientific results

The first scientists to investigate nuclear radiation were unaware of its effects on their health, and many died as a result. When the first atomic bombs were exploded, scientists were not aware of the potential effects on health. They discovered that nuclear radiation can have long-term effects, causing genetic mutations which affect subsequent generations.

It is important for the findings of studies into the effects of radiation on humans to be published. This means that scientists can find out about what other scientists are doing. They can try to repeat experimental results and check the results, which is called **peer review**.

6 **Explain why experimental findings should be checked by peer review.**

7 **Some pigeons were found to be contaminated with caesium-137, a radioisotope of caesium with a half-life of about 30 years. They were almost certainly irradiated too. Suggest why the pigeons were at greater risk from contamination than from irradiation.**

Check your progress

You should be able to:

Describe the amplitude, wavelength, frequency and period of a wave →	Use the wave equation $v = \lambda \times f$ to calculate wave speed →	Rearrange and apply the wave equation
Realise that waves can be transverse or longitudinal →	Give examples of longitudinal and transverse waves →	Compare transverse and longitudinal waves
Describe how sound waves travel through air or solids →	Describe how to measure the speed of sound waves in air →	Use the wave equation to explain why the speed of sound is different in different media
Understand that waves transfer energy or information →	Give examples of energy transfer by waves (including electromagnetic waves) →	Describe evidence that, for e.g. water ripples, it is the wave and not the water itself that travels
Understand that waves can be absorbed, transmitted or reflected at a surface →	Describe examples of reflection, transmission and absorption of waves (including electromagnetic waves) at material interfaces →	Describe how different substances may absorb, transmit, refract or reflect electromagnetic waves in ways that vary with wavelength
Name the main groupings of the electromagnetic spectrum →	Compare the electromagnetic waves in terms of wavelength and frequency →	Describe how radio waves are produced
Describe the hazardous effects of gamma rays, X-rays and ultraviolet radiation →	Explain the risks associated with the use of ionising and ultraviolet radiation →	Evaluate the risks and consequences of exposure to radiation
Give examples of the uses of the main groupings of the electromagnetic spectrum →	Describe examples of energy transfer by electromagnetic waves →	Explain why each type of electromagnetic wave is suitable for the application
State that the number of protons in an element is the atomic number and the total number of protons and neutrons is the mass number →	Understand that isotopes of an element have the same number of protons but different numbers of neutrons →	Use nuclear notation to show subatomic particles in an isotope
Recognise that some isotopes called radioisotopes are unstable and decay →	List some uses of radioisotopes in medicine →	Describe how specific radioisotopes are used medicine
Recognise that radioisotopes have a half-life →	Explain the meaning of half-life of a radioisotope →	Calculate the half-life of a radioisotope
List the three types of ionising radiation →	Describe the structure of each type of ionising radiation →	Explain the properties of each type of radiation
Explain the meaning of background radiation →	List different sources of background radiation →	Explain why background radiation varies in different areas and in different times
Recognise the symbols used in a nuclear equation →	Write nuclear equations involving alpha and beta decay →	Write balanced nuclear equations for different types of nuclear reaction
Define radioactive →	List the hazards of radioactive contamination →	Compare and contrast irradiation and contamination

Worked example

The table below shows the electromagnetic spectrum.

A	microwave	infrared	visible light	B	X-rays	gamma rays

1 **State the names of the waves labelled A and B.**

> A = radio waves   B = ultraviolet waves

Both answers are correct. Use a mnemonic to remember the correct order.

2 **X-rays are dangerous to humans. Explain how they can also be used in medical therapy without lasting harm.**

> We can use them for X-rays to see our bones and for treating cancer by killing the cancer cells.

This answer is a good start but is incomplete. It doesn't give a full explanation. The answer should also say that we can use them by controlling the exposure dose.

3 **Compare X-rays and microwaves, and explain why microwaves are safe to use for communication whereas X-rays are not.**

> X-rays have much shorter wavelengths than microwaves. X-rays are ionising radiation, which means they can damage human cells. Microwaves are not ionising and so are safe to use for communications.

This is a good answer, but could be improved by including a reference to X-rays being higher energy than microwaves.

4 **Complete the wave front diagram to show the refraction of light from air to water.**

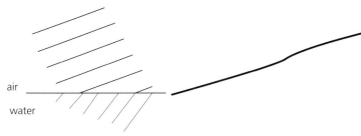

The wave fronts being closer together is correct, but there is one crucial thing wrong. When waves go from a less dense medium to a denser medium, they are refracted **towards** the normal. The diagram shows them being refracted **away** from the normal.

5 **Draw a ray diagram to show how a magnifying glass produces an enlarged virtual image of an object.**

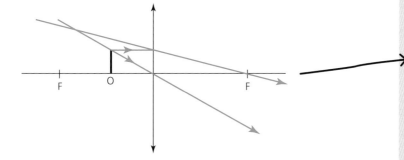

The rays are correct but there should be a line vertically upwards from the principal axis to where the rays cross, annotated to show it is the virtual image and a label to show that the observer is on the right.

End of chapter questions

Getting started

1 Which of the following is a longitudinal wave? `1 Mark`
   a Sound wave   **b** Water wave   **c** Light wave   **d** Radio wave

2 Which is a correct unit of frequency? `1 Mark`
   a metres   **b** watts   **c** hertz   **d** metres per second

3 Explain what is meant by the **amplitude** of a wave. `2 Marks`

4 A water wave in a ripple tank has a frequency of 4 Hz. Calculate the time period (T) of the wave using the equation $T = 1/f$. `1 Mark`

5 A microwave has a wavelength of 1 cm. What type of wave, other than a microwave, might have a wavelength of 1 m? `1 Mark`

6 Describe the structure of an atom using a diagram. `1 Mark`

7 Define the half-life of a radioactive element. `1 Mark`

8 Give two sources of background radiation. `2 Marks`

Going further

9 Name the parts of the electromagnetic spectrum labelled A and B in the diagram. `1 Mark`

| radio waves | microwave | A | visible light | ultraviolet | B | gamma rays |

10 Name the two types of electromagnetic radiation that are used to cook food. `1 Mark`

11 Describe two practical applications for

   a microwaves

   b gamma rays. `2 Marks`

12 What is the speed of a water wave if it has a wavelength of 8 cm and a frequency of 2 Hz? `2 Marks`

13 Define the atomic number of an element. `1 Mark`

14 Name the instrument is used to measure activity of a radioactive source. `1 Mark`

15 Sodium can be represented by the notation $^{23}_{11}$Na.

   a What are the numbers 23 and 11 and what do they stand for? `1 Mark`

   b Describe what an isotope is. `1 Mark`

More challenging

16 What is background radiation? `2 Mark`

17 Describe the difference between irradiation and contamination. `2 Mark`

18 $^{219}_{86}Rn$ decays to $^{x}_{y}Po$ by emitting an alpha particle.

Write a balanced nuclear equation for the decay.

2 Marks

19 The activity of a radioactive sample took 60 minutes to decrease from 400 Bq to 50 Bq. Work out its half-life.

2 Marks

20 Explain why a ray of light travelling from air to water is refracted towards the normal and, if it then passes from the water into glass, is refracted even further towards the normal.

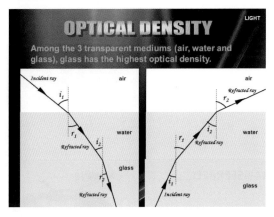

Most demanding

21 The graph below shows an idealised graph of activity against time for a radioisotope.

a Describe how you would expect a graph to differ from this if you measured the activity of the same radioisotope over time.

2 Marks

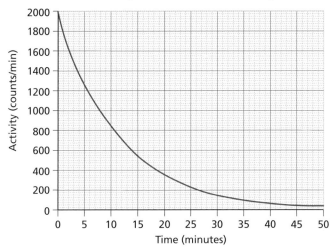

b Calculate the half-life for this sample.

2 Marks

22 Describe the characteristics of the alpha and beta particles and gamma rays.

2 Marks

23 Explain how the evidence from Geiger and Marsden's scattering experiment led to the development of the nuclear model of the atom.

4 Marks

Total: 39 Marks

ENERGY

ENERGY

- A mass raised above the ground stores gravitational potential energy.
- A moving object has kinetic energy.
- A stretched spring transfers energy in stretching.

WE CAN MEASURE HOW MUCH ENERGY IS TRANSFERRED AND HOW QUICKLY

- Energy can be stored and also transferred from one store to another. Energy changes are measured in joules (J) or kilojoules (kJ).
- The energy values of different foods can be compared.
- The power ratings of appliances are measured in watts (W) or kilowatts (kW).

TEMPERATURE AND ENERGY

- Temperature tells us how hot something is.
- When there is a difference in temperature between two objects, energy is transferred from the hotter object to the colder one.
- Energy transfer tends to reduce the temperature difference.

TRANSFER OF THERMAL ENERGY

- Thermal energy is transferred by conduction, convection and radiation.
- In conduction and convection energy is transferred by the movement of particles.
- Radiation is the only way energy can be transferred in a vacuum.

IN THIS CHAPTER YOU WILL FIND OUT ABOUT:

HOW CAN WE CALCULATE THE AMOUNT OF ENERGY STORED OR TRANSFERRED?

- Gravitational potential energy = mass × acceleration due to gravity × height.
- Kinetic energy = 0.5 × mass × (velocity)^2.
- Energy transferred in stretching = 0.5 × spring constant × (extension)^2.

WHAT IS THE CONNECTION BETWEEN ENERGY TRANSFER AND POWER?

- Energy is transferred by heating, by electric current in a circuit, and when work is done by a force.
- We can measure the rate at which energy is being transferred or the rate at which work is done – this is called power.

WHAT IS THE CONNECTION BETWEEN ENERGY CHANGES AND TEMPERATURE CHANGE?

- We can calculate the energy stored in or released from a system when its temperature changes.
- The rate of cooling of a building is affected by the thickness and the thermal conductivity of its walls. Insulation can be used to reduce the transfer of energy by conduction and convection.

WHAT IS THE ENVIRONMENTAL IMPACT OF DIFFERENT ENERGY RESOURCES?

- Fuels such as coal, oil, gas and nuclear fuel are not renewable. Supplies will run out.
- The use of fossil fuels is changing as more renewable energy resources are used for transport, electricity generation and heating.
- Most renewable resources do not generate a predictable (reliable) amount of electrical power.
- There are different environmental issues for each different energy resource.

Investigating kinetic energy

Learning objectives:

- describe how the energy stored by an object changes as its speed changes
- calculate kinetic energy
- consider how energy is transferred.

Formula 1 racing cars reach speeds of 300 km/h or more. This means the energy stored is very large. If the car is involved in a collision this energy store may be reduced to zero very rapidly, causing lots of damage.

Kinetic energy

Energy must be transferred to make things move. A car uses energy from petrol or diesel to move (Figure 5.1). The greater its mass and the faster it goes, the more energy is transferred to the car and the higher the rate at which fuel is used.

1. **Why does an adult have more kinetic energy than a child when running at the same speed?**

2. **What is the 'fuel' for a child running around a playground?**

Figure 5.1 The engine applies a force that transfers energy from a store in the fuel to kinetic energy

Calculating kinetic energy

The energy stored by a moving object can be increased by:

- increasing the mass of the object, m in kg
- increasing its speed, v in m/s.

We can calculate the **kinetic energy** (E_k) of an object by using
kinetic energy = 0.5 × mass × (velocity)^2

$$E_k = \frac{1}{2}mv^2$$

DID YOU KNOW?

Hollywood star Idris Elba smashed an 88-year-old record by driving at an average speed of 180.361 mph over a measured mile across the Pendine Sands in Wales in May 2015. The award-winning star beat the 1927 record set by Sir Malcolm Campbell.

> Example: A car of mass 1600 kg is travelling at a steady speed of 10 m/s.
>
> **a** Calculate the car's kinetic energy.
>
> **b** The car's speed increases to 20 m/s. Calculate how much the energy stored increases.
>
> **a** E_k at 10 m/s $= \frac{1}{2}mv^2 = \frac{1}{2} \times 1600$ kg $\times 10^2$
> $= \frac{1}{2} \times 1600$ kg $\times 100 = 80\ 000$ J.
>
> **b** E_k at 20 m/s $= \frac{1}{2}mv^2 = \frac{1}{2} \times 1600 \times 20^2$
> $= \frac{1}{2} \times 1600 \times 400 = 320\ 000$ J.
>
> The increase in the car's $E_k = 320\ 000 - 80\ 000 = 240\ 000$ J.

Doubling the speed has increased the car's E_k by a factor of 4. Note that speed is squared in the equation for E_k.

3 a Meena is riding her bicycle at 2 m/s. She has a mass of 50 kg. Calculate her kinetic energy.

b Meena doubles her speed. What happens to her kinetic energy?

We can convert from km/h to m/s by

- multiplying by 1000 (there are 1000 m in a km)
- dividing by 3600 (there are 3600 seconds in an hour).

For example, $300 \text{ km/h} = \dfrac{(300 \times 1000 \text{ m})}{3600 \text{ s}} = 83.3 \text{ m/s}$

> **REMEMBER!**
>
> Take care when calculating kinetic energy using $\frac{1}{2}mv^2$. Only the speed is squared. Start by squaring the speed.

4 A car of mass 1200 kg increases its speed from 10 m/s to 30 m/s. By how much has its E_k increased?

5 Change a speed of 240 km/h to m/s.

Dropping a ball

If a ball is held 2 m above the ground it has **gravitational potential energy**, relative to a ball on the ground. Allowing it to fall transfers energy from a gravitational potential energy store to a kinetic energy store as it drops. As the ball bounces back up (Figure 5.2), the kinetic energy decreases as energy is transferred back to the gravitational potential **energy store**. The ball does not return to its original height though, because some of the energy is transferred to the surroundings by heating.

> **KEY INFORMATION**
>
> Energy is transferred from one energy store to another. Before the ball is dropped it has a store of gravitational potential energy. As the ball falls, energy is transferred to a store of kinetic energy.

> **REMEMBER!**
>
> Energy can also be stored in a stretched spring.
>
> energy stored $= \frac{1}{2}ke^2$
>
> where k is the spring constant and e is the extension.

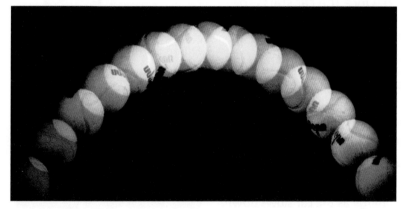

Figure 5.2 Time-lapse photo showing the path of a ball that is dropped and bounces off a surface

6 At what point does the ball in the photo

a have most gravitational potential energy?

b have most kinetic energy?

7 Describe the changes to energy stores when a ball is thrown upwards.

8 A ball with a mass of 2 kg is dropped from a height of 20 m. Assuming all of the GPE transfers to E_k, calculate the speed of the ball as it hits the ground (g = 10 N/kg).

Work done and energy transfer

Learning objectives:

- recall what is meant by work done
- use the relationship between work done and force applied
- identify the transfers between energy stores.

The total energy in a system is always conserved. If the amounts of energy you calculate before and after an energy transfer appear to be different, this means you have overlooked a store of energy. Often, that 'missing' store will be heat.

Work done by a force

You saw in Chapter 2 that work is only done by a **force** when an object **moves**.

More work is done when

- the force is bigger
- the object moves further – its displacement is bigger.

Remember the example of Sam's car breaking down. Sam and his friends pushed the car together to make it move. They were all doing work.

Consider the energy transfers involved. Once the car starts to move, it has kinetic energy. The amount of energy depends on how hard the friends push (the size of the force) and for how far (the distance moved).

> **REMEMBER!**
>
> Work is only done when a force causes a displacement of the object (that is, movement along the line of action of the force).

Figure 5.3 These men are doing work

1. Suggest what store of energy is used by the friends to cause work to be done as they push the car.

When the friends let go of the car and stop pushing, the car continues to move but slows down and stops.

2. Explain why the car slows down when the friends let go. Think about the forces involved.

3. Explain what happens to the kinetic energy as the car slows down.

4. Explain the energy transfers that take place. How is energy conserved?

> **REMEMBER!**
>
> One joule of work is done when a force of one newton causes a displacement of one metre.

Calculating work done

Remember that the equation that links work, force and distance is:

work done = force × distance moved along the line of action of the force

where work, W, is in joules, force, F, is in newtons and distance, s, is in metres.

$$W = F \times s$$

Figure 5.4 The crane does work as it lifts the container upwards

When a dockside crane lifts a loaded container into the air the force moved is the weight of the container.

Example: A dockside crane in a container port lifts a loaded container a distance of 30 m. The loaded weight of the container is 300 000 N. Calculate the work done by the crane.

Work done = force × distance moved along the line of action of the force.

Work done = 300 000 N × 30 m = 9000 000 J.

5 The container used in the example is unloaded. The empty container weighs 40 000 N. How much work does the crane do if the empty container is lifted a height of 30 m?

6 Calculate the gravitational potential energy of the container at a height of 30 m when it is

a loaded and **b** empty.

7 Describe the energy transfers that take place when the loaded container is lifted from the ground to a height of 30 m.

8 If the container was dropped from a height of 30 m, what can you say about the kinetic energy at the instant just before the crane hits the ground?

Using energy to find out other quantities

Now that we know a number of different equations for calculating energy, we can use those equations and the conservation of energy to calculate quantities such as the size of a force or the speed of a moving object.

Example: A Formula 1 car of mass 750 kg is travelling at 80 m/s. The driver applies the brakes to bring the car to a complete stop. The car travels 100 m with the brakes applied. Calculate the braking force.

E_k of car $= \frac{1}{2}mv^2$

$\qquad = \frac{1}{2} \times 750 \text{ kg} \times (80 \text{ m/s})^2 = 2400\ 000 \text{ J}.$

Work has to be done to reduce the kinetic energy of the car and bring it to a stop. The force that does the work is the friction force between the brakes and the wheel. The work done by the braking force is 2400 000 J.

$W = F \times s$, where F is the braking force and s is the distance moved during braking. We can rearrange this to make F the subject of the equation.

$F = \dfrac{W}{s}$

$\quad = \dfrac{2400\ 000 \text{ J}}{100 \text{ m}} = 24\ 000 \text{ N}.$

Remember that energy must be conserved for all energy transfers.

DID YOU KNOW?

The amount of energy dissipated as a Formula 1 car brakes is enough to melt or burn ordinary braking materials. The brakes have to be made from a very pure form of carbon. The brakes can be seen to glow as they reach temperatures of around 1200°C.

Figure 5.5 A Formula 1 car breaking at high speed.

9 Explain what happens to the kinetic energy of the Formula 1 car as it brakes.

10 What can you say about the temperature of the breaks as the car comes to a halt?

11 Modern Formula 1 cars use systems that can transfer some of the kinetic energy into stored energy in a battery that the car can use when it accelerates again. Describe the energy transfers involved as the car travels quickly, slows down (using its brakes and its energy storage system) and then accelerates again.

Specific heat capacity

Learning objectives:

- understand how things heat up
- find out about heating water
- find out about specific heat capacity.

If you eat a jam sponge pudding soon after taking it out of the oven the jam seems to be hotter than the sponge, even though they have been cooked at the same temperature. This is because at the same temperature the jam stores more energy than the pudding around it.

Hot and cold

It takes more energy to get some things hot than others. Different materials need different amounts of energy to raise the temperature by a given amount. Imagine a 1 kg block of copper and a 1 kg block of steel. From experiments we can show that:

- it takes 380 J of energy to raise the temperature of 1 kg of copper by 1 °C
- it takes 450 J of energy to raise the temperature of 1 kg of steel by 1 °C.

The amount of energy needed to change the temperature of an object depends on:

- its mass
- what it is made of
- the temperature change.

1 The same mass of two different substances is heated. The amount of thermal energy transferred is the same in each case. Why does one material have a bigger increase in temperature?

Hot water

It takes a lot of energy to raise the temperature of 1 kg of water by a certain amount; more than for most other substances.

Specific heat capacity (c) is a measure of how much energy is required to raise the temperature of 1 kg of a substance by 1 °C.

You can calculate the amount of energy stored in a system when it is heated using the equation:

change in energy stored = mass × specific heat capacity × change in temperature

$\Delta E = mc\Delta\theta$

where ΔE is in J, m is in kg, c is in J/kg°C and $\Delta\theta$ is in °C.

Example: Calculate the change in energy stored when 2 kg of water is heated from 20 °C to 80 °C.

Substance	c in J/kg °C
Water	4200
Copper	380
Steel	450
Concrete	800

$\Delta E = mc\Delta\theta$

$= 2 \text{ kg} \times 4200 \text{ J/kg°C} \times (80 \text{ °C} - 20 \text{ °C})$

$= 504\ 000 \text{ J}$

$= 504 \text{ kJ}$

2 How much energy is needed to heat 1 kg of copper by 20 °C?

3 How much energy is given out when the temperature of 2 kg of steel falls by 30 °C?

Water has a very high specific heat capacity. This means it can absorb a large amount of thermal energy from a hot object for a given temperature change of the water. Water is used to cool many car engines. The energy stored in the engine decreases and the energy stored in the water increases. Energy is then transferred from the energy store in the water to the store in the air surrounding the radiator.

Water can also release a lot of energy without a large temperature decrease. This makes it a very useful way of transferring large amounts of thermal energy around a house in a central heating system.

Figure 5.6 Water is used to cool many car engines

4 Explain why a hot-water bottle is so effective at warming a bed.

5 What is meant by specific heat capacity?

6 How much energy is needed to raise the temperature of 3 kg of steel by 15 °C?

More about specific heat capacity

Example: 0.5 kg of copper at 90 °C is added to 2 kg of water at 10 °C. Calculate the final temperature of the copper and water (T).

Assume that the decrease in energy stored by the copper = increase in energy stored by the water.

Change in energy stored by copper

$= 0.5 \text{ kg} \times 380 \text{ J/kg°C} \times (90 \text{ °C} - T)$

Change in energy stored by water

$= 2 \text{ kg} \times 4200 \text{ J/kg°C} \times (T - 10 \text{ °C})$

$190 \times (90 - T) = 8400 \times (T - 10)$

$(8400 + 190)T = 17\ 100 + 84\ 000$

$T = 101\ 100/8590$

$T = 11.8 \text{ °C}$

7 A night storage heater contains 50 kg of concrete. The concrete is heated during the night when electricity is cheaper, gradually emitting stored energy during the day. How much thermal energy is required to warm the concrete from 10 °C to 30 °C? Suggest why concrete is chosen.

8 A 1 kg steel block at 80 °C is added to 0.5 kg of water at 10 °C. Calculate the final temperature of the block and the water.

Energy and power

Learning objectives:

- recall that energy cannot be created or destroyed, only transferred
- describe the energy transfers in different domestic appliances
- describe power as a rate of energy transfer
- calculate the energy transferred.

KEY WORDS

power
kilowatt-hour

Remember that energy cannot be created or destroyed, only transferred. This means we have to take into account where the energy ends up in designed vehicles or electrical appliances.

Energy transfers in electrical devices

You saw in Chapter 3 that energy is transferred whenever we use an electrical device. Different appliances transfer energy in different ways. For examples, they may transfer energy from the a.c. mains supply or from stores such as batteries. Some of this energy is transferred in ways that we find useful, for example an electric kettle used to boil water transfers energy to the water. However, some energy is also transferred in ways that are less useful. The kettle also makes noise and transfers some heat to the surroundings.

Figure 5.7 An electric kettle

1 **List all the possible energy transfers you can think of when an electric kettle is used to boil water.**

2 **A kettle is used to water that came at 10°C from a kitchen tap. Name the quantities that we need to know or measure in order to determine how much energy is used to heat the water up to its boiling point.**

3 **When all the water has reached its boiling point, if the kettle continues to heat the water where is the energy transferred?**

Power and energy transferred

Remember that we can determine the energy transferred in an electrical device. This can be thought of as the work done by the power supply on the device when the current flows.

Energy transferred = power × time

(in joules, J)   (in watts, W) (in seconds, s)

$$E = Pt$$

Remember too that if we know the potential difference across

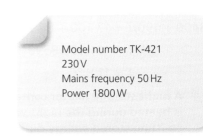

Model number TK-421
230 V
Mains frequency 50 Hz
Power 1800 W

Figure 5.8 The electrical information label on a kettle

an electrical component or device and can measure the current flowing, we can determine the power:

$$\text{Power} = \text{potential difference} \times \text{current}$$

(in watts, W)   (in volts, V)   (in amps, A)

Example:

A washing machine that has a power rating of 500 W and operates at a potential difference of 230 V is used for 60 minutes. Calculate **a** the current needed to operate the washine machine and **b** the total energy transferred by the washing machine.

a   Rearrange $P = VI$ so that I is the subject:

   $I = P/V = 500 \text{ W} / 230 \text{ V} = 2.2 \text{ A}$

b $E = Pt$

   $= 500 \text{ W} \times (60 \times 60) \text{ s}$

   $= 1800\,000 \text{ J (or 1.8 MJ)}$

All modern electrical devices should have a label like that in Figure 5.8, which show the mains supply voltage, the frequency of the alternating current and the power it uses.

KEY INFORMATION

The numbers shown in a label on an electrical device are found using a series of tests made by the manufacturer. A device called a joulemeter is used to measure the energy the device uses over set periods of time. These measurements are used to calculate the power.

④   **Figure 5.8 is the label for an electric kettle. Use the equation for power to calculate the current the kettle uses.**

⑤   **If it takes this kettle 90 seconds to boil a particular amount of water, how many joules of energy will it take from the mains supply?**

⑥   **Why is the amount of energy transferred to the water in the kettle not the same as the amount as you calculated in question 5?**

DID YOU KNOW?

Homes and offices use electricity at 230 V, but hospitals and schools receive it at 11 000 V. Large factories receive it at 33 000 V.

The kilowatt-hour

We can see that even for fairly low-power devices such as a washing machine or a kettle, the amount of energy they use in joules can add up to be very large numbers. To make it easier to measure the total energy used in a home or factory, and to determine how much the energy used costs, we use a unit called the kilowatt-hour.

1 kilowatt-hour (kWh) = a power of 1000 watts used for 1 hour

Example: The washing machine used in the earlier example used 500 W for 60 minutes. Calculate the energy used in kilowatt-hours.

$$E = Pt$$

In kilowatt-hours:

$$E = 0.500 \times 1 = 0.5 \text{ kWh}$$

⑦   **What is 1 kWh in joules?**

Dissipation of energy

Learning objectives:

- explain ways of reducing unwanted energy transfer
- describe what affects the rate of cooling of a building
- understand that energy is dissipated.

KEY WORDS

conduction
energy dissipation
radiation
thermal conductivity

Thermograms (Figure 5.9) are infrared photographs in which colour is used to represent temperature.

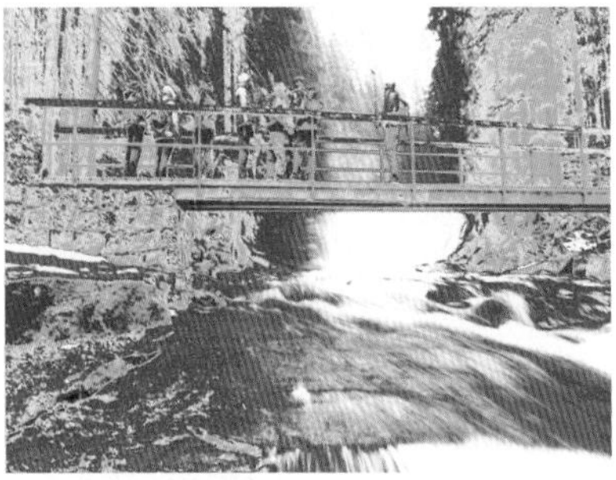

Figure 5.9 White represents the hottest area and blue the coolest

Reducing energy transfer

Sometimes the transfer of thermal energy is useful, such as in cooking, but on other occasions we might want to reduce it. For example, pushing a supermarket trolley with stiff wheels needs a lot of work to be done against frictional forces. This means the wheels transfer some energy to the surroundings as thermal energy. This energy is wasted and we would want to reduce this energy transfer.

Lubrication – oiling the moving parts of a machine reduces the friction force so less energy is wasted as thermal energy.

We might want to reduce thermal energy being transferred so that a parcel of fish and chips stays hot for longer or so that a block of ice cream stays frozen until we get it home.

Thermal insulation – surrounding a hot object with an insulating material reduces the rate at which energy is transferred away from it so the hot object cools more slowly (Figure 5.10). Clothing made of wool is a good insulator. Air is trapped between the wool fibres. Wool and air are bad **conductors** of thermal energy.

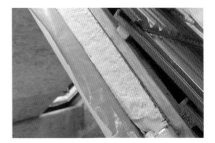

Figure 5.10 Why is this a good insulator?

1. **The wheels of a scooter do not move freely. Describe how unwanted energy transfers in the wheels can be reduced.**
2. **Explain why a wrapping of newspaper is as good at keeping fish and chips hot as it is at keeping a block of ice cream cold.**

Insulating a building

A building needs to be well insulated so that less energy is needed to keep the building warm. Loft and cavity wall insulation reduce the rate of energy transfer from inside a building to the colder outside.

Look at Figure 5.11. White, red and yellow represent the hottest areas. Black, dark blue and purple represent the coldest areas.

DID YOU KNOW?

The foam blocks used for cavity wall insulation in new houses have shiny foil on both sides. This further reduces energy transfer, as shiny objects reflect **radiation** rather than absorbing or emitting it.

The diagram of thermal energy losses from a house (Figure 5.12) shows that it is important to insulate the walls and roof.

Insulation reduces the amount of energy transfer by **conduction**. The lower the **thermal conductivity** of the insulating material and the thicker the layer, the more the rate of energy transfer by conduction is reduced.

For any building, the rate of energy transfer into (heating) or out of (cooling) the building is affected by the thickness and thermal conductivity of its walls.

Figure 5.11 The wheels of the car are red because they are hot

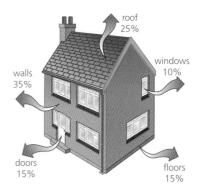

Figure 5.12 Thermal energy loss from a house

3 Looking at Figure 5.12, where is most thermal energy lost? Explain how you could reduce this unwanted energy transfer.

4 Explain, using examples, how an eco home that has no heating system can stay warm.

Energy dissipation

A system is an object or group of objects. The total energy in a closed system is always constant. Energy is never created or destroyed.

Work done against the frictional forces acting on a moving object cause energy to be transferred from the object. This energy transfer raises the temperature of the surroundings by such a small amount that it is of no use. This is wasted energy – energy is transferred to a store where it cannot be used. Some energy is always **dissipated** when it is transferred.

5 Explain why are we unable to reclaim thermal energy arising from energy due to friction or air resistance.

6 A car engine is designed to transfer energy from fuel into kinetic energy, making the car move. Name the other energy transfers that are likely to take place.

7 Look at the thermal image in Figure 5.11. Describe some of the features you can see. Use technical terms such as *thermal energy*, *thermal conductivity* and *dissipated* in your description.

Energy efficiency

Learning objectives:

- explain what is meant by energy efficiency
- calculate the efficiency of energy transfers
- find out about conservation of energy.

KEY WORDS

conservation of energy
energy efficiency

Electric cars have an efficiency of about 85% compared with about 15% for a petrol car. This means an electric car can transfer a greater portion of energy to produce movement from the original energy store. But batteries have to be charged – and the fossil fuel plant supplying the electric current is only about 35% efficient.

Useful energy output of a system

It is not possible for the useful energy output of a system to be greater than the total input energy. The law of conservation of energy also says that when a system changes, there is no change to the total energy of the system.

Even so, not all of the total energy input to a system is stored or usefully transferred. Some energy is always dissipated. This reduces the amount of energy that is usefully transferred.

For example, as an electric car accelerates, the engine transfers energy from the energy store of the battery to the energy store of the moving car. Some of the input energy is wasted by transfer of thermal energy by heating the wheels and the surrounding air.

1. **What effect does the waste energy from a light bulb have on the surroundings?**

2. **Suggest why is an electric vehicle more efficient than a petrol or diesel vehicle.**

Calculating energy efficiency

Efficiency is an indication of how much of the energy supplied to a device is transferred as a useful output. If all of the energy supplied was transferred usefully the transfer would be 100% efficient.

Energy efficiency = $\dfrac{\text{useful output energy transfer}}{\text{total input energy transfer}}$

OR

Energy efficiency = $\dfrac{\text{useful power output}}{\text{total power input}}$

Figure 5.13 The least efficient light bulbs are being replaced with more energy-efficient alternatives, including LED light bulbs

MATHS

To convert from a decimal to a percentage, multiply the decimal by 100.

Quite a lot of energy transfers are not very efficient; a lot of energy is transferred in a way that isn't useful.

Example: Tina is an athlete. She applies a force of 75 N for a distance of 100 m using 44 000 J of energy stored in food. What is her efficiency? Give your answer as a percentage.

Useful work done = force × distance = 75 N× 100 m = 7500 J

$$\text{Efficiency} = \frac{\text{useful energy output}}{\text{total energy input}}$$

$$= \frac{7500 \text{ J} \times 100}{44\ 000 \text{ J}} = 17\%$$

When you exercise, you get hot – your body temperature increases. Most of the energy stored in food is transferred to energy stored by your body.

3 For every 100 J of energy supplied to a motor, 80 J of useful work is done. Calculate the efficiency of the motor. Give your answer as a percentage.

4 For every 500 J of energy in coal, 135 J are transferred to a room as heat from a coal fire.

  a Calculate its efficiency.

  b Suggest why coal fires are inefficient.

5 Suggest why a kettle is not 100% efficient.

6 The efficiency of a television is 0.65. Calculate the useful energy output if the total energy input = 200 J.

Conservation of energy

Energy cannot be created or destroyed, only transferred from one store to another. In a closed system (one in which no energy can enter or leave) the *total* amount of energy put into the system equals the *total* amount of energy output. We say that energy is conserved. This is the law of **conservation of energy**. However, only some of the energy output is useful to us. The rest is dissipated as wasted energy. This affects the efficiency of a machine.

7 What is meant by 'conservation of energy'?

8 Explain why heating a material does not increase only the thermal energy store of the material.

9 When sound transfers energy from the store in a vibrating cymbal to your eardrums, not all the energy transferred is stored by your eardrums. Suggest how some of the energy is wasted.

HIGHER TIER

10 An electric car is 85% efficient. The electricity for the car is supplied by a coal power station with an efficiency of 35%. Determine how much energy is needed from the energy store of the coal for the car to provide 100 J of useful energy. Suggest how each energy transfer could be made more efficient.

DID YOU KNOW?

25% of all carbon dioxide emissions in the UK are as a result of heating and lighting our homes.

COMMON MISCONCEPTION

You often hear phrases like, '*Conserve energy*; turn off the lights'. However, to scientists, *conservation of energy* means that there is no net change to the total energy of a system.

PRACTICAL

Investigating ways of reducing the unwanted energy transfers in a system

KEY WORDS

conduction
energy transfer
insulation
thermal radiation

Learning objectives:

- use scientific ideas to make predictions
- analyse data to identify trends
- evaluate an experimental procedure.

Energy will always be transferred from warmer places to cooler ones. Sometimes this is useful, as in a domestic heating system. However on other occasions we need to stop that transfer, or at least slow it down.

These pages are designed to help you think about aspects of the investigation rather than to guide you through it step by step.

Developing a hypothesis

Tazim's group are investigating insulation materials and they are trying to predict which will work well. They are going to use the material to pack around a hot cooking pot that will be put into a wooden box with a close-fitting lid. The pot also has a lid. The liquid in the pot needs to be kept as hot as possible.

They are investigating the use of:

- expanded polystyrene
- wood shavings
- air.

One of the ways that thermal energy is transferred is by conduction.

1. Tazim thinks that all the materials will have the same insulating effect, because only metals are good thermal conductors. **Is he right?**

2. Write a list of all the factors that may affect the thermal insulation properties of the box around the hot cooking pot.

3. Write a hypothesis connecting one of these factors to the temperature of the liquid in the pot.

4. Plan a method that would enable the hypothesis to be tested. Include in this an indication of the variables to be kept the same, the variables to change and the variables to measure.

Analysing the results

The students then set up an experiment to investigate the cooling of the cooking pot when insulated with different materials. They left a similar pot on the bench to act as a control. The results are shown in the table.

Thermal insulator	Temperature of the pot (°C)					
	Start	1 hour	2 hour	3 hour	4 hour	5 hour
Control	90.0	38.0	26.5	25.5	25.0	25.0
Air	90.0	43.5	28.0	25.5	25.5	25.0
Polystyrene	90.0	55.0	43.5	37.5	30.0	26.5
Wood shavings	90.0	52.5	40.0	32.5	28.0	25.5

5 Draw a graph of how the temperature of the pot changes with time for each insulator.

6 What feature on the graph indicates which material is best at reducing energy transfer?

7 Explain why the graph lines levelled out.

8 Suggest how you could calculate the rate of cooling from the graphs.

9 Suggest why the rate of cooling changed from during the first hour to during the fifth hour.

Evaluating the experiment

Think about their experiment and the evidence it produced. The students are sharing ideas about how effective the experiment was.

10 These are some of the comments made. Respond to each of these, justifying your point of view:

a 'This experiment didn't work because all the pots ended up nearly cold.'

b 'To make it a fair test we should have used the same mass of liquid in each experiment.'

c 'The control was pointless – it's just using air as an insulator.'

d 'If you draw a straight line from the starting temperature to the final temperature for each of the experiments they have nearly the same gradient, showing that there's little difference between the types of insulation.'

11 a Show that the energy transferred to the surroundings in the first hour was about 1.33 times more when air was used as the insulator compared with polystyrene.

b Calculate what this value would be for the second hour.

KEY CONCEPT

Energy transfer

Learning objectives:

- to understand why energy is a key concept in science
- to use ideas about stores and transfers to explain what energy does
- to understand why accounting for energy transfers is a useful idea.

KEY WORDS

chemical
dissipate
energy
store
thermal
transfer

Young children often love to run around and play on swings. After a while they'll get tired. 'I've run out of energy!' they'll say, and flop down. A few minutes later they're up again, announcing 'I've got my energy back!' and run off again.

What is energy?

The concept of energy is one of the most important ideas in science. We use it to explain what's happening when a torch is turned on – and when the batteries run flat. We talk about an energy crisis, and whether we have enough energy to keep our lamps lit and our cars on the road. It's important in chemistry because when reactions take place energy is transferred, and it's important in biology because cells need energy to carry out important processes.

However, we sometimes find it difficult to explain what we mean by energy. It's easier to understand what stores energy, rather than what energy is.

1. Decide which of these is an energy store:

    a   a ball rolling down a ramp

    b   a stretched string

    c   a hot object

    d   a mixture of oxygen and fuel.

2. For each of a to d in Question 1, suggest if and how energy might be transferred from one store to another and used for something useful.

Transferring energy

You may find that people use names for energy, such as electrical, kinetic or gravitational potential. Actually it's more useful to identify where the energy is. This tells us more. We can then work out how it's been transferred.

Think about a wind-up torch (Figure 5.15). When you turn the handle you transfer energy from your muscles to the energy

Figure 5.15 Energy is transferred into this torch when it is wound up and out of it when it used to project light

store in the torch's battery. The energy store in your body decreases while the the energy store in the battery increases. When you turn the torch on, the energy store in the battery decreases and an electric current transfers energy in the bulb. The internal energy of the bulb increases (it increases in temperature), and the bulb transfers energy by light waves to the surroundings. Since the bulb is hot, it dissipates energy to the surroundings, increasing the internal energy of the surroundings. When the battery is flat, its energy store is zero and all the energy has been transferred to the surroundings.

3 Draw a flow diagram to represent where energy has been transferred from and to.

4 Identify which energy store increases and which decreases when:

a in a bicycle, being ridden

b in a match, being struck.

Accounting for energy

Energy does not disappear when it is transferred to other stores. It is still there but it is sometimes hard to see where it is being stored. For example, a charged battery is storing energy. When the battery is flat, the energy has been transferred to the surroundings.

Figure 5.16 Accounting for energy is rather like checking on the number of bricks in a set

The physicist Richard Feynman suggested that one of the ways of understanding accounting for energy was to compare it to a set of child's building blocks (Figure 5.16). The parent knows how many blocks there are in the set. If there is a block missing when you put them away, you look for it. Energy is similar. When you start with a certain amount of energy in a system, it is all still there, but you may have to look for it.

Coal stores energy. When the coal is burned, the energy store of the coal decreases and energy is transferred as heat. In a steam engine (Figure 5.17), energy is transferred from the store in the coal to the water (as steam) in the boiler. The steam turns the wheels and makes the train move, so there is an energy store associated with the movement of the train. At the end of the journey the coal is burnt, the steam used and the train has come to rest, but the energy is still there – the energy has been transferred to the surroundings.

Because scientists think this is an important idea, they go to a lot of trouble to measure the amounts of energy (look at the labels on prepared food), to account for the energy transfers and to calculate the efficiency from this (which can be given as a percentage).

Figure 5.17 Energy is being transferred here; can it all be accounted for?

5 How does the story of the child's bricks explain the concept of conservation of energy?

6 Energy is conserved within a system. In the case of the steam engine, what does the system include?

MATHS SKILLS

Calculations using significant figures

Learning objectives:

- substitute numerical values into equations and use appropriate units
- change the subject of an equation
- give an answer to an appropriate number of significant figures.

KEY WORDS

substitute
rearrange an equation
subject of an equation
significant figures

People have been trying to invent a perpetual motion machine for centuries. Perpetual motion means moving forever. But where there are energy transfers, some energy is always dissipated. This is why the idea of perpetual motion is an impossible dream.

Calculating changes in energy

Example: A diver dives into water from a board 10.0 m above the water surface. The mass of the diver is 50.0 kg. The gravitational field strength is 9.8 N/kg.

a) Calculate the change in gravitational potential energy of the diver as she falls from the board to the surface of the water.

b) Calculate the diver's speed when she hits the water.

a) Use $E_p = mgh$

$$E_p = 50.0 \text{ kg} \times 9.8 \text{ N/kg} \times 10.0 \text{ m}$$
$$= 4900 \text{ J}$$

b) As the diver falls, the potential energy due to the height of the diver above the water is transferred to the energy stored by the diver due to movement.

The energy transferred in this way = 4900 J

Use $E_k = 0.5 \, mv^2$

You need to **rearrange the equation** to find v (make v the **subject of the equation**).

Multiply both sides by 2: $2E_k = mv^2$

Divide both sides by m: $\dfrac{2E_k}{m} = v^2$

So: $v = \sqrt{\dfrac{2E_k}{m}}$

Substituting the values for E_k and m:

$$v = \sqrt{\dfrac{2 \times 4900}{50}}$$
$$v = \sqrt{196}$$
$$v = 14 \text{ m/s}$$

Figure 5.18 An idea for a perpetual motion machine. Such a machine could not work because it would violate the law of conservation of energy.

1 Calculate the change in gravitational potential energy of a diver of mass 70.0 kg who dives from a board 2.0 m above the water.

2 Calculate the gravitational potential energy gained by a ball of mass 50.0 g thrown to a height of 10.0 m.

Significant figures

The answer to a calculation can only have the same number of **significant figures** as the data provided.

> Example: A diver stands on a board 5.0 m above water. The mass of the diver is 50.0 kg. The gravitational field strength is 9.8 N/kg. Calculate the diver's speed when he hits the water. Give your answer to two significant figures.
>
> Increase in energy due to movement = decrease in gravitational potential energy
>
> $= mgh$
>
> $= 50.0 \text{ kg} \times 9.8 \text{ N/kg} \times 5.0 \text{ m}$
>
> = 2450 J (Do not round to two significant figures yet.)
>
> Energy stored by movement (kinetic energy), $E_k = 0.5\ mv^2$
>
> Rearranging as before, $\dfrac{2E_k}{m} = v^2$
>
> $v = \sqrt{\dfrac{2E_k}{m}}$
>
> $= \sqrt{\dfrac{2 \times 2450}{50}}$
>
> $= \sqrt{98}$
>
> = 9.899, or 9.9 m/s, to two significant figures

KEY INFORMATION

You should keep at least one extra significant figure in your calculations to avoid rounding errors. Only round to the required number of significant figures when you have calculated the answer.

KEY INFORMATION

To round a number to two significant figures, look at the third digit. Round up if the digit is 5 or more, and round down if the digit is 4 or less.

3 A spring of spring constant $k = 350$ N/m is extended by 9.0 cm. Calculate the energy transferred in stretching, E_e, stored in the spring. Give your answer to two significant figures.

Two-step problems

Example: A lift raises four people with a combined weight of 3500 N to the third floor of a building in 25.0 seconds. The height gained is 15 m. Calculate the power required.

You need to use: Power = $\dfrac{\text{work done}}{\text{time taken}}$, or $P = \dfrac{W}{t}$

You have the time taken, but not the work done. You must approach this problem in two steps. First, calculate the work done, then **substitute** that value into the equation for power.

Work done = force × distance moved along the line of action of the force

The force used (the weight that is lifted) is 3500 N.

Work done = 3500 N × 15 m

$\qquad$ = 52 500 J, or 52.5 kJ

Substituting this value for work done into the power equation:

Power = $\dfrac{52500 \text{ N}}{25.0 \text{ s}}$

$\qquad$ = 2100 W, or 2.1 kW

MAKING LINKS

A set of readings taken with the same instrument should all have the same number of significant figures. So if the extension of a spring is measured with a ruler as 4.1, 4.2, 5.9 and 6 cm, the table of data should list 6 cm as 6.0 cm.

Check your progress

You should be able to:

describe how energy can be stored by raising an object up or by stretching or compressing it

→

use the equations for gravitational potential energy and energy transferred in stretching

→

apply the equations for gravitational potential energy and energy transferred in stretching in a variety of contexts, and change the subject of these equations

describe how a moving object stores energy

→

know that kinetic energy is related to mass and velocity squared and use the formula to calculate it

→

use the equation for kinetic energy to solve problems, including changing the subject of the equation

state that some materials require more energy than others to increase a certain mass by a certain temperature rise

→

describe what is meant by the specific heat capacity of a material and use the equation for specific heat capacity

plan an experiment to measure the specific heat capacity of a material

→

calculate temperature changes, masses or specific heat capacities given the other values

evaluate an experiment to measure the specific heat capacity of a material

recognise that some energy transfers are unwanted

→

describe how lubrication and insulation can be used to reduce unwanted energy transfers

calculate energy efficiency

describe how some energy transfers are more useful than others

→

explain how thermal conductivity affects the rate of energy transfer across a material and affects the rate of cooling of a building

recognise that in a closed system there may be energy transfers that change the way energy is stored, but there is no net change to the total energy

Worked example

Jo's group is investigating the energy changes that take place when a toy car runs down a ramp.

1 The mass of the car is 500 g, g is 10 N/kg and the vertical height of the top of the ramp is 20 cm. Calculate the GPE of the car at the top of the ramp.

$GPE = mgh = 500 \times 10 \times 20 = 100\ 000\ J$

> This answer correctly uses the formula to multiply the variables together but hasn't converted the mass or the height into standard units. It should be 0.5 kg × 10 N/kg × 0.2 m = 1 J

2 The pupils use a speed detector to measure the speed of the car when it gets to the bottom of the ramp. They find out it is travelling at 0.8 m/s. Calculate its kinetic energy at the bottom of the ramp.

$KE = \dfrac{1}{2}mv^2 = \dfrac{1}{2} \times 0.5 \times 0.8 \times 0.8 = 0.16$

> This answer correctly uses the formula and has converted g to kg. The speed (only) is squared but there is no indication of the correct unit at the end.

3 **a** How could they calculate the percentage efficiency of the system at transferring the potential energy stored into the energy due to movement?

b Explain why it will be less than 100%.

$Efficiency\ could\ be\ found\ by\ dividing\ output\ by\ input,$

$so\ \dfrac{KE}{GPE}.$

$Nothing\ is\ perfect\ and\ efficiency\ is\ always\ less\ than\ 100\%$

> This is correct in that it is the output divided by the input but it is important to use the **useful** output. Furthermore, the question asked for the efficiency as a percentage, so the answer has to be multiplied by 100.

> This is true but is not an explanation. The reason it is not 100% is because not all of the potential energy stored has been transferred to the energy stored by the car. Some energy is dissipated to the surroundings, raising the temperature of the car body and the surrounding air.

4 Jo says that if the ramp was 100% efficient then doubling the height of the top of the ramp would double the speed at the bottom. Referring to the relevant formulae, suggest whether she is correct.

$GPE = mgh\ and\ KE = 1/2mv^2.\ Increasing\ h\ will\ increase\ GPE$
$and\ this\ will\ increase\ KE\ which\ will\ increase\ v\ so\ Jo\ is\ correct.$

> This quotes the correct formulae and identifies that an increased h will mean an increased GPE. In fact, doubling h will double the GPE which will double the KE (if it's 100% efficient). However, KE = $1/2mv^2$ and the squaring means that although the speed will increase, it won't double (it will actually go up by a factor of about 1.4). If the question includes a quantitative approach (it refers to doubling) it's not enough to give a qualitative response (say **how much** it increases).

End of chapter questions

Getting started

1 Sally is choosing a new electric kettle. One is rated at 1.5 kW and the other at 2 kW. What does this show? `1 Mark`

    a The first one is smaller.

    b The second one is a newer design.

    c The first one will keep the water hot for longer.

    d The second one will transfer energy more quickly.

2 Write down the equation for efficiency. `2 Marks`

3 What is meant by a non-renewable resource? `2 Marks`

4 When energy is being wasted we say it is

    a diffusing

    b propagating

    c dissipating

    d refracting `1 Mark`

5 Describe the difference between energy transferred in stretching and gravitational potential energy. `2 Marks`

6 Two steel blocks, one with a mass of 100 g and the other with a mass of 200 g, are placed in boiling water for several minutes. Which of these statements is **not** true? `1 Mark`

    a They are both at the same temperature.

    b They are made of the same material.

    c They have the same amount of stored energy.

    d They remain solid.

7 Order these light bulbs from most to least powerful. `1 Mark`

    15 W, 0.1 kW, 60 W, 0.08 kW, 150 W

Going further

8 Which of these does **not** affect the amount of energy needed to heat up a sample of material? `1 Mark`

    a Its colour.

    b Its mass.

    c Its specific heat capacity.

    d The temperature rise.

9 Explain why bubble wrap is an effective insulator. `3 Marks`

10 A hot parcel of fish and chips is taken outside on a cold night. Describe what transfers of energy will take place, identifying where the energy is stored. `3 Marks`

11. Look at the image of the house and suggest what this thermogram of a house shows. `2 Marks`

12. The power of a kettle is 2000 W. Explain what **2000 W** means in terms of energy transfer. `1 Mark`

More challenging

13. Write down what each of the symbols stands for in $\Delta E = mc\Delta\theta$ `2 Marks`

14. Night storage heaters heat up during the night time and release energy during the day. Explain why they are made from a material with a high specific heat capacity. `2 Marks`

15. A student was given some rods made from different materials. He was asked to arrange the rods in order of increasing thermal conductivity. Describe a procedure the student could follow to carry out the task safely by using a fair test. `6 Marks`

Most demanding

16. Explain the difference between thermal transfer of energy and temperature. `2 Marks`

17. Explain why energy is conserved within a closed system. `2 Marks`

18. A student was investigating how the efficiency of a squash ball changed with temperature. The efficiency of a squash ball can be worked out by using the formula:

    gravitational potential energy associated with the squash ball before it is dropped ÷ gravitational potential energy associated with the squash ball when it reaches its maximum height after it bounces.

    The student placed the ball in a beaker of water and heated the water to the desired temperature. She then removed the ball from the water and dropped it from a height of 1m onto a hard surface. Once the ball had bounced, the student measured the height that the ball bounced up to by using a metre ruler.

    Here are her results:

    Mass of squash ball = 25 g

    Gravitational field strength on Earth = 10 N/kg

Temperature (°C)	20	30	40	50	60
Bounce height 1 (cm)	6	28	39	43	45
Bounce height 2 (cm)	18	23	36	40	42

    The student concluded that the higher the temperature of the squash ball, the more efficient it was.

    Discuss whether the student made a valid conclusion and evaluate the limitations of the experiment. `6 Marks`

`Total: 40 Marks`

GLOBAL CHALLENGES

FOSSIL FUELS AND ALTERNATIVE ENERGY RESOURCES

- Fossil fuels are burnt to release the energy stored in them.
- Fossil fuels were formed over millions of years and supplies are running out.
- There are alternative energy resources which have advantages and disadvantages.

ENERGY USE AT HOME

- Most of the devices we use at home depend on energy.
- The energy is produced by generators in distant power stations.

ELECTRICITY IN THE HOME

- Electricity supplied to the home is alternating current (a.c.).
- Care must be taken when using mains electricity as it has a high potential difference (230 V).
- Fuses and circuit-breakers switch off the current if a fault occurs.

IN THIS CHAPTER YOU WILL FIND OUT ABOUT:

WHAT IS THE ENVIRONMENTAL IMPACT OF DIFFERENT ENERGY RESOURCES?

- Fuels such as coal, oil, gas and nuclear fuel are not renewable. Supplies will run out.
- The use of fossil fuels is changing as more renewable energy resources are used for transport, electricity generation and heating.
- Most renewable resources do not generate a predictable (reliable) amount of electrical power.
- There are different environmental issues for each different energy resource.

WHY IS ELECTRICITY TRANSMITTED AT HIGH POTENTIAL DIFFERENCES?

- When the potential difference is high the current is low for the same power.
- A low current means much less energy is wasted.
- Transmitting electricity through the National Grid at 400 000 V minimises energy losses.

HOW CAN ELECTRICITY BE USED SAFELY IN THE HOME?

- Circuit-breakers and fuses are used to cut off the current when there is a short circuit.
- The earth is connected to the Earth so it provides a path for the current if there is a short circuit.
- The higher the power (in W) of an electrical device, the more expensive it is to use it.

Keeping safe on the road

Learning objectives:

* explain the factors that affect stopping distance
* explain the dangers caused by large deceleration.

Road safety campaigns use slogans such as 'Kill your speed not a child!' What difference does reducing speed make in the case of an accident?

REMEMBER!

$$speed = \frac{distance}{time}$$

Driving safely

A car driver cannot begin to stop a car immediately. It takes time for the driver to react to a stimulus. This is called **reaction time**. The greater the speed of the car, the further it travels while the driver thinks (the red line in Figure 6.1).

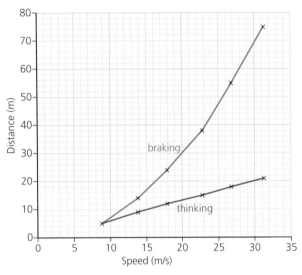

Figure 6.1 How speed affects stopping distance, for a typical car and an alert driver in good conditions

Thinking distance is the distance travelled during the reaction time. It is the distance travelled between the driver seeing a danger and taking action to avoid it, such as braking.

Braking distance is the distance travelled before a car stops after the brakes have been applied. It increases as the speed of the car increases (the green line in Figure 6.1).

Stopping distance = thinking distance + braking distance (Figure 6.2).

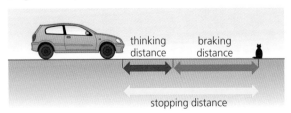

Figure 6.2 Stopping distance

REMEMBER!

Don't confuse thinking distance and braking distance.

1. Laura's thinking distance is 12 m. Use Figure 6.1 to find:
   a How fast is she going?
   b What is her braking distance?
   c What is her stopping distance?

2. Joe is driving at 80 km/h (36 m/s). Use Figure 6.1 to find his stopping distance in m.

Factors that affect stopping distance

Reaction time varies between 0.2 s and 0.9 s, but is typically about 0.7 s. Reaction time and hence thinking distance may increase if a driver is

- tired
- under the influence of alcohol or other drugs
- distracted or lacks concentration.

The braking distance may increase:

- when the road is wet or icy
- the car has poor brakes or bald tyres
- the speed of the car is greater.

> **KEY INFORMATION**
>
> One method of measuring human reaction time is to try catching a ruler as soon as you see it begin to fall. You will need to convert the distance the ruler has dropped into a time measurement.

Figure 6.3

Figure 6.1 shows how important it is to keep a suitable distance from the car in front.

3. In Figure 6.1, how does braking distance increase as speed increases?

4. Explain why a driver should slow down when road conditions are poor.

The dangers caused by large deceleration

Energy is transferred away from a vehicle that is slowing down. Work done by the friction force between the brakes and the rotating wheel reduces the energy of the vehicle. Energy is transferred to the brake pads, which heat up.

Many journeys involve slowing down to rest from a high speed and do so without discomfort or injury. However, it is when the vehicle needs to stop from a very high speed in a short time (a large deceleration) that problems can arise.

If deceleration is very rapid, it means a large braking force is being applied. This can result in the brake pads overheating or the driver losing control of the direction of the vehicle.

Transmitting electricity

Learning objectives:

- describe how electricity is transmitted using the National Grid
- explain why energy is transmitted at high potential differences
- understand the role of transformers.

KEY WORDS

National Grid
step-up
  transformer
step-down
  transformer
efficiency

In the USA, the potential difference used is 110 V instead of 230 V as in the UK. This means the wires have to carry about twice the current to make appliances work.

The National Grid

When electricity was first delivered to homes, each town had its own local power station. If the power station broke down then the town did not receive any electric power.

The **National Grid** is a collection of power cables and **transformers** that connect power stations to factories and houses across Great Britain. Everything is connected up in a grid so that energy can be transferred along many different routes. This means that the electricity supply used in your house can come from lots of different power stations.

DID YOU KNOW?

Before the National Grid, Each power station produced electricity at a different potential difference. This meant that electric appliances, such as light bulbs, would only work in one town. If you moved house you would have to buy new ones.

Figure 6.4 Power cables connected in the National Grid

1. **State an advantage of connecting your house to the National Grid rather than just connecting it up to a local power station.**

Changing the potential difference

The potential difference of the domestic UK mains supply is 230 V. This means that there is a potential difference of 230 V between the live wires and the earth wires in a house.

Energy is transmitted across the country at 400 000 V. The potential difference between a live power line and the earth is very large.

2 Explain why it would not be a good idea for the potential difference to be 400 000 V in a domestic electricity supply.

An electric current passing through the National Grid's power cables heats up the cables (Figure 6.5). Energy is being transferred to the surroundings rather than to houses and factories.

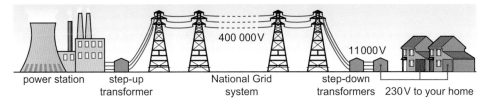

power station   step-up transformer   400 000V   National Grid system   11 000V   step-down transformers   230V to your home

Figure 6.5 The National Grid.

The higher the current, the more energy is wasted and the National Grid becomes less efficient. For the same electrical power, increasing the potential difference reduces the current. So using a high potential difference makes the National Grid more efficient.

3 How does increasing the potential difference make the National Grid more efficient?

Transformers

Step-up transformers increase the potential difference. They are connected between the power stations and the National Grid (Figure 6.5). **Step-down transformers** decrease the potential difference.

4 State where step-down transformers are connected in the National Grid.

Figure 6.6 Step-up transformers are installed close to the power stations

Using energy resources

Learning objectives:

- describe the main energy sources available for use on Earth
- distinguish between renewable and non-renewable sources
- explain the ways in which the energy resources are used.

KEY WORDS

non-renewable resource
renewable resource

Across the world we use over five hundred million trillion joules of energy every year. This has to come from somewhere.

The need for energy

Industrial societies use huge amounts of energy. Much of it is used for the generation of electricity in power stations. Electricity is useful because appliances can use it to transfer energy to many different types of useful energy stores. For example, a kettle can use electricity to transfer energy to the water that it is heating up.

1. **Identify an electrical device that transfers energy to:**

   a the energy store of a moving object

   b the energy stored by an object due to gravity (its gravitational potential energy)

We can also use electricity for transport (such as trains and electric cars) and for heating. However, it is often cheaper and easier to use energy resources directly for these purposes.

2. **Give an example of an energy resource being used to heat something.**

3. **State the energy resource you are using when you ride a bicycle.**

4. **Suggest why we mainly use electricity to power trains but fuel to power aeroplanes.**

Energy resources

Most of the energy resources available to us store energy that has originally come from the Sun. Energy resources include fossil fuels (coal, oil and gas), bio-fuel, wind, hydroelectric, solar, wave, geothermal (from hot, underground rocks), tidal and nuclear.

All of these resources have advantages and disadvantages. For example, in fossil fuels the energy is very concentrated – a small amount of fuel stores a large amount of energy. Bio-fuels (such as wood pellets) are produced from plants and animals. They are not as concentrated as fossil fuels so you need a much larger mass to release the same amount of energy.

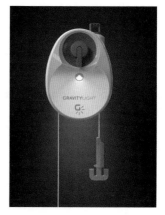

Figure 6.7 A gravity light has been developed that transfers the GPE of a falling 12 kg weight to power a light

DID YOU KNOW?

Tidal energy comes from the gravitational potential energy store of the Moon. Nuclear and geothermal resources store energy that was produced by stars exploding in a supernova.

Reliability is another issue. Some energy resources are available all the time but others are not. You cannot use solar during the night or in bad weather. Rain is needed for hydroelectric power and wind and wave requires it to be windy.

5 Give two ways of generating electricity in which no fuel is burned.

6 Suggest why wave is only useful for a few countries

7 Satellites orbiting the Earth use solar panels to provide them with their energy needs. Suggest why they also carry rechargeable batteries.

Renewable and non-renewable energy resources

Figure 6.8 Wind turbines are usually placed on high hills or out at sea

Renewable resources never run out (at least not for the foreseeable future). They can be replenished as soon as they are used.

- Solar, wind, wave and hydroelectric resources are usually available. The Sun always shines and it always creates wind and rain. However, there may be short periods of time when there is little wind or rain and no waves.

- Any energy extracted from hot rocks from the geothermal resource is replenished by physical processes in the rocks.

- The Moon produces two high tides nearly every day, whether we extract energy from them or not.

8 Wood is a form of bio-fuel. Explain why we can regard wood as a renewable resource.

Non-renewable resources will run out eventually. This is because they are not being replenished at the same rate that we are using them.

9 Identify a non-renewable resource that is not a fossil fuel.

10 Both bio-fuels and fossil fuels are formed from plants and animals. Explain why bio-fuels are renewable resources but fossil fuels are non-renewable.

11 a Describe the difference between energy and energy resource.

b Explain why energy is conserved but an energy resource is not conserved.

Global energy supplies

KEY WORDS

efficiency

Learning objectives:

- analyse global trends in energy use
- understand what the issues are when using energy resources.

• •

The white clouds coming from a power station are not smoke but water vapour coming from the cooling towers. In a coal-fired power station about half the energy stored in coal is lost in this way. We need the electricity, but do we have to have the waste?

Global trends

Figure 6.9 shows how energy resources have been used in the past and how they are likely to be used in the future.

You can see that the amount of energy we need increases every year. This is partly because the population of the world is increasing. Also, more countries are developing technologically and need more energy for industry. China's energy use, for example, grew rapidly between 2000 and 2015.

Although there are environmental problems with fossil fuels, they are likely to provide the world with most of its energy for many years to come.

World energy consumption by fuel (10^{18} J)

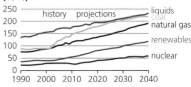

Figure 6.9 The world's use of energy resources

1. **Explain why some of the lines on the graph will eventually stop rising.**

2. **Look at Figure 6.9. Suggest the energy resource that China used the most from 2000 to 2010. Explain your answer.**

3. **Suggest why fossil fuels are likely to provide most of the world's energy for the foreseeable future.**

Energy issues

Scientists have discovered that using some energy resources is having an environmental impact. For example, fuel-burning power stations cause pollution.

They release carbon dioxide into the atmosphere which traps the Sun's energy and contributes to global warming. They also emit sulfur dioxide which causes acid rain.

Nuclear power stations create waste, some of which remains dangerous for thousands of years. There is also the danger of a nuclear accident which could contaminate the area with radioactive materials.

Scientists do not always have the power to make the decisions about energy use – these decisions are made by governments.

DID YOU KNOW?

Mean sea level has risen by about 20 cm in the last 100 years. Most scientists think this is due to global warming. Levels are expected to rise as much as a further 240 cm in the next 100 years.

Governments have to weigh up ethical, social and economic considerations as well as the likely impact on the environment. They also need to make sure they represent the views of the population that elected them.

Ethical considerations are to do with whether something is morally right or wrong. An example is making sure that energy resources are plentiful for the future. Although it will not affect us, it would be wrong to cause problems for future generations.

Social considerations concern how they affect people. Fossil fuel power stations need to be built to power factories and so provide people with jobs.

Economic considerations involve money. Although a particular energy resource is not as harmful to the environment it might be too expensive to produce.

Figure 6.10 A protest sign against plans to extract shale gas from the ground

4 **A local council has plans to extract shale gas from the ground and to burn it as fuel. Suggest some considerations that the council needs to make before they decide whether to go ahead.**

Using energy resources efficiently

One way of preserving energy resources is to use them efficiently. This means you need to find ways to reduce the amount of wasted energy in any energy transfer.

The chart shows the efficiencies of some typical engines and motors.

	Efficiency (%)
Petrol engine	25
Diesel engine	35
Electric motor	80

Fuel-burning engines have a low efficiency. It is impossible to transfer energy without wasting most of it.

You can use this formula to calculate **efficiency:**

$$\text{Efficiency} = \frac{\text{useful power output} \times 100}{\text{total power input}}$$

5 **Suggest why the electric motor is more efficient than the fuel-burning engines.**

6 **The output power of an electric motor is 3 kW. Calculate the input power it needs.**

7 **The power station that produced the electricity for the electric motor is 40% efficient. Use this value and your answer to question 6 to determine whether using an electric motor is more efficient than a diesel engine.**

8 **Besides increasing the efficiency of the engine, what else could you do to increase the efficiency of a car?**

Electricity in the home

Learning objectives:

- recall that the domestic supply in the UK is a.c. at 50 Hz and about 230 V
- describe the main features of live, neutral and earth wires.

KEY WORDS

earth
fuse
live
neutral

A circuit-breaker (Figure 6.11) is a resettable fuse. It has replaced the wire fuse in the main fuse box as it can be reset at the flick of a switch.

Domestic electricity supply

A cell or battery has two terminals, positive and negative. The current is d.c. which means that it always passes in the same direction.

Mains electricity differs in two ways (Figure 6.12):

- The current alternates, that is it changes direction. It has a frequency of 50 Hz.
- It has a much higher potential difference (about 230 V).

Figure 6.11 Circuit-breaker

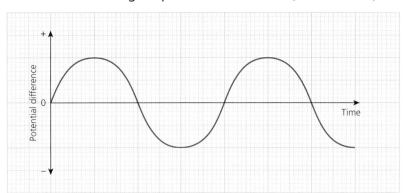

Figure 6.12 The potential difference variation from the mains

1. Describe the difference between a direct and an alternating potential difference.

2. The mains electricity in the USA has a potential difference of 120V and a frequency of 60Hz. Describe how Figure 6.12 would change for the USA.

Connecting a three-pin plug

Live, neutral and **earth** wires can be seen in a plug (Figure 6.13). If the appliance is working properly, there should be no current in the earth wire.

The three wires inside the mains cable are colour-coded:

- brown is connected to the live terminal (L)
- blue is connected to the neutral terminal (N)
- green/yellow stripe is connected to the earth terminal (E).

Figure 6.13 What colour is the earth wire?

3 Explain why most electric wires in the home are covered in plastic.

4 Suggest why the three wires have to be very different colours.

Live, neutral and earth wires

Our bodies are at Earth potential – there is no potential difference between our bodies and the Earth. If the casing of a faulty appliance becomes live, the potential difference between it and Earth is 230 V. If a person touches it, there is a complete circuit and current passes through the person's body to Earth. The person receives an electric shock. If the appliance is earthed it is connected to the Earth or ground (Figure 6.14). Any charge in it flows safely down to the ground through the low-resistance earth wire. This stops a person receiving an electric shock if they touch the live case of a faulty appliance.

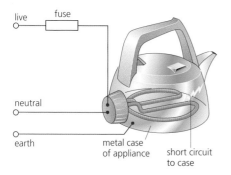

Figure 6.14 The arrangement of wires in a metal-cased appliance

The mains electricity supply usually comes from a power station. Two wires connect a house to a power station – live and neutral.

- The live wire carries a high potential difference into and around the house. The **fuse** in the plug (in Figure 6.13) is always connected to the live wire.
- The neutral wire provides a return path to the local sub-station. The neutral wire is earthed. There is no current in the neutral wire until an electrical appliance is connected.
- The earth wire is a safety wire. It is connected to the metal case of an appliance to prevent it becoming charged if touched by a live wire. It provides a low-resistance path to the ground. There is normally no current in it.

5 Explain why a battery-powered torch has two connections to its power supply but a mains lamp has three.

6 Describe the function of the earth wire. Explain whether the current is high or low when there is a fault and how this makes the appliance safe.

Figure 6.15 Double insulation symbol

DID YOU KNOW?

A double-insulated appliance does not need an earth connection (Figure 6.15). It has a plastic case with no electrical connections to it, so the case cannot become live.

REMEMBER!

A fuse is always connected in the live wire. If the current becomes higher than the fuse's rating then the fuse will melt and switch off the circuit.

Check your progress

You should be able to:

State that vehicle speed and reaction time affect the stopping distance of a vehicle

Identify measures to increase road safety

→

Describe factors that affect a driver's reaction time and a vehicle's braking distance Relate measures to incerese road safety to ideas about forces and energy

→

Interpret a graph that relates speed to stopping distance for different vehicles Calculate braking forces using ideas of stopping distance and energy transfer

state that various resources are used as fuels and to generate electricity

→

describe the advantages and disadvantages of fossil fuel, nuclear and renewable energy resources

→

evaluate and justify the use of various energy resources for different applications

Recall that the National Grid is a system of cables and transformers linking power stations to consumers

→

Describe how step-up and step-down transformers change the potential difference in the National Grid

→

Explain why electrical power is transmitted at high voltages in the National Grid

State that high potential differences are used to reduce power transmission losses

→

Describe how when the potential difference is increased the current decreases for the same power transmitted

→

Explain how power transmission losses are related to the square of the current

Identify live, neutral and earth wires by their colour-coded insulation

→

Explain why a live wire may be dangerous even when a switch in the main circuit is open

→

Explain the dangers of providing any connection between the live wire and earth or our bodies

Worked example

1. **What name is given to a device which will change a.c. from one potential difference to another?**

   a Transformer

   b Translator

   c Power supply

   d Generator

   c

   > the only device that changes one potential device to another is a transformer (it transforms the potential difference). Power supply is a general term for anything which supplies power; a power supply may include a transformer but is specifically the transformer that changes to potential difference.

2. **Explain the difference between the input and output of a step-up transformer.**

   a step-up transformer increases the voltage.

   > this is correct but doesn't include enough detail to gain all of the available marks. A step-up transformer increases the potential difference but it also decreases the current.

3. **Explain why power is converted to a higher potential difference for distribution over a wide area.**

   converting the potential difference reduces the energy losses.

   > this is true, but it doesn't explain why. If the potential difference in increased the current is decreased and this means that there is less energy transfer as heat.

4. **Explain what would happen if the power was transmitted at a lower potential difference.**

   at a lower potential difference the current would be higher, the energy losses more and less energy would reach consumers a long way from the power station.

   > this is a good response and covers the main points. If energy losses are higher, less power would end up with the user.

End of chapter questions

Getting started

1 Describe what we mean by the **National Grid**. `2 Marks`

2 Write the colour of the insulation on the earth wire in a three-pin plug. `1 Mark`

3 Describe what is wrong with the wiring in the plug in the diagram above. `2 Marks`

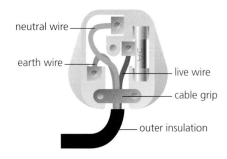

neutral wire
earth wire
live wire
cable grip
outer insulation

4 Which of these shows how to calculate the percentage energy efficiency of an appliance? `1 Mark`

  a (Useful output/input) × 100

  b (input/useful output) × 100

  c (Waste output/input) × 100

  d (input/waste output) × 100

5 Ryan says that burning wood is not sustainable, as once the wood is burnt, it's gone. Mary isn't so sure; she's seen an advert for bundles of firewood, saying that it came from a sustainable source. Explain how wood can be used as a fuel sustainably. `2 Marks`

Going further

6 Describe **two** factors that affect the stopping distance of a car. `2 Marks`

7 When a vehicle is travelling at speed it has kinetic energy. Explain what happens to this energy when the driver applies the brakes. `2 Marks`

8 This graph shows the use of global energy resources. `6 Marks`

  a What type of fuel is the most popular?

  b What does the graph show about the use of fossil fuels?

  c What does it show about the global demand for energy?

World energy consumption by fuel
(10^{18} J)

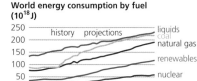

history   projections
liquids
coal
natural gas
renewables
nuclear

250 — 200 — 150 — 100 — 50 — 0

1990 2000 2010 2020 2030 2040

More challenging

9 Explain how a person gets an electric shock if they are charged and then earthed.

`1 Mark`

10 Explain how a fuse acts as a safety device.

`2 Marks`

11 Any electrical appliance that has a metal body has to be earthed. Explain what this means and why it makes the appliance safer.

`4 Marks`

12 Which one of these shows a correct relationship?

`1 Mark`

    a Stopping distance = thinking distance + braking distance

    b Braking distance = thinking distance + stopping distance

    c Braking distance = stopping distance + thinking distance

    d Thinking distance = stopping distance + braking distance

13 The power supply for a laptop computer contains a transformer. Explain what the purpose of the transformer is.

`2 Marks`

Most demanding

14 In certain places, the National Grid transmits electricity at a potential difference of 44 kV. Evaluate the use of a high potential difference when transmitting power.

`3 Marks`

15 A generator on an island produces electricity at 750 V and 12 A. The power distribution lines have a resistance of 50 Ω. If the power loss in the lines is given by I^2R, determine how much power would be saved by transforming it to 2.25 kV before transmission. Assume the transformers are 100% efficient.

`6 Marks`

16 Which of these statements is incorrect?

`1 Mark`

    a Transformers don't work on d.c. – if you supply a d.c. current there's no output

    b Batteries supply a lower frequency output than the mains

    c With the correct design a transformer can convert any a.c. potential difference to any other a.c. potential difference

    d When a step-down transformer converts 240V a.c. to 12V a.c., the output still has the same frequency as the input.

`Total: 38 Marks`

Appendix – Equations

It is important to be able to recall and apply the following equations using standard S.I. units:

Equation Number	Word Equation
1	density (kg/m³) = mass (kg)/volume (m³)
2	distance travelled (m) = speed (m/s) × time (s)
3	acceleration (m/s²) = change in velocity (m/s)/time (s)
4	kinetic energy (J) = 0.5 × mass (kg) × (speed (m/s))²
5	force (N) = mass (kg) × acceleration (m/s²)
6	work done (J) = force (N) × distance (m) (along the line of action of the force)
7	power (W) = work done (J)/time(s)
8	**momentum (kgm/s) = mass (kg) × velocity (m/s)**
9	force exerted by a spring (N) = extension (m) × spring constant (N/m)
10	gravity force (N) = mass (kg) × gravitational field strength, g (N/kg)
11	(in a gravity field) potential energy (J) = mass (kg) × height (m) × gravitational field strength, g (N/kg)
12	charge flow (C) = current (A) × time (s)
13	potential difference (V) = current (A) × resistance (Ω)
14	energy transferred (J) = charge (C) × potential difference (V)
15	power (W) = potential difference (V) × current (A) = (current (A))² × resistance (Ω)
16	energy transferred (J, kWh) = power (W, kW) × time (s, h)
17	wave speed (m/s) = frequency (Hz) × wavelength (m)
18	efficiency = useful output energy transfer (J)/input energy transfer (J)

It is important to be able to recall and apply the following equations using standard S.I. units:

Equation Number	Word Equation
19	change in thermal energy (J) = mass (kg) × specific heat capacity (J/kg°C) × change in temperature (°C)
20	thermal energy for a change in state (J) = mass (kg) × specific latent heat (J/kg)
21	(final velocity (m/s))^2 – (initial velocity (m/s))^2 = 2 × acceleration (m/s^2) × distance (m)
22	energy transferred in stretching (J) = 0.5 × spring constant (N/m) × (extension (m))^2
23	**force on a conductor (at right angles to a magnetic field) carrying a current (N) = magnetic field strength (T) × current (A) × length (m)**
24	potential difference across primary coil (V) × current in primary coil (A) = potential difference across secondary coil (V) × current in secondary coil (A)

Glossary

A

absorption process in which matter takes in energy, e.g. when an atom takes in energy from an electromagnetic wave

acceleration rate at which an object speeds up, calculated from change in velocity divided by time; symbol a, unit metres per second squared, m/s^2

activity the rate at which unstable nuclei decay in a sample of a radioactive material; unit becquerel, Bq

air resistance force produced by the collision of molecules in air with a moving object; the force acts to oppose the direction of movement

algebraic equation an equation that shows a relationship between variables, using letters to represent the variables

alpha decay radioactive decay process in which an alpha particle is emitted by an unstable nucleus

alpha particle a particle (two neutrons and two protons, same as a helium nucleus) emitted by an atomic nucleus during radioactive decay

alternating current (a.c.) electric current that continually changes direction

ammeter device that measures electric current

ampere SI unit of electric current, symbol A; an electric current of 1 A is equal to 1 C of charge passing through a point in a circuit in 1 s

amplitude maximum displacement of a wave or oscillating object from its rest position

anomaly a value in a set of results which is judged not to be part of the variation caused by random uncertainty

atom the basic 'building block' of an element; a positively charged nucleus surrounded by negatively charged electrons

atomic number number of protons in the nucleus of an atom of an element

average speed distance travelled by an object over a measured time interval

B

background radiation nuclear radiation that is present in the environment as a result of the radioactive decay of certain elements; it is produced from natural sources (e.g., from radon gas in the Earth's crust) and from artificial sources (e.g., as a result of testing nuclear weapons)

balanced forces when two or more forces act on a body, and the resultant force is zero, then the forces are said to be balanced

bar chart a chart used to present data in which bars of equal width represent the set of values and the length of each bar is proportional to the value; often used when the independent variable is qualitative

becquerel unit of activity for a radioactive isotope, symbol Bq

beta decay radioactive decay process in which a beta particle is emitted by an unstable nucleus

beta particle fast-moving electron that is emitted by an atomic nucleus in some types of radioactive decay

boiling the change of state in which all the particles in a liquid have enough energy to break free and become a gas; happens at a fixed temperature for a given liquid

bonds forces of attraction between particles, such as between atoms, ions or molecules

braking distance distance travelled by a vehicle after the brakes have been applied before coming to a complete stop

C

change of state process in which one state of matter changes to another, e.g., solid melting to form liquid, or gas condensing to form liquid

circuit diagram visual representation of electrical components connected by wires, using standard symbols

circuit symbol visual representation of an electrical component; a standard symbol exists for each type of electrical component

closed system system that is not acted upon by any external forces and does not exchange energy with its surroundings

commutator (split-ring) electrical connector consisting of two semi-circular metal contacts, which is connected to a rotating coil in a dynamo (to produce direct current) or a motor (to use direct current)

components (forces) the result of breaking down or resolving a single force into two separate forces acting in perpendicular directions, often horizontally and vertically

compression a region of a longitudinal wave where the particles are closer together

condensation the change of state in which the particles in a gas slow down and move closer together to form a liquid; happens at a fixed temperature for a given liquid

conduction (electrical) the process by which electrical charge passes through a material

conduction (thermal) the transfer of heat (internal energy) due to the vibration of molecules; its rate depends upon temperature difference between two regions

conductivity (thermal) quantity that measures the rate at which thermal energy is conducted through a material; the higher the thermal conductivity, the higher the rate of thermal energy transfer

conductor material or object that allows electric charge to flow through it

conservation of energy a fundamental principle of physics: energy cannot be created or destroyed, only transferred, stored or dissipated. This means that the total energy of a closed system is constant

conservation of mass a fundamental principle of physics: mass cannot be created or destroyed by physical changes or chemical reactions; the total mass of a system is constant

conservation of momentum a fundamental principle of physics: the total momentum of a system of objects after a collision is the same as the total momentum before the collision

constant of proportionality in a directly proportional relationship between two variables, x and y, of the form $y = kx$, the constant k is the constant of proportionality

contact force force that acts at the point of contact between two objects (e.g., friction or the normal reaction)

contamination (radioactivity) the unwanted presence of materials containing radioactive atoms

continuous data a type of quantitative data in which the values can take on any value within a certain range

control variable quantity in an experiment that is kept constant while the independent variable is changed and the dependent variable is measured

correlation a link or association between two variables, so that when one changes so does the other one

coulomb SI unit of electric charge, symbol C

count rate the number of decays recorded each second by a detector (e.g. Geiger-Muller tube)

crumple zone an area of a car that is designed to deform and crumple in a collision; this increases the time taken to change the car's momentum in a crash, reducing the force on people in the car

current (electric) flow of electric charge; the size of the electric current is the rate of flow of electric charge; symbol I, unit amps (A)

D

deceleration negative acceleration, when an object slows down

density measure of the amount of substance per unit volume; symbol ρ, unit kilograms per metre cubed, kg/m^3

dependent variable quantity in an experiment that is measured for each change in the independent variable

diode circuit component with a low resistance if it is connected one way around in a circuit, or a very high resistance if it is connected the other way around; a diode allows current in one direction only

direct current (d.c.) flow of electric charge in one direction only

directly proportional relationship a relationship of the form y proportional to ($\propto$) x; plotting a graph of y against x will produce a straight line through the origin

displacement distance moved in a particular direction; it is a vector quantity and is equal to the area under a velocity–time graph; symbol s, unit metres, m

dissipation the spreading out of energy into the environment, so that it is stored in less useful ways

distance quantity that measures how far an object moves but not the direction; it is a scalar quantity; symbol s, unit metres, m

distance–time graph graph with distance on the y-axis and time on the x-axis; the gradient of a distance–time graph is equal to the speed

dose (radiation) quantity that measures the amount of ionising radiation received (e.g., by a human body); measured in sieverts (Sv)

dynamo device that produces a direct current using the generator effect (e.g. from the rotation of a coil in a magnetic field)

E

earth (electrical) electrical connection between the metal case of an electrical appliance and the ground, used as a safety device to prevent the case becoming charged if touched by a live wire

Earth's magnetic field the magnetic field around the Earth, which affects the magnet in a compass needle

efficiency useful output energy transfer divided by the total input energy transfer – may be expressed as a percentage or as a decimal

elastic deformation process in which an object (e.g., a spring) is stretched by a force and returns to its original size or length when the force is removed

elastic potential energy energy that is stored in an object as a result of the object being stretched or compressed

electric charge fundamental property of matter that results in an electric field around an object; objects can be electrically positive, negative or neutral (no overall charge); symbol Q, unit coulomb, C

electric current flow of electric charge; the size of the electric current is the rate of flow of electric charge; symbol I, unit amps, A

electrical power amount of energy transferred each second; symbol P, unit watts or joules per second, W or J/s

electromagnet magnet formed by an electric current flowing through a solenoid (coil of wire) with an iron core – the magnetic field of an electromagnet can be switched on and off by switching the current on and off

electromagnetic (EM) spectrum electromagnetic waves ordered according to wavelength and frequency – ranging from radio waves to gamma rays

electron a particle that orbits the nucleus in all atoms; electrons have a negative electric charge

energy efficiency *see* efficiency

energy level stable state of a physical system, e.g., electrons orbiting the nucleus of an atom can exist in only particular energy levels and be moved between them

energy store the energy associated with fuel, a heated object (thermal energy), moving object (kinetic energy), a stretched spring (energy transferred in stretching) and an object raised above ground level (gravitational potential energy)

energy transfer process in which energy is moved from one store to another

equilibrium situation in which there is no resultant force acting on an object; any forces that are acting balance each other in magnitude and direction

equivalent resistance the overall resistance of an arrangement of two or more resistors

estimate best guess of the value of a quantity that cannot be measured precisely, based on scientific knowledge and observation

evaporation the change of state in which the particles at the surface of a liquid have enough energy to break free and become a gas; happens at all temperatures

extension the increase in length of an object when a force is applied

F

filament bulb an electric light that contains a thin coil of wire called the filament; the heated filament emits light

Fleming's left-hand rule shows which way a current-carrying wire tries to move when placed in a magnetic field – First finger shows Field, seCond finger shows Current, thuMb shows Movement

force 'push' or 'pull' on an object that can cause the object to accelerate

free body diagram drawing showing the magnitude and direction of all the forces acting on an object, and in which the object is represented by a point

freezing the change of state in which the particles in a liquid stop moving around and become fixed in place to form a solid; happens at a fixed temperature for a given solid

frequency number of waves passing a set point in one second, symbol f, unit Hz

frequency table a table showing a count (tally) of frequencies of objects or events

friction force acting at points of contact between objects moving over each other, to resist the movement

G

gamma rays ionising electromagnetic radiation with shortest wavelengths in the electromagnetic spectrum

gas state of matter in which all the particles of a substance are separate and move about freely

gas pressure the total force on a unit area of surface, caused by collisions between the gas particles and the surface

gradient the slope of a graph $= \dfrac{\text{change in } y\text{-axis values}}{\text{change in } x\text{-axis values}}$

gravitational field strength quantity that measures the 'pull' of the force of gravity on each kilogram of mass; symbol g, unit newtons per kilogram, N/kg

gravitational potential energy energy that an object has because of its position; e.g., increasing the height of an object above the ground increases its gravitational potential energy

H

half-life the average time it takes for half of all the nuclei present in a sample of a radioactive element to decay, or the time it takes for the count rate (or activity) to halve

hazard anything that may cause injury (e.g., the risk of contamination by radioactive materials when they are used in a scientific experiment)

hertz unit of frequency, symbol Hz

histogram a chart used to present the distribution of data, in which bars represent the set of values and the length of each bar is proportional to the value; the bars may not be of equal width if the class intervals are not equal, and so it is the area of each bar rather than the height that is proportional to the frequency of values in each class

hypothesis an idea for, or explanation of, a phenomenon in science that can be tested through study and experimentation

I

independent variable quantity in an experiment that is changed or selected by the experimenter

induced magnet material that is magnetic only when it is placed in the magnetic field of another magnet, e.g., the iron core within a solenoid

inelastic deformation process in which an object (e.g., a spring) is stretched by a force and permanently deformed so that it does not return to its original size or length when the force is removed

inertia natural tendency of objects to resist changes in their velocity

inertial mass measure of how difficult it is to change the velocity of an object

infrared radiation electromagnetic radiation with a range of wavelengths longer than visible light but shorter than microwaves; emitted in particular by heated objects

insulator (electrical) material that does not allow electric charges to pass through it (e.g., wood)

insulator (thermal) material that does not easily allow the transfer of thermal energy

intercept point at which the line of a graph crosses one of the axes

internal energy total kinetic energy and potential energy of all the particles in a system

inversely proportional relationship a relationship of the form $y \propto 1/x$

ionisation process in which electrons split away from their atoms; some radiation is harmful to living cells because it is ionising

irradiation process in which an object is exposed to radiation; this does not make the object itself radioactive

isotopes atoms of an element containing the same number of protons but different numbers of neutrons

J

joule SI unit of energy, symbol J

K

kilogram SI unit of mass, symbol kg

kinetic energy energy an object has because of its movement; kinetic energy is greater for objects with greater mass or higher speed

L

latent heat energy needed for a substance to change state without a change in temperature (e.g., the latent heat of vaporisation is the energy needed to turn a sample of liquid water into gas)

light-dependent resistor (LDR) electric circuit component with a resistance that decreases as the intensity of the light falling upon it increases

limit of proportionality the point beyond which the extension of an elastic object is no longer proportional to the force applied

line of best fit line on a graph that most closely matches all the data points to show a trend or pattern

linear relationship relationship between quantities in which increases in one quantity result in proportional increases or decreases in the other quantity; a graph of a linear relationship produces a straight line

liquid state of matter in which the particles of a substance are close together and attract each other but have a limited amount of movement; a liquid has a definite volume but will spread out to fill its container

live wire conducting wire connection that carries the alternating current from the supply

longitudinal wave wave motion in which the vibrations of the particles of the medium are parallel to the direction of energy transfer (e.g., sound waves)

M

magnetic field area around a magnet or current-carrying wire, where there is a force on magnetic materials or current-carrying wires

magnetic flux density quantity that measures the amount of magnetic flux (field lines) in an area perpendicular to the direction of the magnetic flux; symbol B, unit tesla, T

magnitude size of a quantity

mass quantity that measures the amount of matter in an object; symbol m, unit kilogram, kg

mass number total number of neutrons and protons in the nucleus of one atom of an element

mean the sum of a set of values divided by he number of values in the set

median the middle value of an ordered data set

melting the change of state in which the particles in a solid start moving around and are no longer fixed in place, the solid changes to a liquid; happens at a fixed temperature for a given solid

microwave electromagnetic radiation with a range of wavelengths longer than infrared but shorter than radio waves; used to cook food in microwave ovens, and for satellite communication

mode the most frequent item in a set of data

momentum the product of mass and velocity of an object, symbol p, unit kilogram metres per second, kg m/s

motor effect interaction between a magnetic field due to a magnet and a current-carrying wire that causes a force on the wire and so causes movement of the wire

mutation a change in DNA, sometimes caused by ionising radiation

N

National Grid network of cables and transformers that links power stations to consumers across the country

neutral wire conducting wire connection that allows electric charge to return to its source

neutron a particle inside the nucleus in the atoms of nearly all elements; neutrons have no electric charge

neutron radiation a type of radiation emitted during nuclear fission; fast-moving neutron

newton SI unit of force, symbol N; 1 N is the force needed to give an object of mass 1 kg an acceleration of 1 m/s^2

Newton's first law if the resultant force acting on an object is zero, a stationary object will remain stationary and a moving object will keep moving at a steady speed in a straight line

Newton's second law a resultant force on an object produces an acceleration in the same direction as the force that is proportional to the magnitude of the force and inversely proportional to the mass of the object; in equation form $F = ma$

Newton's third law whenever two objects interact, the forces they exert on each other are equal, opposite and of the same type

newtonmeter device used to measure force

non-contact force force that acts at a distance between two objects that are separated (e.g., force due to an electric, gravitational or magnetic field)

non-linear relationship any relationship between two variables which when plotted on a graph does not produce a straight line

non-renewable resource source of energy used by humans that will eventually run out (e.g., fossil fuels are non-renewable fuels)

non-uniform motion movement in which the speed of an object changes

nuclear equation equation that uses symbols to show the elements involved in a nuclear decay, including the atomic numbers and mass numbers

nuclear model model of the the atom with a small central nucleus, surrounded by orbiting electrons

nuclear radiation radiation emitted from the nucleus, either as electromagnetic waves or as moving particles

nucleon any particle in the nucleus (proton or neutron)

nucleus very small volume at the centre of an atom that contains all the protons and neutrons, and so concentrates nearly all the mass of an atom

O

ohm SI unit of electrical resistance, symbol Ω; a component with a resistance of 1 Ω allows a current of 1 A when a potential difference of 1 V is applied

order of magnitude description of a quantity in terms of powers of ten; e.g., a distance of 100 m (= 10^2 m) is two orders of magnitude larger than a distance of 1 m

P

parallel (circuit) electric circuit in which the current divides into two or more paths before combining again

particle model model in which all substances contain large numbers of very small particles (atoms, ions or molecules); it is used to explain the different properties of solids, liquids and gases

pascal SI unit of pressure, symbol Pa; 1 Pa of pressure arises when 1 N of force is applied over an area of 1 m²

peer review process in which scientific experiments, writings and theories are checked and evaluated by other scientists

penetrating power measure of how far different types of radiation can pass into different types of material

period time taken for one complete cycle of an oscillation of a wave, symbol T

permanent magnet object or material that produces its own magnetic field even if it is not within the magnetic field of another object

plum pudding model early model of the structure of an atom, which suggested that an atom was a solid sphere of positive electric charge with negatively charged electrons in it

pole (magnetic) regions of a magnet from which field lines are directed to and from

potential difference (p.d.) a measure of the energy transferred per unit charge as charges move between two points in a circuit – also called the voltage between two points

power (of ten) number of times that ten is multiplied by itself in a quantity, e.g., ten to the power two = 10^2 = 10 × 10 = 100

power (energy transfer) the rate at which energy is transferred or the rate at which work is done; an energy transfer of 1 J/s is equal to a power of 1 W

prefix letter added before the symbol for a unit to show how many powers of ten a quantity contains; e.g., 1 MW = 10^6 W = 1000 000 W, where the prefix M (mega) means 10^6

pressure pressure at any point is the force acting at that point divided by the area over which the force acts; pressure increases if force increases or area decreases

proportional *see* directly proportional, inversely proportional

proton a particle inside the nucleus in all atoms; protons have a positive electric charge

R

radiation energy given out in the form of electromagnetic waves or as moving particles; e.g. in radioactive beta decay a nucleus emits high-speed electrons, and the Sun radiates electromagnetic waves including visible light

radioactivity process in which particles or energy are produced by the reactions of unstable atomic nuclei

radioisotope a radioactive isotope

radio waves electromagnetic radiation with a range of wavelengths longer than microwaves; used for long-distance communication

random (radioactive decay) process in which the time of each particular event cannot be predicted, although a trend or average can be measured across many events; e.g., the decay of a radioactive element

random error estimated amount by which a measurement or calculated quantity is different from the true value, due to results varying in unpredictable ways

range the lowest and highest values measured in an experiment, or for a measuring instrument, the lowest and highest values that the instrument can record

rarefaction a region of a longitudinal wave where the particles are further apart

ray diagram line diagram showing how rays of light travel

rate of change a measure of how quickly one variable changes in comparison with another variable

reaction time time it takes a vehicle driver to respond to a danger on the road; the 'thinking distance' is the distance the vehicle travels during this reaction time

rearrange an equation to make another variable the subject of the equation

reflection process in which a surface does not absorb any energy, but instead bounces it back towards the source; e.g., light is reflected by polished surfaces

refraction change of direction of a wave when it hits a boundary between two different media at an angle; e.g., when a light ray passes from air into a glass block

renewable resource store of energy that can be replaced or reused over a short time, e.g., biofuels from crops that can be grown again from seed

repulsion repelling force that acts between two objects that tends to push them further apart, e.g. the force that arises between two positive electric charges

resistance ratio of the potential difference across an electrical component to the current through the component symbol R, unit ohms, Ω

resolution (forces) splitting a single force into two components acting in different directions, to simplify a calculation

resultant force the single force that would have the same effect on an object as all the forces that are acting on the object

round to approximate a number by expressing it to fewer significant figures

S

satellite any natural or artificial object orbiting around a larger object

scale a set of evenly spaced marks on a measuring instrument, alternatively a factor used to enlarge of reduce a number, quantity or measurement by a given amount

scalar quantity measurable quantity that has only a magnitude, not a direction (e.g., mass)

scatter diagram graph used to find a relationship between two quantitative variables

series (circuit) electric circuit in which all components are connected one after the other in a single line

SI unit standard units of measurement, one per quantity, used by all physicists; all SI units are derived from seven 'base' units that have precise definitions

significant figures digits within a measured quantity that have meaning; e.g., a measurement made using a 30 cm long ruler with divisions marked in millimetres can only have three significant figures, such as 17.4 cm; it is meaningless to state 17.42 cm because the ruler is not that precise (note: it may be possible on some rulers to estimate a measurement to the nearest 0.5 mm)

sketch graph a line graph that shows the general shape of the relationship between two variables

solenoid a coil of current-carrying wire that generates a magnetic field

solid state of matter in which the particles are held together in a fixed structure by bonds

spark a sudden flow of charge (a discharge, or electric current) when a conductor connects two static charges of opposite charge

specific heat capacity the energy needed to raise the temperature of 1 kg of a substance by 1 °C ; symbol c, unit J/kg °C

specific latent heat the energy needed to change 1 kg of a substance completely from one state to another state without any change in temperature; symbol L, unit J/kg

specific latent heat of fusion the energy needed to change 1 kg of a substance completely from solid to liquid without any change in temperature

specific latent heat of vaporisation the energy needed to change 1 kg of a substance completely from liquid to gas without any change in temperature

spectrum a series of waves with a range of frequencies, for example the visible spectrum and the electromagnetic spectrum

speed the distance travelled by an object per unit of time; unit metres per second, m/s

spring constant quantity that tells you how much an object (such as a spring) will stretch by if a force is applied to it, as long as the object obeys Hooke's law; symbol k, unit newtons per metre, N/m

standard form a form in which numbers are recorded as a number between 1 and 10 multiplied by a power of ten

state of matter form that particles of a substance take depending on temperature; different states include solid, liquid and gas

step-down transformer transformer that changes an alternating potential difference across the primary coil to a lower potential difference across the secondary coil

step-up transformer transformer that changes an alternating potential difference across the primary coil to a higher potential difference across the secondary coil

stopping distance total distance a vehicle travels before coming to a complete stop; stopping distance = thinking distance + braking distance

subject of an equation the variable in the equation that is on its own on the left of the equals sign

sublimate the change of state in which a solid changes to a liquid without going through the liquid state

systematic error consistent amount by which a measurement differs from the true value each time it is measured, due to the experimental technique or the set-up; e.g., an instrument not correctly calibrated, or background radiation in the measurement of radioactive decay

T

tangent on a graph, a straight line that touches a curve at only one point

terminal velocity constant velocity that occurs when the gravitational force acting downwards on a body falling through a fluid is exactly balanced by the upwards force due to the resistance of the fluid

tesla SI unit of magnetic flux density, symbol T

thermal conductivity measure of the ability of a material to conduct energy from a hotter place to a colder place

thermal energy internal energy present in a system due to its temperature, which itself is due to the random motion of the particles within the system

thermal radiation, *see* infrared radiation

thermistor a ntc (negative temperature coefficient) thermistor is an electric circuit component with a resistance that decreases as its temperature increases

thinking distance distance a vehicle travels during the time it takes a vehicle driver to respond to a danger on the road

time period time taken for one complete oscillation of a wave, symbol T

tracer a radioactive substance that is put into the body or fluid (such as in a pipe), so that the path of the substance can be followed by monitoring the radiation it emits

transformer device that transfers energy between circuits using induction: it can be used to increase (step up) or decrease (step down) the potential difference of an alternating current

transmission movement of energy or information from one position to another; e.g., microwaves are used to transmit mobile phone signals to and from an aerial (signal mast)

transverse wave wave motion in which the vibrations of the particles of the medium are perpendicular to the direction of energy transfer (e.g., water waves or electromagnetic waves)

U

ultraviolet radiation electromagnetic radiation with a range of wavelengths shorter than visible light but longer than X-rays; emitted in particular by the Sun

unbalanced forces when two or more forces act on a body, and the resultant force is not zero, then the forces are said to be unbalanced

uniform motion movement of an object in a straight line at a constant speed

V

vaporisation the change in state from liquid to gas

vector quantity measurable quantity that has both a magnitude and a direction (e.g., velocity)

velocity speed at which an object is moving in a particular direction; symbol v, unit metres per second, m/s

velocity–time graph graph with velocity on the y-axis and time on the x-axis; the gradient of a velocity–time graph is equal to the acceleration; the area under a velocity–time graph is equal to the displacement

visible light electromagnetic radiation with a range of wavelengths shorter than infrared but longer than ultraviolet; detectable with the human eye

volt SI unit of potential difference, symbol V; 1 V is the potential difference between two points on a conducting wire when an electric current of 1 A dissipates 1 W of power between those points

voltage *see* potential difference

voltmeter device that measures potential difference

W

watt SI unit for power, symbol W; a power of 1 W is equal to 1 J of energy transferred in 1 s

wave a disturbance (oscillation) that transfers energy or information from one point to another

wave front an imaginary line that joins all the points on a wave that are moving up and down together at the same time

wavelength distance between a point on one wave to the equivalent point on the adjacent wave

weight measure of the force of gravity on an object

work done work is done when a force acts on an object and the object moves along the line of action of the force; symbol W, unit joules, J or newton-metres, Nm

X

X-ray ionising electromagnetic radiation with a range of wavelengths shorter than ultraviolet and can have similar wavelengths to gamma rays; used in X-ray photography to generate picture of bones or teeth and in CT scans

Index